Senators
William S. Cohen and
George J. Mitchell

MEN *of* ZEAL

*A Candid Inside Story of
the Iran-Contra
Hearings*

VIKING

VIKING
Published by the Penguin Group
Viking Penguin Inc., 40 West 23rd Street, New York, New York 10010, U.S.A.
Penguin Books Ltd, 27 Wrights Lane, London W8 5TZ, England
Penguin Books Australia Ltd, Ringwood, Victoria, Australia
Penguin Books Canada Ltd, 2801 John Street, Markham, Ontario, Canada L3R 1B4
Penguin Books (N.Z.) Ltd, 182–190 Wairau Road, Auckland 10, New Zealand

Penguin Books Ltd, Registered Offices: Harmondsworth, Middlesex, England

First published in 1988 by Viking Penguin Inc.
Published simultaneously in Canada

1   3   5   7   9   10   8   6   4   2

Grateful acknowledgment is made for permission to reprint excerpts from the following
copyrighted works:

"Two Leaks, but by Whom?" from *Newsweek*, July 27, 1987. © 1987, Newsweek, Inc.
All rights reserved. Reprinted by permission.
"The Ollie We Knew" by David Halevy and Neil C. Livingstone in *The Washingtonian*,
July 1987. By permission of the authors.
"An Autopsy" by Theodore Draper in *The New York Review of Books*, December 17,
1987. By permission of the author.
"True or False" from *The Birds of Pompeii* by John Ciardi, published by The University
of Arkansas Press, © Judith Ciardi, 1985. Reprinted by permission.

Photo Credits:

Dennis Brack / Black Star: 2, 3, 5, 8, 23, 32, 37, 42, 44
Bill Fitz-Patrick / The White House: 6
UPI / Bettmann Newsphotos: 1, 11, 13, 15, 17, 24, 27, 29, 30, 34, 35, 38, 39, 41, 45, 46
The Washington Post: 20
Wide World Photos: 4, 7, 9, 10, 12, 14, 16, 18, 19, 21, 22, 25, 26, 28, 31, 33, 36, 40,
43, 47

Photo insert researched and edited by Vincent Virga,
and designed by Vincent Virga with Francesca Belanger.

LIBRARY OF CONGRESS CATALOGING IN PUBLICATION DATA
Cohen, William S.
Men of zeal.
Includes index.
1. Iran-Contra Affair, 1985–   . I. Mitchell,
George J. (George John), 1933–   . II. Title.
E876.C63   1988   973.927   88-40108
ISBN 0-670-82252-3

Printed in the United States of America by Arcata Graphics, Fairfield, Pennsylvania
Set in Plantin
Designed by Francesca Belanger

ACKNOWLEDGMENTS

Transforming one's thoughts and experiences into words is a uniquely personal undertaking. Yet the writing of this book would not have been possible without the encouragement and assistance of a number of people.

We are grateful to literary agent Bill Adler, who suggested that a book describing our observations and reflections would contribute to the American people's understanding of the Iran-Contra affair. Our heartfelt thanks must go to Richard Arenberg for his review of the manuscript and sound advice in its organization. We thank Britt Snider for his insightful comments and contributions; Cynthia Waters for the long weekends she devoted to typing hundreds of handwritten (and often illegible) pages into a letter-perfect manuscript; and James Kaplan, Timothy Woodcock, and Arthur Liman for their thoughtful comments.

A special expression of gratitude must go to our editor, Nan Graham, whose good cheer and enthusiasm for the project never abated and whose unerring eye helped provide focus to a massive amount of material; and to Christine Pevitt, vice president and editor in chief of Viking Penguin, for her confidence in us and her belief in the importance of making our views and insights public.

We are, of course, deeply indebted to Senators Robert Dole and Robert Byrd, who had the confidence in us to appoint us to the Senate Select Committee, thus placing us in the eye of a major political storm.

v

Finally, we wish to express our gratitude to the people of Maine, who have extended to us their patience, trust, and support, especially during this time of challenge to us and to the nation.

CONTENTS

AUTHORS' NOTE

Throughout the book, for the sake of convenience, we refer to the Senate Select Committee on Secret Military Assistance to Iran and the Nicaraguan Opposition and the House Select Committee to Investigate Covert Arms Transactions with Iran simply as the Committee.

Also, because the White House refused to declassify the names of the countries that contributed to the Nicaraguan Opposition, we are compelled to refer to them by number. For the same reason, we are required to refer to the CIA Chief of the Central American Task Force simply as C/CATF.

WHO'S WHO

United States Senate
  Select Committee on Secret Military Assistance
  to Iran and the Nicaraguan Opposition

DANIEL K. INOUYE, D-Hawaii   Chairman
WARREN RUDMAN, R-New Hampshire   Vice Chairman

Democrats

GEORGE J. MITCHELL, Maine
SAM NUNN, Georgia
PAUL S. SARBANES, Maryland
HOWELL T. HEFLIN, Alabama
DAVID L. BOREN, Oklahoma

Republicans

JAMES A. McCLURE, Idaho
ORRIN G. HATCH, Utah
WILLIAM S. COHEN, Maine
PAUL S. TRIBLE, JR., Virginia

ARTHUR L. LIMAN   Chief Counsel

United States House of Representatives
Select Committee to Investigate Covert Arms Transactions with Iran

LEE H. HAMILTON, D-Indiana   Chairman
DANTE B. FASCELL, D-Florida   Vice Chairman

Democrats

THOMAS S. FOLEY, Washington
PETER W. RODINO, JR., New Jersey
JACK BROOKS, Texas
LOUIS STOKES, Ohio
LES ASPIN, Wisconsin
EDWARD P. BOLAND, Massachusetts
ED JENKINS, Georgia

Republicans

DICK CHENEY, Wyoming   Ranking Republican
WILLIAM S. BROOMFIELD, Michigan
HENRY J. HYDE, Illinois
JIM COURTER, New Jersey
BILL McCOLLUM, Florida
MICHAEL DeWINE, Ohio

JOHN W. NIELDS, JR.   Chief Counsel

GEORGE W. VAN CLEVE   Chief Minority Counsel

ABRAMS, ELLIOTT   Assistant Secretary of State for Inter-American Affairs.

BECKLER, RICHARD   Attorney for John Poindexter.

BELNICK, MARK A.   Arthur Liman's Executive Assistant.

BUCKLEY, WILLIAM   CIA Station Chief in Lebanon, taken hostage in Beirut in March 1984. Known to have been tortured; died in captivity in June 1985.

BUSH, GEORGE   Vice President of the United States.

BYRD, ROBERT C.   U.S. Senator (D-West Virginia), Senate Majority Leader. Appointed Senate Democratic members of Iran-Contra Committee.

CALERO, ADOLFO   Leader of the Nicaraguan Democratic Force (FDN), the largest of the Contra organizations.

CASEY, WILLIAM   Director of Central Intelligence, 1981–87. Died May 6, 1987.

CASTILLO, TOMAS   See FERNANDEZ, page xiv.

CAVE, GEORGE   Retired CIA officer, paid consultant to CIA. Participated in sessions with the Iranians as a translator.

CHANNELL, CARL R. (SPITZ)   Private fund-raiser whose tax-exempt organization, the National Endowment for the Preservation of Liberty, raised funds for the Contras. Pleaded guilty to conspiracy to commit tax fraud, April 29, 1984.

CLARRIDGE, DUANE (DEWEY)   CIA official. Chief, CIA Latin America Division, August 1981 to October 1984. Chief, Europe Division, from October 1984 to February 1986.

CLIFFORD, CLARK   Former Secretary of Defense.

CLINES, THOMAS   Former CIA official, associate of Richard Secord, international arms dealer.

COOPER, CHARLES   Assistant Attorney General, Office of Legal Counsel.

DOLE, ROBERT   U.S. Senator (R-Kansas), Senate Minority Leader. Appointed Senate Republican members of Iran-Contra Committee.

EAGLETON, THOMAS   Former U.S. Senator (D-Missouri). Participated in the selection of Chief Counsel for the Senate Iran-Contra Committee.

EARL, ROBERT   Deputy to Oliver North on the National Security Council staff, Marine Lieutenant Colonel.

FERNANDEZ, JOSEPH F. CIA Station Chief in Costa Rica. Known in Central America by his alias, "Tomas Castillo."

FURMARK, ROY New York businessman. Friend of William Casey. Previously worked for Adnan Khashoggi. Served as contact point with Manucher Ghorbanifar.

GATES, ROBERT CIA Deputy Director.

GEORGE, CLAIR CIA Deputy Director for Operations during the Iran-Contra affair.

GHORBANIFAR, MANUCHER Iranian businessman. Intermediary between National Security Council staff and Iranian contacts.

GREEN, THOMAS C. Attorney for Richard Secord. Also represented Oliver North and Albert Hakim in November 1986.

HAKIM, ALBERT Richard Secord's business partner in the "Enterprise." Naturalized U.S. citizen of Iranian birth. Negotiated the "Hakim Accords."

HALL, FAWN Secretary to Oliver North.

HASENFUS, EUGENE Sole survivor of the C-123 cargo plane shot down over Nicaragua on October 5, 1986.

INMAN, BOBBY Former Director of the National Security Agency and former Deputy Director of the CIA.

JACOBSEN, DAVID P. American hostage in Lebanon, kidnapped in May 1985 and released in November 1986.

JENCO, LAWRENCE Catholic priest, American hostage in Lebanon, kidnapped in January 1985 and released on July 26, 1986.

KHASHOGGI, ADNAN Saudi Arabian businessman who financed the shipments of weapons from Israel to Iran.

KIMCHE, DAVID Director General of the Israeli Foreign Ministry.

LEDEEN, MICHAEL National Security Council consultant. Informal channel between National Security Adviser McFarlane and the Israelis.

MCFARLANE, ROBERT C. (BUD)   National Security Adviser, 1982–85. Also led mission to Teheran in May 1986.

MEESE, EDWIN   Attorney General.

NIDAL, ABU   Terrorist. North cited a threat from Nidal as the reason he accepted a security fence from Secord.

NIMRODI, YAACOV   Former Israeli defense official, arms dealer.

NIR, AMIRAM   Adviser to Israeli Primer Minister Peres on counterterrorism.

NORTH, OLIVER   Lieutenant Colonel, U.S. Marine Corps. Assistant Deputy Director for Political-Military Affairs of the National Security Council 1981–86.

OWEN, ROBERT   Messenger between Contra leaders and North. Contracted with the Nicaraguan Humanitarian Assistance Office of the U.S. State Department to work with the Contras.

POINDEXTER, JOHN   Vice Admiral, U.S. Navy. National Security Adviser from December 1985 to November 25, 1986. McFarlane's Deputy previously.

POLGAR, TOM, SR.   Investigator for the Senate Iran-Contra Committee. Former CIA Station Chief.

REAGAN, RONALD   President of the United States.

REGAN, DONALD   White House Chief of Staff, 1985–87.

REYNOLDS, WILLIAM BRADFORD   Assistant Attorney General, Civil Rights Division. Discovered the "diversion memo" in North's files.

RICHARDSON, JOHN   Meese's Chief of Staff. Present when Bradford Reynolds located the "diversion memo" in North's files. Took notes of some interviews during November 1986 Meese investigation of Iran-Contra events.

ROBINETTE, GLENN A.   Former CIA employee hired to arrange for the construction of a security fence around North's home.

RODRIGUEZ, FELIX   Alias "Max Gomez," former CIA operative recruited by North for resupply operation in Central America.

SCHWIMMER, ADOLPH (AL)   Adviser to Israeli Primer Minister Peres. Arms dealer who helped set up Israeli and U.S. Iranian contacts on arms deal.

SCIARONI, BRETTON   Sole professional staff member of the President's Intelligence Oversight Board. Author of legal opinion that Boland Amendments did not apply to the National Security Council.

SCOWCROFT, BRENT   National Security Adviser under President Ford. Member of the Tower Board.

SECORD, RICHARD V.   Retired Major General, U.S. Air Force. Operated the "Enterprise" with partner Albert Hakim.

SHULTZ, GEORGE   Secretary of State.

SIGUR, GASTON   Assistant Secretary of State for East Asian and Pacific Affairs since March 1986.

SINGLAUB, JOHN K.   Retired U.S. Army Major General. Solicited funds for and sold arms to the Contras.

SOFAER, ABRAHAM   State Department Legal Adviser. Threatened to re-sign if false statements were not removed from congressional testimony prepared for Casey about the November 1985 HAWK shipments.

SPORKIN, STANLEY   CIA General Counsel.

SULLIVAN, BRENDAN   Attorney for Oliver North.

TAMBS, LEWIS   Ambassador to Costa Rica.

THOMPSON, PAUL   National Security Council Counsel.

VANCE, CYRUS   Former Secretary of State.

WALSH, LAWRENCE   Independent Counsel investigating the Iran-Contra affair. Former federal judge.

WEINBERGER, CASPAR   Secretary of Defense during the Iran-Contra affair.

WEIR, REVEREND BENJAMIN   American hostage in Lebanon, kidnapped May 8, 1984, and released September 15, 1985, after shipment of 508 U.S. TOW missiles to Iran by Israel.

WILSON, EDWIN   Former CIA agent, arms dealer who supplied explosives to Libya's Qaddafi.

ZUCKER, WILLARD   Hakim's attorney/banker in Switzerland. Met with Mrs. Oliver North in Philadelphia.

CHRONOLOGY

11/14/79   U.S. imposes embargo on arms shipments to Iran.

9/19/83   President signs finding authorizing covert aid intended to pressure the Sandinistas to negotiate a treaty with nearby countries.

10/23/83   Bombing of U.S. Marine barracks in Beirut, killing 241 Marines.

12/83 $24-million cap on Contra funding imposed by Congress.

12/14/83   U.S. begins "Operation Staunch," urging allied governments to "stop transferring arms to Iran."

1/20/84   U.S. government officially lists Iran as a sponsor of international terrorism.

4/7/84   Disclosure of mining of Nicaraguan harbors. Public criticism of U.S. involvement undermines congressional support for assistance to the Contras.

5/84   McFarlane meets with Ambassador of "Country Two," who agrees to provide $1 million per month as contribution to the Contras.

Spring '84 According to North, he and Casey first discuss the "fall-guy plan," to provide "plausible deniability" to North's superiors.

6/25/84 National Security Planning Group (NSPG) meeting to consider options for funding Contras (President, Bush, Shultz, Weinberger, Casey, Meese, McFarlane present). Casey urges President to seek third-country funding. Shultz quotes Jim Baker that such would be an impeachable offense. Meese recalls William French Smith opinion providing authority for such. No decision made. Neither President nor McFarlane reveals Country Two contribution already agreed to.

Summer '84 At Casey's suggestion, according to North, North recruited Secord to assist in buying weapons for the Contras with the third-country funds being received.

10/12/84 Boland II becomes law.

2/85 Country Two agrees to contribute additional $24 million. President informed by head of state.

Spring '85 First two arms shipments arranged by Secord and North reach Contras.

4/23/85 House rejects administration's Contra-aid request.

5/1/85 President announces imposition of economic sanctions against Nicaragua.

5/3/85 Ledeen (with McFarlane's approval) meets with Israeli Prime Minister Peres and expresses interest in sharing intelligence on Iran. Hostages discussed, according to Israelis.

6/19/85 Ghorbanifar and Furmark meet Israelis in Israel to propose sale of 100 TOWs to Iran. Ghorbanifar agrees to set up meeting with Iranian official.

7/8/85 President's speech to American Bar Association. Calls Iran part of "confederation of terrorist states . . . a new international version of Murder Inc. America will never make concessions to terrorists." Refers to Iran, Libya, North Korea, Cuba, and Nicaragua as "outlaw states run by the strangest collection of misfits, Looney

Tunes and squalid criminals since the advent of the Third Reich."

7/8/85   Israelis meet in Hamburg with Ghorbanifar, Khashoggi, and Iranian representative to discuss sale of 100 TOWs, with sale to be followed by release of the American hostages.

7/8/85   Singlaub arms shipment received by Contras. Last arms shipment by dealer other than Secord, and last time funds were handled by Calero rather than by the "Enterprise."

7/18/85   McFarlane meets with the President at the hospital, where he is recuperating from surgery. Regan present. No notes. McFarlane testified that the Israelis were informed that the President was unwilling to allow the U.S. to supply arms directly to Iran.

8/2/85   Kimche meets with McFarlane in Washington to seek explicit U.S. position on sale of 100 TOWs. McFarlane agrees to present issue to the President.

8/6/85   Meeting with the President, McFarlane, Bush, Shultz, Weinberger, and Regan. Permission for the sale of 100 TOWs to Iran by Israel is discussed. Shultz and Weinberger opposed. McFarlane testified that the President called him several days later and authorized the Israelis to proceed. (The President told the Tower Board that he had authorized the sale, then said that he had not authorized the sale, and finally said that he had no recollection one way or the other.)

8/8/85   President signs bill authorizing $27 million in humanitarian assistance to the Contras.

8/10/85   North meets with Castillo and Tambs in Costa Rica to discuss establishment of secret air base for resupply of Contras in Nicaragua.

8/20/85   96 TOWs delivered by Israel to Iran. No hostages are released.

Fall '85   North meets with representative of Country Three at Hay-Adams Hotel to request funds for Contras. Country Three eventually donates $2 million.

9/4–5/85   Ledeen meets in Paris with Israelis and Ghorbanifar. Ghorbanifar indicates that one hostage will be released in exchange for an additional 400 TOW missiles.

9/15/85   408 TOW missiles delivered to Tabriz, Iran. McFarlane is given the choice of the release of any hostage other than Buckley.

9/15/85   Benjamin Weir is released.

10/10/85   White House spokesman Speakes reading statement following capture of hijackers of the *Achille Lauro:* "From the outset the United States Government made . . . clear to all the governments involved our firm opposition to negotiations with terrorists or concessions to them."

11/15/85   McFarlane meets with Israeli Defense Minister Rabin at White House and conveys President's authorization for further arms sale, with U.S. replenishment of Israeli stocks.

11/17/85   McFarlane informs President about shipment of 80 HAWKs just before they leave for summit meeting in Geneva.

11/18/85   Problem develops with flight clearances for shipment of HAWKs to Iran, and North recruits Secord to go to Europe to resolve it.

11/24–25/85   First 19 HAWK missiles delivered by CIA plane from Israel to Teheran. Remaining HAWKs rejected by Iran. No hostages released.

12/4/85   Poindexter succeeds McFarlane as National Security Adviser.

12/5/85   In one of his first acts as National Security Adviser, Poindexter presents finding to President, who signs it. (Regan, present at the briefing, has no memory of President's signing it.) Finding retroactively authorizes HAWK shipment and indicates exchange for hostages.

12/6/85   North tells Israeli officials at meeting in New York that U.S. wants to use profits from upcoming arms sale to Iran to fund activity in Nicaragua (according to Israeli Historical Chronology submitted to the Committee).

12/7/85   White House meeting; President, Shultz, Weinberger, McFarlane, Poindexter, John McMahon, and Regan present. Strong opposition to arms sale expressed by Shultz and Weinberger.

12/8/85   McFarlane meets in London with Kimche, Secord, North, Nimrodi, and Ghorbanifar. McFarlane is unhappy with Ghorbanifar's arms-for-hostage approach. North is unhappy with McFarlane's negative reaction, raises specter of hostage deaths if plan doesn't go forward.

12/12/85   Poindexter visits Central America.

12/13/85   On return from Central America, Poindexter briefs President on secret airstrip in Costa Rica.

1/2/86   Nir meets with Poindexter and North in Washington to propose new arms sale involving 4,000 TOWs, the release of all American hostages and 20–30 Hizballah prisoners held by the Southern Lebanon Army.

1/3/86   North and Sporkin meet to draft new finding to authorize CIA participation in new arms sales (and inclusion of "third parties" in draft North prepared).

1/6/86 Poindexter tells President of new plan in presence of Bush, Regan, and Donald Fortier. Poindexter presents President with draft finding. President, not realizing that it was intended for discussion, reads and signs the finding.

1/7/86 At National Security Council meeting, with President, Bush, Shultz, Weinberger, Meese, Casey, Poindexter, and Regan present, Weinberger and Shultz object strenuously. President's signing of the finding the previous day is not mentioned.

1/15/86 North gives National Security Agency–provided KL-43 encryption devices to key members of the Contra resupply operation. This equipment and accompanying classified codes allowed secure communications among North, Secord, and others over open telephone lines.

1/17/86 President signs new finding in presence of Bush, Poindexter, Regan, and Fortier. Finding is identical to the draft finding signed on 1/6 except for the insertion of the words "third parties," thereby allowing for the use of the "Enterprise."

1/22/86 North, Secord, and Nir meet with Ghorbanifar in London. Ghorbanifar, according to North testimony, suggests diversion in bathroom meeting. At London meeting, delivery schedule for 1,000 TOW missiles agreed upon.

2/17/86 First 500 TOWs shipped, returning with 17 rejected HAWKs from November 1985 shipment.

2/25/86 North, Secord, and Ghorbanifar meet with Iranian official in Frankfurt. Hakim, under disguise, serves as translator. Eventually agreement reached that sale of 1,000 missiles will lead to release of "a couple of hostages."

2/27/86   Second load of 500 TOWs delivered to Iran. No hostages released.

3/7/86   North, Cave, Ghorbanifar, and Nir meet in Paris. Ghorbanifar indicates that Iranians are not interested in additional TOWs, but seek 240 HAWK spare parts.

4/1/86   First air resupply to the Nicaraguan Democratic Force (FDN) accomplished.

4/4/86 (approx.)   North prepares extensive report for Poindexter, summarizing the Iran initiative and indicating the use of the profits for the Contras in Nicaragua. This is the "diversion memo" found in North's files in November 1986.

4/11/86   First successful air resupply mission into southern Nicaragua accomplished.

4/20/86   North and Secord meet at the air base in Central America with James J. Steele, Felix Rodriguez, and the military leadership of the FDN. Complaints about the age and reliability of the aircraft expressed.

5/1/86   Rogriguez meets with Bush. Scheduling memo states: "To brief the Vice President on the status of the war in [a Central American country] and resupply of the contras."

5/6/86   North, Nir, Cave, and Ghorbanifar meet in London to discuss pricing of spare-parts shipment. Agreement that HAWK parts would be brought on a plane with McFarlane for meeting with high Iranian officials in Teheran. Remainder of HAWK parts would be delivered after release of hostages took place.

5/16/86   National Security Planning Group (NSPG) meeting with the President to discuss third-country humanitarian assistance. Shultz instructed to prepare list of potential third-country donors. No one mentions Country Two and Country Three funds already received by the Contras.

5/25/86   McFarlane mission arrives in Teheran.

5/28/86   McFarlane breaks off Teheran negotiations and party leaves Teheran without the release of hostages, having delivered one pallet of HAWK parts.

6/16/86   Shultz first learns of Country Two solicitation from McFarlane.

6/25/86   House approves $100 million for Contras.

7/4/86   Israelis and Ghorbanifar fail in effort to convince Iranians to arrange release of hostage in time for Statue of Liberty celebration.

7/26/86   Father Jenco is released, as arranged by Ghorbanifar and Israelis.

7/29/86   North memo to Poindexter predicts hostage will be killed if HAWK parts not delivered to Iran.

7/30/86   Poindexter indicates President approved shipment of HAWK parts.

8/8/86   240 HAWK missile parts shipped to Iran.

8/8/86   North, Ghorbanifar, and Nir meet in London to discuss continued initiative. North agrees to sequential deliveries of arms and hostages, subject to ratification by administration.

8/8/86   Abrams meets Brunei representative in London and solicits $10 million. Funds never reach Contras: North or Fawn Hall transposes account number given to Brunei by Abrams.

8/8/86   Rodriguez meets with Donald P. Gregg, Bush's National Security Adviser, and voices allegations about Secord group overpricing, Edwin Wilson connections, etc. Rodriguez makes clear to Gregg (reflected in his notes) that North is involved. Gregg testified that he never told Bush this.

8/25/86   Secord and Hakim meet with the "Second Channel" in Brussels.

9/9/86   Another American, Frank Reed, Director of the Lebanese International School, is taken hostage in West Beirut.

9/12/86   Joseph Cicippio, Chief Accountant at the American University, is abducted in West Beirut, raising the number of American hostages in Lebanon to five.

9/19–20/86   Meeting in Washington with Iranians from Second Channel. Iranians tour White House with North.

9/25/86   Costa Rican officials hold press conference announcing discovery of secret airstrip in Costa Rica.

10/5/86   Hasenfus flight shot down over Nicaragua.

10/6–8/86   Meetings with Second Channel in Frankfurt. North leaves Hakim to negotiate with the Iranians. Agreement reached on nine-point so-called Hakim Accords.

10/7/86   Casey is informed by Roy Furmark, a business associate of Khashoggi, one of the principal financiers of the arms sales, that investors in the arms sales and Ghorbanifar are upset and threatening to go public.

10/13/86   According to North, Casey tells him sometime be-
(to 11/4)   tween October 13 and November 4, 1986: ". . . this whole thing was coming unravelled and that things ought to be 'cleaned up.' " North testified that in response to this instruction he began shredding documents.

10/28/86   500 TOWs delivered to Iran under the "nine-point plan."

10/29/86   North, Hakim, Cave, and Secord meet with Second Channel in Mainz, Germany, to discuss release of one or two hostages and completion of nine-point plan.

11/2/86   David Jacobsen is released.

11/3/86   *Al-Shiraa*, Lebanese newspaper, reports U.S. had sold arms to Iran.

11/86   According to North, shortly after disclosure of the arms sales, he and Casey discuss implementing the "fall-guy plan." According to North, Casey tells him that he (North) might not be "big enough" to be the "fall guy" and indicates that "it's probably going to go higher." Casey suggests: "Poindexter might have to be a fall guy."

11/6/86   President, in his first public statement on the subject of the reports of U.S. arms sales to Iran, states they have "no foundation."

11/13/86   President states, in an address to the nation: "We did not—repeat—did not trade weapons or anything else for hostages nor will we."

11/19/86   President's news conference. President denies third-country involvement in arms sales, asserts U.S. involvement only after January 17 finding, asserts that only 1,000 TOWs were shipped, and that everything "sold could be put in one cargo plane."

11/20/86   Shultz meets with President to inform him of misstatements at press conference and that he was receiving misinformation from subordinates. Shultz testified, "Not the kind of discussion I ever thought I would have with the President of the United States."

11/20/86   Meeting held in Poindexter's office to review Casey statement prepared for testimony before the House and Senate Intelligence Committees on November 21. Casey, Meese, Poindexter, North, Cooper, Thompson, and Gates attend. At North's suggestion, statement is changed to say "no one in the U.S. Government" knew at the time that the November 1985 shipment contained arms. The "oil drilling equipment" story agreed to at the meeting was false, as North admitted in his testimony. It was removed from Casey's testimony at the insistence of State Department Legal Adviser Abraham Sofaer.

11/21/86　President authorizes Meese to commence an inquiry into the arms-sales matter.

11/21/86　North instructs Fawn Hall to alter series of documents. North, Earl, and Hall shred documents.

11/21/86　Poindexter tells North that the President was never told of the diversion of Iran arms-sale funds to the Contras.

11/21/86　Casey and Poindexter appear before the Intelligence Committees. Poindexter tells the Committees that the U.S. had disapproved of the Israeli arms shipments to Iran and that until the day before (11/20) he had believed that administration officials did not know of them until after they had occurred.

11/21/86　Poindexter destroys December 1985 retroactive presidential finding.

11/22/86　Diversion memo discovered by Reynolds and Richardson. Meese is told at lunch at Old Ebbitt Grill.

11/22/86　Casey and Poindexter have lunch for two and a half hours. Poindexter testified that he remembers nothing about what was discussed.

11/22/86　Meese meets with Casey at Casey's home. According
(6:00 P.M.)　to Meese's later testimony, he does not ask about diversion.

11/23/86　Meese interviews North. North conceals existence of the "Enterprise"—Secord's companies and Swiss bank accounts—telling Meese that funds went directly from Israelis to Calero's accounts.

11/23/86　Later that evening North shreds additional documents at his office, working until at least 4:15 A.M.

11/25/86　Meese press conference revealing diversion of funds from arms sale to Iran to Contras.

11/25/86   National Security Council security officer secures North's office.

11/25/86   Fawn Hall smuggles documents out of North's office.

12/1/86   Senate Select Committee on Intelligence begins preliminary inquiry.

12/13/86   Meeting with Second Channel in Frankfurt. This is first meeting at which State Department is represented. As a result Shultz learns of the nine-point plan.

12/14/86   Shultz reports nine-point plan to the President. Shultz testified that the President was "stunned and furious." Poindexter testified that the President had approved the plan.

12/19/86   Independent Counsel appointed.

1/6/87   Senate Select Committee created.

1/7/87   House Select Committee created.

1/24/87   Three hostages kidnapped in Lebanon (Alann Steen, Jesse Turner, Robert Polhill).

1/27/87   President's State of the Union Address: "The goals were worthy. . . . But we did not achieve what we wished, and serious mistakes were made in trying to do so."

1/29/87   Senate Select Committee on Intelligence issues report on preliminary inquiry.

2/26/87   Tower Board issues report. This special commission created by President Reagan interviewed many of the participants and gathered most of the significant documents. The report, at the time the Iran-Contra Committee began its investigation, provided the basis for most of what was then known about the affair.

3/4/87   President's Oval Office Speech on Iran: "A few months ago, I told the American people I did not trade arms for hostages. My heart and my best intentions still tell me that's true, but the facts and the evidence tell me it's not."

4/29/87   Channell pleads guilty to conspiracy and tax fraud, naming North and Richard R. Miller as coconspirators.

5/5/87   Joint hearings of Congressional Select Committees begin.

5/6/87   Miller pleads guilty to conspiracy and tax fraud.

8/3/87   Public hearings of Select Committees conclude.

8/12/87   President's address to the nation: "Our original initiative got all tangled up in the sale of arms, and the sale of arms got tangled up with the hostages. . . . I let my preoccupation with the hostages intrude into areas where it didn't belong."

11/17/87   Select Committees submit final report.

3/11/88   McFarlane pleads guilty to four counts of withholding information from Congress.

3/16/88   Indictments returned against North, Poindexter, Hakim, and Secord.

MEN *of* ZEAL

Introduction

As he nears the end of his eight years in office, President Ronald Reagan remains personally popular. Just a year ago, his presidency was in danger of sinking in an unfolding scandal of lies, deception, and lawbreaking by high-ranking officials in his administration. An effort to secure the release of American hostages held in Lebanon included selling weapons to Iran—a terrorist nation the President had consistently denounced. Most Americans, once they learned of this secret action, reacted with disbelief and anger.

No one questioned President Reagan's motives in exploring with rational elements in Iran—if they existed—opportunities for establishing better relations between the two countries. Few faulted him for pursuing every effort to bring American hostages home safely. But secretly providing arms to a terrorist nation violated the clear and unambiguous policy of the United States. The President's plan to sell weapons to the nation he had called "Murder Inc." could only end in disaster. Even if it succeeded and all of our hostages were returned, the United States would be charged by our allies with hypocrisy and lose its position of moral leadership in the fight against global terrorism.

When Attorney General Edwin Meese disclosed, on November 25, 1986, that money derived from the sale of weapons to Iran had been diverted to support the Nicaraguan Contras, after Congress had prohibited such assistance, President Reagan's ability to continue to govern seemed in doubt. The President said that he had no knowledge of the diversion, that it had been done without his authority. Moreover, he said he was not aware of funds being solicited for lethal aid for the Contras. An absence of knowledge could provide no safe haven for the President. For, even if he had no knowledge of the diversion or the fund-raising activities for the Contras, two questions remained. Had the President failed to manage the affairs of his office to take care that the laws of the land were faithfully executed? Or had an extraordinary usurpation of power taken place within the White House by members of the staff of the National Security Council?

The congressional Intelligence Committees initiated preliminary investigations. President Reagan tried to stem the growing controversy by establishing a special review commission to determine exactly what had happened within his administration.[1] The House and Senate each established a select committee to investigate whether any existing laws had been violated and new laws were needed.

We were asked to serve on the Senate Select Committee and agreed to do so. We were both born and raised in Maine and had lived there most of our lives. We both attended public high schools and then graduated from Bowdoin College, a small liberal-arts college in Brunswick, Maine. We are both lawyers. We both represent Maine in the United States Senate. So we have much in common. We also differ, however. One of us is a Republican, the other a Democrat. We disagree on a number of legislative issues. But our policy disagreements have never been personally disagreeable. As we approached the crucible of the Iran-Contra investigation, we knew there would be pressure from both sides to be partisan, to attack the President strongly or defend him. Surely we would not agree on everything in this complex matter. But we were determined to lay aside any political differences in the search for the truth. If the President and his men had ignored or violated our laws, their political affiliation could not mitigate the damage done to the nation's well-being. If the President had merely made errors in judgment, then his political paralysis was a price that neither he nor the nation could afford to pay.

Our mandate was to discover the facts and lay before the American people the origins and operations of two secret but parallel programs that the Reagan administration had pursued in Iran and Nicaragua. It was not an easy assignment. The truth was buried under layers of duplicities, camouflaged by the secret activities of retired General Richard Secord, Albert Hakim, Lieutenant Colonel Oliver North, and deceased CIA Director William Casey. The task was complicated by the House and Senate Select Committees' agreement to hold joint hearings. The investigatory process was burdened with public and back-room partisan wrangling, deadlines for the completion of the investigation, and the independent counsel's investigation of possible crimes.[2]

The public watched a parade of witnesses come before the Committee and swear to tell the truth, among them a dynamic Marine officer who helped turn the National Security Council staff into an operational arm of the CIA; a secretary who altered, shredded, and smuggled documents in an effort to conceal the secret "initiative"; an aggressive retired Air Force general and his Iranian-born business partner, who helped transport weapons to Iran and to the Nicaraguan Contras and set up Swiss bank accounts to hide profits that were to be used for future covert activities; a pipe-smoking admiral who claimed to have authorized a diversion of profits from the sale of weapons to Iran because it was a mere technicality and the President needed "plausible deniability" of the activity; a Secretary of State whose advice was rejected and whose diplomatic functions were undertaken by amateurs; and always there was the "brooding omnipresence" of the deceased Director of the CIA.

Many questions were not asked or could not be answered. Although the Committee scrutinized more than three hundred thousand documents, others, some crucial, were reduced to confetti in shredding machines or to ashes in burn bags. Many of the more than five hundred witnesses called before the Committee appeared to offer candid testimony, but others suffered from curious cases of accommodating amnesia. Some participants, such as CIA Director William Casey, were dead and thus beyond the reach of any mortal subpoena. Top officials were in flat contradiction on key facts. Some were lying, others merely mistaken. There were vast evidentiary ellipses that may never be filled. New doubts or theories may emerge as some new revelation comes forth from an unexpected source. More documents will materialize. Enterprising reporters will follow leads that went stale or dead for congressional investigators.

Nevertheless, the Committee's report, signed by a majority of its members, documented a pattern of executive secrecy and deceit that was dangerous to and incompatible with our democratic form of government. However high-minded the President's motives may have been in trying to obtain the release of American hostages and hold the Nicaraguan Contras together, there existed among some members of his administration an excess of zeal, and contempt for those who held different views, that threatened the sanctity of the rule of law. Left unchecked, the secret arms sales and Swiss bank accounts would have continued to fund policies and activities that many Americans, if they ever knew about them, might have found offensive to our nation's ideals and interests.

Comprehensive as the Committee's report was, the full story of the Iran-Contra affair has not been told. As much as a vigorous press can learn, as close as the eye of the camera can get, as effective as congressional investigations can be in unlocking secrets, much of what was taking place behind the Committee's closed doors and why it was taking place were necessarily hidden from the public. Yet the private discussions and decisions profoundly affected the nature of our public deliberations and final judgments.

Why did the Committee select Secord to be the lead witness? How did North come to write the terms of his own appearance before the Committee? What was it like to confront a military hero—one whose charismatic personality fired the hearts and minds of millions of Americans? What apprehensions did we experience in challenging a secretary who was just following (albeit eagerly) instructions to alter and shred classified documents? How did we react to the flood of mail, telegrams, and telephone calls that poured into our offices? Did television help the investigation or transform it into a theatrical stage on which the Committee stumbled?

Serving on the Committee presented us with the opportunity not only to interrogate witnesses and weigh evidence, but to observe the dynamic flow of events and personalities as well: the stratagems and posturing of witnesses, attorneys, Committee members, correspondents; the impact of television commentators; the subtle internal struggles to shape the course and conduct of the hearings. We also shared insights with our colleagues, who were as much on trial before the viewing public as any witness.

We decided to write this book because we believe that the Iran-Contra affair was a significant event in our nation's history. Congress and the American people were lied to, laws were bent and broken, power was abused. One result of public disclosure of these events has been a series of personal tragedies: careers shattered, indictment for serious crimes, the possibility of prison sentences. Another result was a demonstration of the remarkable resiliency of American democracy. Errors were exposed, mistaken policies ended, and culpable persons punished, all without upsetting the fragile balance of power so necessary to democracy—and all through the rough-and-tumble of an open, competitive political process.

Although the democratic balance of power was not altered, it was severely tested. Burning with patriotic zeal, intoxicated by the power and trappings of high public office, convinced beyond any doubt of the rightness of their cause, bristling with contempt for those who lacked their power and certainty, especially those in the Congress, a handful of men tried to use the powerful machinery of the United States government to achieve their mission.

The experience proved so congenial, particularly the escape from the chains of accountability, that it led them to organize a permanent enterprise—a government within the government—to undertake such activities in the future. No more would they need bother with a vacillating, indecisive, meddlesome Congress or an

American public that often didn't know what it needed or even wanted. The danger to the republic was clear to them, so clear that extraordinary measures were necessary. The regular process was too slow, too uncertain, too filled with nonbelievers. And if others couldn't see the danger as clearly as they could—well, one day these doubters would, and a grateful nation would remember and honor those they had condemned.

But they failed. Despite their power, their dedication, their energy, their secrecy—despite all that and more—they failed. This was in part because their patriotism was misguided, their schemes harebrained, their methods amateurish. But another reason they failed was that in the American democracy power flows from the people to the government. It cannot be imposed from above. Ultimately no major policy can be sustained over time unless the American people understand and support it. Operations conceived and executed in secret may carry out publicly supported policies, but they cannot substitute for them.

The Iran-Contra affair was, finally, a lesson in democracy. Coming as it did in the year in which Americans celebrated the two-hundredth anniversary of their Constitution, it was remarkably well timed. Given the recurring human failure to heed the teachings of history, it is a lesson to be understood, emphasized, and repeated. We wrote this book to make our contribution to its understanding.

It was a challenge in writing this book to distinguish our feelings as the hearings unfolded from the views we hold in retrospect. At the time we felt as though we were strapped to the front seat of a roller coaster, with no control over the momentum of the hearings or over the sudden rush of unanticipated events. The evidence gathered by the Committee often seemed out of logical or temporal sequence. Caught up in the emotion of the moment, at times disappointed that our position did not prevail, concerned—on occasion disheartened—about the way the hearings were going, we both were uncertain of the Committee's accomplishments. A knot of anxiety tied itself around us daily.

The Committee faced difficult choices and was forced to compromise. At times, we felt the compromises to be unwise. But the apparent alternative—to forgo a witness or to engage in a lengthy legal battle for his testimony—seemed equally unwise. Our doubts grew, subsided, returned.

The same difficulty marked the writing of the Committee's report. As we worked and reworked numerous drafts, we were pulled by partisan forces from left and right. We tried to resist the use of inflammatory language or the leap to conclusions that were unsupported by the evidence. Chairman Daniel Inouye, Vice Chairman Warren Rudman, and Arthur Liman, the Senate Committee's counsel, were constant positive forces who reinforced the legitimacy and integrity of the Committee's work. They refused to permit either the investigation or the report to be derailed by partisan considerations. They preached the need for conciliation and compromise, and they practiced it.

Each of us can point to areas that were not fully explored: Israel's role in initiating the opening of the relationship with the so-called Iranian moderates; the Vice President's participation in the discussions leading up to and following the presidential "finding" of January 17, 1986; a complete accounting of the complicated financial transactions by the Secord and Hakim "Enterprise"; the many conflicts in the testimony of key witnesses; the activities of CIA Director William Casey. But the Committee's inability to answer every question should not obscure the fact that it did answer most questions.

Throughout the investigation and in the report, we tried to maintain a decent respect for the office of the President and to present an objective analysis of the facts as we found them. Obviously our opinions about various witnesses differed, as did our approaches to examining them. While we have attempted in the succeeding pages to convey our thoughts in a combined editorial fashion, we provide our individual reflections, in italicized passages, where appropriate.

But we remain united on the importance of the issues raised by the Iran-Contra affair, the lessons to be learned from it, and the need to avoid a repetition. We offer our recollections on what we observed, experienced, and thought during a difficult period in our history and a crucial episode in the constant struggle to keep our government a republic.

A final note of caution to the reader. The views expressed in this book are refracted through our personalities and predispositions. Other members of the Committee, no doubt, viewed events and witnesses differently. There are at least twenty-six versions of what happened during the Iran-Contra investigation. Each bears its own stamp of truth.

PART I

The greatest dangers to liberty lurk in insidious encroachment by men of zeal, well-meaning but without understanding.

—Supreme Court Justice Louis Brandeis,
in his 1928 dissent in *Olmstead* v. *United States*[3]

The Mandate

The Senate Committee on Secret Military Assistance to Iran and the Nicaraguan Opposition was created by a resolution of the Senate passed on January 6, 1987, the first day of the 100th Congress. The House Select Committee was created the following day. By that time the nation had been jolted by a series of improbable, but apparently true, revelations.

In mid-November 1986 we learned that the United States had sold arms to Iran. This had been done despite publicly stated U.S. policies that we would sell arms neither to Iran nor to its current adversary, Iraq. The Arms Export Control Act of 1976 prohibited the sale of U.S. arms to nations that had sponsored repeated acts of terrorism, and Iran had been so designated by the Secretary of State in 1984.

President Reagan stated that the sales were to provide the "bona fides" necessary for a diplomatic opening to Iran. But this explanation, from a president who came to office critical of the way his predecessor had dealt with Iran over the U.S. hostages, did not ring true with most Americans. They suspected the real reason lay in the President's consuming desire to free the hostages. But to deal with hostage-takers would be a violation of Reagan's own policy—and a long-standing policy of the United States. So the President and his men had clung to a rationalization of a diplomatic overture to Iran that widened the credibility gap they had opened with the public. Neither the press nor the Congress was satisfied;

the implausibility of the administration's explanations nagged at their faith in the President.

Initial explanations were not only implausible, but conflicting and disingenuous as well. The public came to believe the administration was playing games with the facts. The President announced at a press conference on November 19, 1986, that there was no third-country involvement in the arms sales to Iran. Twenty minutes later, a correction was issued by the White House. Israel had been involved.

Indeed, we learned that the United States had approved two shipments of U.S. arms from Israel to Iran in 1985. The U.S. role in those shipments was unclear, but they apparently had been undertaken with the approval, or at least the acquiescence, of the President. This, too, appeared to violate the Arms Export Control Act, which, among other things, prohibited the President from consenting to retransfers of U.S. weapons to countries to which the U.S. would not itself sell. Iran was one such country.

Moreover, Congress had never been advised either of the 1985 Israeli shipments, which the President apparently had approved, or of the 1986 sales, expressly authorized by the President, which were carried out by the United States. These failures in themselves appeared to violate U.S. law.

Under the Arms Export Control Act, Congress is to be advised by the President when he approves a retransfer from one country to another of U.S. arms valued at $14 million or more. It appeared that the U.S. arms sold by Israel to Iran may have exceeded this amount.

Similarly, the 1986 U.S. sales to Iran were carried out utilizing personnel and equipment controlled by the CIA, in accordance with a formal presidential determination called a "finding," which authorizes the initiation of a covert action. In 1980 Congress had enacted a statute that established a procedure by which covert operations undertaken by the CIA are approved and reported to Congress. No such operation can be undertaken unless the President "finds" that it is important to the national security. The purpose is to establish presidential accountability for all such operations. The statute also assumes that these findings will be reported to the Senate and House Intelligence Committees prior to the initiation of the covert action in question. It also implicitly recognizes that such notice may come after the covert operation has been initiated, but where prior notice has been withheld, the Committees must nonetheless be notified "in a timely fashion."

In the case of the arms sales to Iran, no notice of the finding was provided to the Congress until after the operation had been disclosed in the press, some eleven months later, making a mockery of the notion of notice "in a timely fashion." Indeed, it is apparent that, had the operation not been disclosed by the press, the Congress would have remained in the dark indefinitely.

However provocative these failures were to the Congress, the public's perceptions were shaped most by the Attorney General's announcement on November 25, 1986, that the proceeds of the arms sales to Iran had been used to fund the Nicaraguan resistance at a time when U.S. military assistance to the resistance was prohibited by law and when most Americans opposed such aid.

The "diversion," as the Attorney General termed it, clearly was intended to avoid the strictures of the law, whether it technically violated them or not. The arms sales to Iran had been troubling to most Americans. Now it was clear that the money from these sales had been used to fund the controversial war in Nicaragua when the U.S. government was itself barred from doing so.

Moreover, the "diversion" announcement suddenly confirmed what had long been suspected, that the White House staff was orchestrating covert assistance to the Nicaraguan resistance. This caused both Congress and the press to hark back to recent events and re-examine the assurances from the administration that it had not provided illegal assistance to the Contras: the denials of U.S. involvement in the resupply flight to the Contras that was shot down in October 1986; the denials of soliciting financial and military assistance from foreign countries; the denials that the White House staff was involved.

Whereas the President's support for the Contras had not wavered from the beginning of his administration, Congress had imposed legal restraints that varied over time, in response to events in Central America and to public opinion. The United States had provided both lethal and humanitarian aid from 1981 to October 1984, when all aid was cut off by the Congress. But a year later Congress authorized the provision of humanitarian assistance and the exchange of intelligence with the resistance. In December 1985 intelligence agencies were further authorized to provide communications equipment, related training, and intelligence "information and advice." Ten months later, in October 1986, funding for lethal as well as humanitarian assistance was resumed.

Although some in Congress suspected that members of the administration were in some way involved in keeping assistance flowing to the Contras, whatever legal restrictions may have been applicable at the time, there was no concrete evidence available to support random newspaper articles that alleged White House improprieties. When members of Congress did ask, they received categorical denials from officials at the White House whom they trusted, and did not, as a rule, press the administration any further.

To realize now that they had been lied to, that the White House had deliberately flouted the will of Congress and the law of the land, as expressed in the various restrictions on aid to the Contras, compelled both Democratic and Republican members of Congress to demand a full accounting of the facts. There was a growing perception that the diversion may have been only a part of a larger and continuing pattern of deception and disregard for the law.

Thus the Senate and House Committees were given separate but similar mandates, covering both the Iran arms sales and the assistance to the Nicaraguan resistance: Investigate; air the facts;

tell us what went wrong, and what lessons we should draw from this. And do it quickly, because it is apparent even now that this affair is consuming an inordinate amount of the nation's time and attention.

Congress required the Committees to submit their reports in ten months, by the end of October 1987.

Here Come the Judges

The leaders of the Senate, Robert Byrd (D-West Virginia) and Robert Dole (R-Kansas), announced on December 4, 1986, that they intended to appoint a separate select committee to investigate the Iran-Contra scandal. As soon as they made the announcement, competition for a position on the Select Committee began discreetly—and in earnest.

Congressional investigations of a president and his administration do not occur often. Because the political stakes in such an investigation are high, so is the attention devoted to it by the national media. To a congressman or senator, network coverage means an opportunity for nationwide exposure, an opportunity to step from relative political anonymity, reinforce one's standing at home, and enhance one's future national prospects. There is, of course, a darker and more dangerous side to such exposure. Politicians tend to forget the adage that whom the gods would destroy, they first make famous. Exposure invites scrutiny, and scrutiny invites criticism as well as praise.

Robert Byrd, destined to become the Senate's Majority Leader once the 100th Congress convened in January, is a skilled politician and plays his cards close to his vest. He was not eager to identify the six Democratic senators he was to appoint to the Senate panel.

Robert Dole, soon to be the Minority Leader, was looking for some signal from Byrd. Would the Democratic membership be dominated by high-profile liberals, who would not be inclined to spare the rod to Ronald Reagan? If so, then Dole would want to respond in kind and fill his five slots with conservative votaries who would turn the investigation into a political circus.

Neither leader expressed this calculation publicly (or privately), of course. No threats were made. Both Dole and Byrd are seasoned politicians who know that things that go unspoken do not always go unheard. Body language is often louder than a shout.

Some Senate Democrats were eager to break out the long knives and deliver incapacitating, if not fatal, thrusts to the Republican Party's wounded Caesar. But Byrd knew that the line between political opportunity and calamity is a thin one that can turn on a headline or a perception. Ronald Reagan, whatever his personal or political weaknesses, remained a popular leader. The American people wanted the truth told, not exploited by opponents seeking political advantage.

Dole was under similar pressure from conservative Republicans. The President had broken an article of faith with them by dealing with a terrorist nation. But they were not about to allow what they conceded was an act of folly to undo the President's agenda or legacy.

Byrd and Dole reviewed their lists as coaches might scan their lineups. In athletics, height, weight, and speed are measured against the opponent's anticipated starting team. Reserves and substitutes are set aside for contingencies. But Byrd and Dole gave no indication of which members they were considering for their starting rosters. In the end, both leaders decided that experience and balance—philosophic and geographic—would be essential for a successful investigation.

GJM: *The telephone rang just as I was walking out the front door. As I walked back in to get it, I looked at the clock. It was ten minutes before eight in the morning. I hoped the call would be from Senator Byrd. I knew that he was going to announce that morning the six*

Democratic members of the Senate Committee. I had told him of my interest in serving on the Committee, and a lot of the speculation in the press included me. But there were plenty of other senators who were interested and qualified. Senator Byrd is a man who can keep a secret. Neither I nor any other senator—I was sure—knew what he would do. But I did know that it was now down to the wire. If this call wasn't from Byrd, I thought, I wouldn't be appointed.

"Hello?"

"George?"

"Yes."

"This is Robert Byrd."

He told me that he was going to appoint me to the Committee. He said he was influenced by my experience as a United States attorney and a federal judge. He said he had considered appointing me chairman of the Committee but had decided in favor of Dan Inouye. He was concerned that appointing me chairman might appear partisan, because I had just completed a two-year term as chairman of the Democratic Senatorial Campaign Committee. Although Inouye had held the same position, his term had occurred a long time ago.

I agreed with Byrd then, and still do. While I would have liked to be chairman, I recognized that it made sense to appoint Inouye. Had I been in Byrd's position, I would have done the same thing. Inouye had participated in the Watergate investigation. He is one of the most respected members of the Senate, with a reputation for fairness and lack of partisanship. He went on to justify Byrd's decision by doing a very good job in a difficult situation.

For myself, I was happy to be on the Committee. It was icing on the cake when Byrd told me I would be the second-ranking Democrat, after Inouye.

As I walked out the door, I knew I was starting a year of challenge and hard work, but I looked forward to it. As I drove to the Capitol, I thought that this appointment would change my life, for better or worse. It did.

Byrd named four other members to the Senate Committee:

• Sam Nunn, chairman of the Senate Armed Services Committee. Nunn is a conservative senator from Georgia who possesses a well-earned reputation as the Senate's leading expert on military affairs. Viewed as a possible presidential candidate, Nunn was also a supporter of Contra aid.

• Paul Sarbanes, a Rhodes scholar and liberal from Maryland. Sarbanes served on the House Judiciary Committee during the Nixon impeachment proceedings. A member of the Senate Foreign Relations Committee, he is highly regarded for possessing an incisive and analytic mind. Sarbanes opposed aid to the Contras.

• Howell Heflin, a conservative from Alabama and former chief justice of the Alabama Supreme Court. Chairman of the Senate Ethics Committee, he is widely respected for his integrity and fairness. Heflin supported the Contra-aid program.

• David Boren, a Rhodes scholar and former governor of Oklahoma. Boren is a Western conservative and is inclined to be generous in the support of presidential powers. He was also a strong supporter of the Contra-aid program.

Bob Dole wanted to appoint an essentially conservative membership but not one weighted with ideological extremists. Dole turned to perhaps the most capable, experienced trial lawyer in the Senate—Warren Rudman. Highly intelligent, tough-minded, and independent, Rudman is a veteran of the Korean War, having served in combat on Pork Chop Hill. He possesses two outstanding qualities—he is absolutely fair and absolutely fearless. Some of his colleagues have dubbed him (affectionately, we hasten to add) "Sledgehammer." During his first term, Rudman denounced a conservative-inspired effort to free the medical profession from the regulatory restraints of the Federal Trade Commission. "The medical profession," Rudman thundered during the Senate debate, "is trying to perform a frontal lobotomy on the American people." Rudman's speech was a key factor in helping to defeat the measure. Liberals were surprised and pleased by Rudman's vigorous opposition to a conservative cause. Shortly thereafter, however, a liberal public-interest group criticized Rudman (who had refused to accept political-action-committee contributions) for not leading the effort to reform the financing of political campaigns. Rudman's response was swift and unambiguous. He called the head of the organization, blasted him for his organization's "cheap-shot" tactics, and advised him that the members of the group were no longer welcome in his Senate office. "Sledgehammer," a hard, heavy blunt instrument that hurts when it hits you, was well earned.

Dole knew that Rudman would not tolerate a partisan attack upon President Reagan, but neither would he condone a "whitewash." George Bush supporters were quick to note that Dole, also a candidate for president, liked Rudman's residency as much as his talent. New Hampshire was going to be important in 1988, and Dole's appointment of Rudman would make him some useful friends in the state.

In addition to Rudman, Dole named:

• James McClure, a conservative from Idaho. McClure serves as chairman of the Steering Committee, a group of conservative Republican senators who periodically meet with President Reagan to review the conservative agenda. As a general rule, Steering Committee members are among the President's strongest supporters. McClure favored aid to the Contras.
• Orrin Hatch, a conservative senator from Utah, who is a senior member of the Judiciary Committee and a member of the Intelligence Committee. Hatch was a strong supporter of Contra aid.
• Paul Trible, a young conservative from Virginia who had been an assistant U.S. attorney before serving two terms in the House of Representatives. Trible also supported aid to the Contras.

WSC: *I had indicated to Bob Dole a conditional interest in serving on the Committee. I had mixed emotions about wanting to serve. I was soon to become the vice chairman of the Senate Intelligence Committee, a position I knew would consume an extraordinary amount of time. The Intelligence Committee was in the process of conducting a preliminary inquiry into the Iran-Contra affair. The documentary and testimonial evidence we had already discovered during closed sessions was disturbing. It was clear that White House officials had lied to and misled Congress, and that the Intelligence Committee was not being told the complete truth. Memories were too conveniently faulty. Evidence was incomplete or missing. The Committee had elicited many contradictions and inconsistencies from key administration officials. A number of those subpoenaed to appear before the Committee invoked their Fifth Amendment privilege against self-incrimination. I could detect the odor of a cover-up. I had witnessed one before—Watergate.*

As a freshman member of the House of Representatives in the 92nd Congress, I had served on the House Judiciary Committee. After listening to all of the evidence, I had helped draft several articles of impeachment against Richard Nixon. But it was that very experience that caused me to hesitate in expressing an interest in serving on the Select Committee.

My career in politics had changed dramatically as a result of the impeachment hearings. Most of the change had been positive, but many party loyalists made it clear at the time that I was not considered a "team player" and could not expect the Republican Party to forget either my words or my deeds. My future in higher national office, according to them, would be limited.

While I believed that my participation in the Intelligence Committee hearings made me better prepared than many other members to conduct a comprehensive search for the truth, I also knew that I would once again—even though I had supported aid to the Contras—be charged with "party disloyalty" if I criticized the administration's actions.

Rumors were floated daily about who the Democratic members on the Select Committee might be. My colleague George Mitchell was frequently mentioned as a candidate. Ordinarily his appointment would have reduced my chances for service on the Committee, since it is rare to have two senators from the same state serve on the same committee.

David Boren (D-Oklahoma) was also a prime candidate. Boren was about to become chairman of the Senate Intelligence Committee. I indicated to Bob Dole that if the new chairman of the Intelligence Committee was to be named, I thought it would be appropriate for the vice chairman to serve as well. Dole obviously agreed on the need for symmetry.

Although the Committee had no formal authority until the Congress reconvened in January, Inouye made a decision in December that would affect every aspect of the Committee's performance and image. Within days of his own appointment, he announced his intention to designate Senator Rudman as vice chairman of the Committee. Under the rules of the Senate, a committee is under the control and direction of the chairman, almost always the member of the majority party with the most seniority. In the chairman's absence, his authority is assumed by the next senior member of the majority. With the exception of the Intelligence Committee, there is no vice chairman. The minority-party members, the most senior of whom is designated simply as the "ranking minority member," have no leadership role on the committee. The ranking member of the minority party does not share in setting the agenda for the Committee, defining the scope of a hearing, or selecting witnesses. The chairman may seek the ranking member's advice, but is free to disregard it.

Inouye's designation of Rudman as vice chairman made him the presiding officer in the event that Inouye was voting on the Senate floor, attending to other Senate business, or otherwise absent. Of much more significance, it conveyed to the Republican members a signal that they would be full partners in the Committee's operations. This decision established an attitude of bipartisanship that dominated the Senate Committee and distinguished it from that of the House throughout the proceedings. Inouye reinforced his commitment to a nonpartisan approach to the hearings by creating a "unitary" staff. Inouye's experience on the Watergate Committee persuaded him that staffs divided along party lines, who work at cross-purposes in separate office space, could only serve to polarize the Committee itself. Senate counsel and staff members would share the same working space (ninth floor of the Hart Senate Office Building) and serve the Committee, not the Democratic majority or the Republican minority.

Inouye also moved quickly to select someone for the all-important position of counsel to the Committee. He assigned Senators Mitchell and Heflin the specific task of locating and hiring "the best possible person for the job."

From mid-December through January the search was conducted, with the help of Paul Sarbanes, a member of the Committee, and Senator Tom Eagleton, a Missouri Democrat who had earlier served as that state's attorney general.

The Committee was looking for a lawyer skilled in investigation, with substantial courtroom experience; a person whose integrity was beyond challenge; someone with a knowledge of politics and political affairs, but not identified as a partisan political figure; and, finally, someone who could work with eleven senators amid the tumult and controversy that was certain to accompany this investigation.

Several hundred persons were considered, some applying on their own, others through prominent sponsors—senators, governors, ambassadors.

Prominent lawyers—among them former Secretary of State Cyrus Vance, former Attorneys General Griffin Bell and Benjamin Civiletti, Edward Bennett Williams, former Secretary of Defense Clark Clifford, former Secretary of Health, Education and Welfare Joseph Califano—made recommendations.

Each of the twelve finalists was invited to a private meeting with the subcommittee in the Russell Senate Office Building. The first was Arthur Lawrence Liman, a fifty-four-year-old lawyer described by *The Washington Post* as "perhaps the top trial lawyer in New York—and one of the best securities and white-collar crime lawyers in the country." A graduate of Harvard College and Yale Law School, where he finished first in his class, Liman has had a distinguished career, rising to become a senior partner at the New York law firm of Paul, Weiss, Rifkind, Wharton & Garrison, one of the largest and most respected firms in the country.

At first glance, he fit the role perfectly: a solid legal background, extensive courtroom experience both as a prosecutor and a defense attorney, and a towering legal reputation. His penetrating intelligence was apparent after just a few minutes of discussion. And he left no doubt that he wanted the job.

As the interviews continued, Liman became the standard against which others were measured. All were distinguished, highly successful lawyers. But none had Liman's unique combination of attributes, including the critical experience of conducting public investigations. Liman had served as counsel to the state commission that investigated the Attica prison riots in New York in 1971. In 1985 he supervised the investigation of charges that the New York City Medical Examiner's office had covered up police brutality. In both cases, Liman had favorably impressed observers with his investigative skill and his ability to manage a complex case under intense public scrutiny.

After more than a month of search and consideration, Liman was recommended to Inouye and Rudman. He had passed one of the most important job interviews of his career.[4] The senators thought they had scrutinized every relevant factor in his personal and professional background.

No one ever paused to consider how he would look or project on television.

A House Divided

On March 18, 1986, Senators Daniel Inouye and Warren Rudman and Congressmen Lee Hamilton and Dick Cheney, the House Committee's chairman and ranking Republican member, announced that the House and Senate Select Committees formed to investigate the Iran-Contra affair had agreed to hold joint hearings. To the general public, this was not a particularly earthshaking event. The decision to conduct hearings as a joint committee, consisting of eleven senators and fifteen representatives, was, however, virtually unprecedented. It presented opportunities and limitations of major proportions.

Less than five hundred feet separate the chambers of the legislative bodies in the United States Congress. But whereas there are surface similarities between the House and the Senate, between representatives and senators, it is only a modest exaggeration to say that the differences are as deep-seated as those that divide the Sunni Muslims from the Shiites.

In the legislative process, the House and the Senate are coequal bodies, with roughly equivalent roles. The rate of pay is the same for members of each body, each individual is technically called a "member of Congress," and each house contributes approximately the same amount to the total legislative output. The House may have an edge in tax matters, because of its constitutional right to initiate all revenue-raising measures; conversely, the Senate's role in foreign affairs is larger because of its treaty ratification and confirmation powers, among others.

It is in the way in which business is conducted in each chamber—and the relative power resting with individual members—that the chasm lies. Proceedings on the House floor are highly regimented, although a casual observer leaning over the visitor's-gallery rail would have difficulty seeing that.

House business is governed by the rigid hand of the Rules Committee, which determines how long a bill can be debated, how many amendments will be allowed, and, in many cases, how successful the bill will be. Measures that bypass the Rules Committee's gauntlet can make their way to the floor, but usually receive abbreviated and unfavorable consideration. A schedule is set and kept.

The rigidity means that an individual member, particularly a new one, may find it difficult to influence the floor action—practically impossible if he is in the minority party. So the average House member, although a celebrity in his home district, receives little notice in Washington or in the nation. He or she is rarely consulted by the national media and has few chances to influence national issues. Service on the Iran-Contra Committee, however, presented an unusual opportunity—many minutes in the limelight before what was hoped would be a large television audience.

In contrast to the House, the Senate looks like a staid debating society. Dark-suited solons raise their voices only occasionally and invariably refer to their adversaries in debate as "my distinguished colleague." The senators sit at individually assigned desks, rather than in randomly selected chairs, as do members of the House. While their attention to the speakers who drone on at astonishing length may not be rapt, it is at least polite. The Senate is a genteel club.

But although decorum may be the outward appearance, the Senate in reality is a chaotic arena where a wily member can prevent almost anything from occurring if he has a strong voice, an intimate knowledge of the parliamentary rules, and unlimited patience. Things move slowly in the Senate, and there is little structure or schedule. Amendments need not be printed in the previous day's *Congressional Record*, as is required in the House, and do not have to be related to the substance of the legislation to which they are attached.

There is another important difference between the bodies. Politics in the House tend to be far more partisan than in the Senate. House Democrats have held a significant majority for most of the past thirty years. They see little benefit in sharing power with Republicans. Virtually every legislative tactic is designed to freeze their political opponents into the role of a sniping, retrogressive, negative-minded, and permanent minority. With absolute control, the Democrats at times succumb to the arrogance of power. Republicans in the House are rarely consulted and barely considered. Republicans have developed a hostility and suspicion bordering on paranoia. Unable to participate in the process, some of them seek only to disrupt it.

In recent years, House Republicans have adopted the tactics of guerrilla warfare. Exploiting the televised coverage of their proceedings, they swoop in on highly emotional issues—abortion, taxes, prayer in public schools, aid to freedom fighters—and attempt to paint Democrats as inveterate big spenders who spinelessly squander our wealth and heritage. It is rare that they win the vote, but they always believe they're beginning to carry the day.

Partisanship is not as flagrant or frequent in the Senate. Significant legislation is usually co-authored by a Republican and a Democrat. Cooperation may be more the product of necessity than statesmanship. Being in the majority guarantees the power to set the legislative agenda, but not the ability to secure the passage of the legislation. Ordinarily, senators are not constrained by time limitations in debating legislation. A senator must give his consent to having a limit set to his right to speak in the Senate. The only other way to limit debate is for the Senate to vote to invoke "cloture," which is not easily achieved or even effective when it is invoked.[5] A handful of determined Senators can sink any measure in parliamentary and verbal concrete. Thus deference and conciliation are indispensable to legislative accomplishment.

If such a vast gulf divides the House and Senate, and such patent rivalries split House Republicans and Democrats, why did either body agree to hold joint hearings, particularly where twenty-six members would be involved? When the Committees were created—with the appointment of fifteen members to the House Committee and eleven to the Senate—it was assumed that they would conduct separate investigations. But as the two committees began to organize and plan their activities, the problems of separate investigations became increasingly apparent. To consider just the most obvious: Would the Committees hold public hearings at the same time, thus competing directly with each other? Which Committee would get which witness first? Would each witness be called before both Committees, or would the list of witnesses be divided between Committees? If they were divided, on what basis would the division be made?

These and a host of other questions soon made it clear—as it should have been from the outset—that the problems of a joint investigation were fewer and more manageable than the problems of separate investigations. Moreover, we concluded that separate investigations would be extremely unpopular with the public. The spectacle of having witness after witness called first to the Senate, then to the House (or the reverse), would have been seen as evidentiary redundance and overkill. The Watergate investigation lasted for seventeen months. During that time, the House of Representatives resisted attempting to compete with the Senate's investigation. At the conclusion of the Senate's hearings, the House Judiciary Committee began a seven-month inquiry to determine whether articles of impeachment should be brought against Richard Nixon. Virtually the same witnesses who had testified before the Senate Watergate Committee testified before the House Judiciary Committee. But their testimony was taken in executive sessions, behind closed doors, until the Judiciary Committee began to debate openly the articles of impeachment.

In the Iran-Contra affair, the length of the investigation would have doubled, while the information elicited would have remained essentially the same. The White House, in turn, would have labeled the hearings the political equivalent of a witch hunt, rather than a serious search for the truth. Editorials and commentaries would have condemned each Committee as egotistical and exploitive.

And so the decision for joint hearings was made and Congress was commended for its exercise in statesmanship. Unfortunately, by the time a consensus developed in both Committees in favor of a joint hearing, there were twenty-six individuals committed and determined to serve on the Committee. Who would volunteer to drop from the Committee? What criteria would the leadership use in rescinding appointments? The dictates of investigative efficiency could not outweigh the political realities. Thus the awkward, repetitious, time-consuming mechanism of a twenty-six-member investigating Committee was created.

The surface waters appeared calm and there seemed to be an unusual camaraderie. Most of us knew, however, that beneath the smooth exterior lurked a powerful, swirling undertow that would pull the hearings in a predictable and irresistible direction.

Deadline Blues
and Designated Hitters

One of the more serious criticisms leveled against the Committee was of its decision to complete its investigation and file a report by August 1, 1987.[6] At the time, the setting of a deadline for the completion of the Committee's work seemed a reasonable and responsible compromise between Democratic members in both the House of Representatives and the Senate, who wanted no time limitations placed upon the Committee, and Republican members, who wanted the hearings completed within two or three months. It escaped no one's attention that an investigation that spilled into 1988 could only help keep Republicans on the defensive during an election year. Both Inouye and Hamilton recommended rejecting the opportunity to prolong and thereby exploit President Reagan's difficulties, determining that ten months would provide time enough to uncover any wrongdoing.[7]

Almost immediately after the Committee's leaders publicly announced the time frame of our investigation, we began to experience unanticipated problems, the most immediate being an inability to acquire security clearances quickly for members of the staff. By the first of March, many staffers were still not cleared and therefore were unable to read or investigate classified matters, leaving Arthur Liman and his key associates with the responsibility for reviewing thousands of documents with very little assistance. The target date for the beginning of the public hearings began to slip.

The delay in granting clearances added irony to frustration. The

30

Tower Report contained extensive portions of many documents that had been declassified by the White House. Our staff found itself in the curious position of being able to read the Tower Report and review the documents contained in it while being barred from reading the very same documents located in a large bank-type vault in our Committee's room on the ninth floor of the Hart Senate Office Building!

We soon recognized the complexity of the issues involved in the structure, mechanics, and financing arrangements of the Iran and Contra programs—and the difficulty that we would have in acquiring needed information. We knew that Swiss authorities, for example, probably would not release the Albert Hakim and Richard Secord bank records and that Israel would be reluctant to provide a full accounting of its activities in the venture.

The existence of a firm deadline for the completion of the hearings demanded that Arthur Liman and the Committee keep the investigation focused on the central questions, events, and characters of the affair. As a result, many side issues raised in the media did not receive the full attention of the Committee.

The time limitations and lack of resources precluded the Committee from giving more than perfunctory treatment to the existence of the "off-the-shelf" covert capability revealed by North. The Committee assumed that the House and Senate Intelligence Committees would explore the activities more fully.

Finally, the Committee's deadline provided a convenient stratagem for those who were determined not to cooperate. Bureaucrats in some agencies appeared to be attempting to thwart the investigative process by delivering documents at an extraordinarily slow pace. But, perhaps most importantly, the deadline provided critical leverage for the attorneys of witnesses in dealing with the Committee on whether their clients would appear without immunity and when in the process they might be called. North and his attorney, as we will see, were able to use the deadline to great advantage.

———

Senator Inouye, again drawing on his experience from the Senate Watergate hearings, knew that junior members of an investigatory committee are called upon last, when few questions remain to be asked and even fewer observations to be made—all of which reinforces their inferior status. He suggested that the responsibility for interrogating witnesses be divided among the members. "Designated hitters" (two Republicans and two Democrats—one each from each house) would be given one hour each to question a "major" witness. Other members would be allotted either ten or fifteen minutes. For "minor" witnesses, designated hitters would have fifteen minutes, the others five. This, in Inouye's words, would provide an equal opportunity in the sunlight.

Inouye and Rudman decided who would be the designated hitters for the list of witnesses. They decided to pair the Senate Committee members so that the talents, methods, and manners of each would provide a philosophical balance and distinctive approach in our search for the facts. Because of the odd number of members, this "team approach" required some flexibility. But basically the teams were as follows:

Inouye and Rudman
Mitchell and Trible
Sarbanes and Hatch
Heflin and Cohen
Boren or Nunn and McClure

Inouye and Rudman also attempted to align designated hitters with witnesses according to the members' expertise. For example, the chairman and vice chairman of the Intelligence Committee, Boren and Cohen, were a logical matchup for CIA witnesses or those witnesses who frequently testified before the Intelligence Committee, such as Elliott Abrams. A former U.S. attorney and federal district judge, Mitchell was assigned to be the designated hitter for North.

The designated-hitter rule initially accounted for the perceived inequitable distribution of time. During the early weeks of the hearings, for example, some members were designated hitters for several witnesses, while others had only five minutes to question each witness. Later, however, those members who appeared to have been slighted earlier were far more active in the examination of witnesses. One Oliver North or John Poindexter was the equivalent of four "nonmajor" witnesses.

The Senate members discovered later that a price had to be paid for adopting the designated-hitter rule.

Senate members wanted opening statements confined to the chairman and vice chairman of the Senate Committee and the chairman and ranking Republican of the House Committee. This in itself, it was argued, would consume an hour of prime time during which goals and theories and timetables could be outlined to the public. We could then proceed with the first witness and demonstrate that we intended to move with determination and dispatch.

But House members objected. They had agreed to the new designated-hitter rule proposed by Senator Inouye, but they were not going to allow the Committee leadership to excise their vocal cords.

Each House member demanded the right to give an opening five-minute statement. This set off the lemming instinct in all of us. If one member rushed before the television cameras, the others had to follow or risk looking wordless or useless.

What can possibly be said in five minutes that the chairman and vice chairman could not say in fifteen? What point did they insist on trying to prove?

First, as mentioned, congressmen individually do not receive the national attention or recognition of Senators; there are simply too many of them. The investigation would provide most with an opportunity that could prove the touchstone of their careers. They wanted to establish their identities at the outset.

Second, and more important, the House Republican members were comfortable with Representative Dick Cheney articulating their collective views, but they did not particularly like what they were hearing from Senator Rudman, the vice chairman of the Senate Committee. Rudman, while a strong supporter of aid to the Contras, made it clear in his public statements that he was going to serve as an investigator during these hearings, not as an apologist for the White House. For some House members, Rudman was seen as too much the prosecutor. His anticipated opening statement, when added to those of Inouye and Hamilton, would result in the score of Democrats, three; Republicans, one. So the first day of our hearings would be baptized with a long march of words.

Prosecutors
or Potted Plants?

One of the early concerns of the Committee was to define the roles of our lawyers. Were they to be auditors running down columns of corporate books, trying to spill out the contents of Swiss bank accounts? Behind-the-scenes archaeologists, picking through tons of factual rubble in search of buried truths? Courtroom interrogators, crossing swords and words with reluctant or immunized witnesses?

Practical necessity dictated that the lawyers be all of the above. The information being assembled was voluminous—more than one million pages of documents had to be reviewed—and field investigations had to be conducted with several witnesses interviewed abroad. Organizing the information intelligently would take months.[8]

Most of the senators and congressmen on the Committee had prior experience in the preparation of criminal or civil litigation. As former trial lawyers, we knew that a mastery of the details of a case was the key to its successful presentation. Exhaustive preparation was indispensable to an effective examination or cross-examination of witnesses. But the fact remained that we were already overburdened with the work of our regular committee assignments. Our days were interrupted by roll-call votes on both important and trivial matters. Weekends were devoted to home-state duties. We could rarely attend, much less conduct, pre-hearing depositions of witnesses. It was also clear to all of us that a few hours of evening work would be totally insufficient to digest the complex set of facts and witnesses, particularly since we were working against our own preset clock. And so we determined that, at least during the initial phases of our hearings, counsel would conduct most of the interrogation.

From the beginning, this did not sit comfortably with some members, who objected to being relegated to a secondary role. We were consulted on issues such as granting immunity to witnesses or deciding whether to proceed with the taking of testimony from Admiral Poindexter or Colonel North before the independent counsel could assemble his facts. But, unless they were the "designated hitters," most members had little idea of what each day's hearings were designed to or would produce. A large and intimidating black briefing book was delivered to our assigned desks each morning. Although most members would prepare questions in the evening for the next day's witness, there was no assurance that one member's area of questioning would not be covered by another before him. We were forced to follow the bouncing ball of interrogation for several hours and then be called upon to ask penetrating, insightful, and nonrepetitive questions. It was almost the equivalent of being handed a playbook on the day of an important televised football game and then being called upon to execute a rush, end run, or pass without ever having attended a practice session.

The underlying resentment and frustrations grew throughout the proceedings, periodically erupting as members perceived our respective counsels as being too timid or too tough, too aggressive or too accommodating.

It became apparent that the public was judging us on the basis of exchanges between our attorneys and the witnesses. We chafed at the condemnation by association. After all, weren't we more than potted plants adorning an unceremonious inquisition?

Up the
White House Ladder

On December 12, 1986, former Federal Judge Lawrence Walsh was appointed to serve as independent counsel[9] for the purpose of determining whether members of the Reagan administration had engaged in violations of our criminal statutes in the sale of weapons to Iran and the raising of funds and acquisition of weapons for the Contras. The tensions between the roles of the independent counsel and the Committee became evident almost immediately.

One of the most effective tools available to prosecutors is the power to confer immunity. Put simply, this is the power to exempt someone from criminal prosecution in exchange for his or her cooperation in a criminal investigation.

For centuries it has been a fundamental principle of English and American law that a person can be required to give evidence in criminal cases. The requirement is indispensable if those who have committed crimes are to be prosecuted and punished.

An exception to that principle is the privilege against self-incrimination, which is set forth in the Fifth Amendment to the Constitution. It provides in part that "No person . . . shall be compelled in any criminal case to be a witness against himself. . . ." The privilege is designed to prevent a person from being convicted of and punished for a crime based on his own compelled testimony. If the possibility of conviction and punishment is removed, then the underlying purpose of the protection no longer exists.

Thus a person can be compelled to testify if the prosecutor first promises not to prosecute and punish him. That is immunity. It is a concept as old as the privilege against self-incrimination. The prosecutor "immunizes" the person, promising in advance not to punish him, even if he admits to having committed a crime.

Immunity is frequently necessary in cases where the only persons with knowledge of a crime, capable of giving testimony about it, are those implicated in the crime. It is commonly granted to minor participants in a crime as a way of getting at the major participants; in the terms of the criminal law, it's "moving up the ladder," getting the testimony of those on the lower rungs to reach those at the top.

When and against whom to use the power of immunity is one of the important decisions made by prosecutors. Because it is unfair to exempt from criminal prosecution someone who has in fact committed a crime—an unfairness that seems to most citizens particularly unjustified if the immunized person's testimony or cooperation is limited in scope and importance—there has developed in the law a more limited form of immunity. Rather than permitting a person to avoid prosecution entirely by giving testimony, limited immunity merely prohibits a prosecutor from using the testimony itself in a subsequent prosecution. This has come to be known as "use" immunity: the prosecutor promises in advance not to use the testimony if the person is later charged with a crime, in exchange for which the person is compelled to testify.

There are important additional conditions. If a later criminal action is brought against the person, the prosecutor is barred from using not only the compelled testimony, but also any evidence derived from that testimony. And at any later trial the prosecutor must prove that the evidence introduced was obtained independently of the compelled testimony.

Thus "use" immunity permits the prosecutor to obtain all relevant evidence in a criminal case, without violating the constitutional right against self-incrimination of the person whose testimony is compelled.

The law permits committees of Congress to confer "use" immunity to compel witnesses to testify at congressional hearings.

Complications arise when the subject matter of a congressional investigation also involves a possible criminal action. That is because there is a continuing tension between the objectives of the prosecutor, conviction and punishment of those who commit crimes, and the objectives of congressional committees, obtaining information necessary to sound legislating and exposing wrongdoing by government officials.

That tension flared into open conflict in the Iran-Contra affair. The mandate of the independent counsel, Judge Walsh, was constrained by subject matter but not by time. He had no deadline, but his scope of inquiry was narrow: to determine whether there were sufficient grounds to bring criminal charges against any of the participants.

By contrast, the mandate of the Committee was constrained by time but not by subject matter. The Committee had agreed to complete its investigation, conduct public hearings, and write and file a report, all by October 30, 1987, less than ten months after it was created. But the Committee's inquiry could and did go far beyond the question of whether a crime had been committed. It looked into the broader questions of how and why certain decisions were made and policies adopted, and who was responsible.

Over the occasional objections of the independent counsel, the Committee conferred "use" immunity on twenty-one witnesses. Most were lower participants on the ladder whom the independent counsel himself granted immunity.

But conflict occurred when the Committee debated whether it should confer "use" immunity on North and Poindexter, by all accounts the "major" participants in the affair. Grants of immunity to them made no sense in an exclusively criminal case. If everyone involved was immunized—both those lower on the ladder and those at the top—the perpetrators would not be punished for any possible crime.

But the objectives of a congressional investigation differ from those of a criminal investigation, and it is not possible for Congress to bring the full story to the public without using immunity if the central figures refuse to testify on Fifth Amendment grounds. That is what the central figures in this case did. North and Poindexter invoked their Fifth Amendment right and refused to testify, before either the independent counsel or the Iran-Contra Committee, on the ground that their testimony might incriminate them.

On March 11, 1987, Judge Walsh made his first trip to Capitol Hill to visit the Senate Committee.

Arthur Liman had warned the Committee that Walsh would ask us not to grant immunity to North or Poindexter. Although none of the members appeared disposed to accept such a request, we felt an obligation to listen to and consider Walsh's arguments. A tall man of patrician bearing and formidable legal reputation, Walsh did not make a persuasive case. He surprised most members by appearing hesitant in his advocacy. He had not yet separated himself from his law practice and had been working on the Iran-Contra investigation on a part-time basis. We were aware of the rules of criminal procedure that would require him to demonstrate that none of the evidence he might present against an individual we had immunized came directly or indirectly from that individual's testimony before us. It is a heavy burden for a prosecutor to bear, but not an impossible one. Walsh and his staff would have to gather information, place it under seal, and be prepared to satisfy a federal trial court that Walsh had acquired the information either prior to or independently of any immunized testimony given to our Committee.

Most members remained silent during Walsh's presentation. Several chose to explain that Congress's responsibility to investigate the affair was as compelling as that of the independent counsel; that we were willing to cooperate and find a middle course, but we could not abdicate our responsibility by failing to compel the testimony of both North and Poindexter.

Several reasons dictated this response. First, many members were not persuaded that Walsh would move quickly in establishing proof that our criminal laws had been violated. Judge Walsh had no idea how long it might take for him and his staff to conclude that there was a basis to indict any of the key people involved in the scandal. Such a determination might not occur until long after our Committee's ten-month life had expired.

Second, assuming sufficient evidence existed to justify indicting North and Poindexter, among others, Walsh could give no guarantee that the American people would ever hear from the two individuals who knew most about what role President Reagan had played in the Iran weapons sale and Contra-aid programs. The rules of evidence governing a criminal trial are stringent. The independent counsel must carry his burden of proof beyond a reasonable doubt. Moreover, a defendant has a constitutional right not to take the witness stand to answer charges brought against him. Finally, even assuming indictments were to be obtained, there was no guarantee a trial would ever occur.

For these reasons, the Committee simply could not forgo testimony from North and Poindexter if it was to carry out its mandate to investigate fully President Reagan's role in or knowledge about events that were paralyzing his administration—to fulfill its constitutional functions of oversight and the providing of information to the public.

We also knew that there were risks involved in rejecting Judge Walsh's request. In the event we proceeded to compel the testimony of North and Poindexter and the independent counsel either could not demonstrate that his evidence was acquired prior to or independently from the congressional testimony, or if those indicted were acquitted by the presiding judge or convened jury, Congress would become the likely scapegoat. We eventually achieved a compromise that permitted us to conduct our investigation while not unduly compromising that of Judge Walsh.

With little dissent (only Congressman Jack Brooks publicly opposed conferring immunity on North), the Committee, after several more meetings, voted to confer "use" immunity on both North and Poindexter. We agreed to defer the taking of a private deposition from Poindexter until early May (and from North until mid-June) and then limit access to that testimony to a small number of Committee members and staff. This restricted access was designed to minimize the possibility of leaks to the public or communication with the independent counsel. Furthermore, the Committee agreed not to compel any public testimony by North or Poindexter until after June 30.

The Committee believed we were acting wisely and fairly—allowing the independent counsel several months to gather his evidence while preserving our right to acquire the information central to our investigation. It was a fair proposal. But, as will be discussed in a later chapter, it did not prove to be a wise one.[10]

Déjà Vu—
All Over Again?

A s the Committee developed its plans for the hearings and pondered the task ahead, the question lingered in all our minds: What effect would this investigation ultimately have upon the President, and, indeed, upon the presidency itself? Would it produce evidence of presidential malfeasance or duplicity? Where was this train taking us?

The headlines spoke relentlessly of Watergate—a code word for presidential mischiefs and maladies that drove Richard Nixon from office. Was it, in Yogi Berra's famous words, *"Déjà vu,* all over again"?

There were similarities to be found in the Watergate experience, some superficial, others substantive.

The Watergate scandal was the product, in part, of an unpopular war that was being waged in Southeast Asia. Daniel Ellsberg had leaked to *The New York Times* classified documents known as the *Pentagon Papers.* Classified information and confidential discussions were regularly being leaked to members of the press. Paranoia had seized the hearts and minds of policymakers in the White House. Richard Nixon authorized: the creation of an internal unit ("plumbers") to plug the leaks springing in the White House; phones to be wiretapped; a political-enemies list to be maintained and utilized by the Internal Revenue Service to harass and intimidate those on the list; secret bombing missions in Cambodia. A plan to burglarize the Democratic Party's headquarters in Washington produced a conspiracy among presidential subordinates and advisers to cover up the attempted break-in. The President suborned perjury. White House officials, with President Nixon's knowledge and acquiescence, authorized the payment of hush money to purchase the silence of the Watergate burglars. The President obstructed justice, offered false and misleading statements as explanations, and resisted releasing tape recordings (one containing an eighteen-and-a-half-minute gap) of White House conversations. John Dean revealed to the Senate Watergate Committee that the White House plan for dealing with Congress was to "take a public posture of full cooperation, but privately . . . attempt to restrain the investigation and make it as difficult as possible to get information and witnesses. A behind-the-scenes media effort would be made to make the Senate inquiry appear very partisan. The ultimate goal would be to discredit the hearings and reduce their impact by attempting to show that the Democrats have engaged in the same type of activities."[11]

There was a war in the Iran-Contra scandal as well, one being fought in our hemisphere but not, at least directly, by Americans. President Reagan and his advisers were also paranoid about leaks. Admiral John Poindexter helped draw a circle of secrecy tightly around a small group of men in the White House in order to preclude any notice to key members of Congress about our dealings with Iran or our financial efforts in behalf of the Nicaraguan Contras. Two Canadian businessmen who had advanced money for the Iranian arms sales threatened Director Casey by demanding the repayment of $10 million as the price of their silence. The threat was conveyed through Roy Furmark, a friend of Casey's and a business associate of Saudi Arabian businessman Adnan Khashoggi.

When the story of the arms deal with Iran and the funding of the Contras by private citizens and foreign governments broke in the press, an attempt was made by the White House staff to construct false chronologies. Official documents were altered, shredded, or removed from the White House. A cover-up was undertaken.

But there were major differences in the scandals, and none more significant than the character of the presidents involved. Richard Nixon was dark, defiant, and uncooperative. He fired Special Prosecutor Archibald Cox, thereby precipitating the resignation of Attorney General Elliot Richardson and his Deputy William Ruckelshaus. He offered edited transcripts of White House conversations and what were cynically described as "modified, limited handouts" as explanations. He invoked executive privilege and urged his advisers and subordinates to perjure themselves before Congress.

By contrast, Ronald Reagan confessed ignorance and offered openness. He urged his officials to tell the truth, produced thousands of pages of documents, waived all claims of executive privilege, and allowed an examination of portions of his personal diary.

More than what he offered to the congressional Committees and the independent counsel investigating his administration was what he represented to the American people. In spite of what some would call his folly and others his failure, he remained an essentially genial and likable man. The American people had not fully recovered from the reverberations of Watergate. They were shocked and disappointed over the disclosure of the arms sale but not angry enough to want to consider removing the President from office. A foreign-policy mistake did not demand a political beheading. Although the American people will not tolerate a president's flouting the law, neither will they accept a punishment greater than the perceived transgression. "Perception" is a critical word.

In spite of some of the parallels to Watergate, Ronald Reagan's transgressions were never deemed to be impeachable offenses—"high crimes and misdemeanors."[12]

First, impeachment represents the most extreme sanction (short of execution or imprisonment) that a nation can impose upon its highest elected official for violating his oath of office. A seventeenth-century Lord Chancellor of England observed that the impeachment process was like "Goliath's sword, to be kept in the temple and not used but on great occasions." The selection of presidents occupies a unique position within our political system. It is the one act in which the entire country participates, and the result is binding upon all of the states for four years. The outcome is accepted. The occupant of that office stands as a symbol of our national unity and commitment. So, if the judgment of the people is to be reversed, if the majority will is to be undone, if that symbol is to be replaced through the action of elected representatives, then it must be for substantial offenses supported by facts, not by surmise.

During the impeachment inquiry of President Richard Nixon, the House Judiciary Committee made an exhaustive analysis of the phrase "high crimes and misdemeanors." Some members of the Committee argued that the phrase must be interpreted as meaning statutory crimes. The Judiciary Committee concluded, however, that the constitutional provision was designed to prevent the chief executive from engaging in the gross abuse of the tremendous power vested in his office, to protect the people against the subversion of the rule of law and of fundamental liberties no matter how silent or subtle that subversion might be.[13]

One constitutional scholar has noted, for example, that if the President of the United States were to refuse to appoint any member of the Catholic faith to a government position, there would be no violation of our criminal laws, but surely there would be a violation of the Constitution, which declares that there shall be no religious test for office.[14] The example is exaggerated, but it makes clear that the impeachment process involves an assessment of acts that strike at the very core of our constitutional and political system.

The sale of weapons to Iran constituted a foreign-policy error of major proportions, but did not appear to involve the President in violation of a criminal statute. There was no evidence that President Reagan knew about the diversion of profits from the arms sale to the Contras. Most Committee members doubted from the very beginning that Poindexter or North would contradict the President's often repeated declaration that he was unaware of the diversion scheme. Congressman Lee Hamilton stated during an interview on national television that if the President in fact had knowledge of the diversion, he might have committed an impeachable act. Hamilton's statement raised an important issue. Was knowledge of the diversion itself a serious breach of the President's constitutional responsibilities? Or would lying about having such knowledge have constituted an offense that would have warranted removing the President from office?

William F. Buckley, Jr., a conservative columnist and commentator, suggested, for example, that it would have been far preferable for President Reagan to have known of the diversion plan (from the beginning), have asked for and received a formal opinion from the Justice Department, and, once satisfied of the plan's legality, authorized it to proceed. In fact, Buckley urged the President to state that he would have approved the diversion had he been told and had the Justice Department said it was legal.[15] Had this occurred, it is doubtful that many members of Congress would have declared that the President's conduct constituted an impeachable offense—unless it could be shown that the Justice Department's opinion was a patent sham and known to be so.

What about soliciting and sending aid to the Contras, in violation of the Boland Amendments? First, even though Congress clearly intended to prohibit further U.S. military aid to the Contras, there was disagreement among Committee members as to whether Congress can constitutionally prohibit a president himself from soliciting other nations to assist in such a cause. But even if a president may solicit such assistance, it is unclear whether his subordinates may do so in the face of a legislative prohibition, particularly if such solicitations result in their receiving and controlling money that they then use for a purpose specifically barred by law.

The evidence concerning President Reagan's knowledge of the solicitation of assistance from foreign governments and private U.S. citizens was ambiguous and contradictory. Bud McFarlane, for example, took pains to persuade the Committee that at no time did anyone in the White House actually solicit funds for the Contras. North and Elliott Abrams would be called upon to outline the plight of the Contras to wealthy U.S. citizens, such as Ellen Garwood, William O'Boyle, and Joseph Coors, who were dedicated to stopping the cancer of communism. Then these individuals would be asked to meet with Carl R. "Spitz" Channell, a conservative fund-raiser, who would collect their checks and presumably help to send humanitarian and military assistance to the Contras.[16] This was what Senator Rudman referred to as the "old one-two punch."

With respect to foreign countries, White House officials maintained that the President had never "solicited" contributions from a foreign head of state. At most, he would indicate to a visiting head of state the nature of his foreign-policy concerns, specifically his desire to support the Contras. That such expressions of concern resulted in immediate financial assistance by that foreign leader was disingenuously treated as coincidental.

Once several Committee members publicly expressed doubt that Congress could prohibit the President from soliciting private or foreign assistance, the statements emanating from the White House shifted immediately. The President declared that, of course, he knew about the solicitations: "It was my idea in the first place." At the same time, the President stated he did not know any of the details of the fund-raising activities; nor did he know that any money solicited for charitable purposes was being used to purchase weapons.

The exact state of the President's knowledge about the fund-raising activities was never resolved. But even if the Committee had established that the President had been fully informed, it is doubtful that Congress would have considered that a "high crime and misdemeanor."

On more than one occasion during the course of our hearings, administration witnesses, along with several Committee members, charged that the confusion, secrecy, and deception surrounding the Contra-aid program was caused by Congress's vacillation in providing assistance from one fiscal year to another.

Since 1981 the White House had offered a variety of rationales for aid to the Contras: interdicting the flow of weapons from Nicaragua to El Salvador; harassing the Sandinistas to prevent them from consolidating power and exporting their revolution; forcing the Sandinistas to eliminate all foreign forces, reduce the size of their military, and democratize their political system. Congress had cast a skeptical eye at each rationale proffered by the administration. It suspected that the administration's true purpose was identical to that of the Contras—the overthrow of the Sandinista regime itself. Nevertheless, while yielding to domestic political pressure to discontinue assistance to the Contras, Congress was unwilling to bear responsibility for the loss of Central America to communist military and political forces. It hedged, offering aid in the form of bandages instead of bullets, terminating military assistance even as it, at one point, authorized the State Department to solicit other countries to provide funding for humanitarian purposes.

The administration seized upon every congressional gesture or ambiguity as a loophole through which it could drive armored trucks and personnel carriers. It failed to comply with the spirit if not the letter of the Boland Amendments, but the evasions were facilitated by Congress's unwillingness to terminate all forms of assistance.[17] Whereas Congress may be entitled to complain about the administration's misuse of the National Security Council (NSC) staff and improper solicitations of foreign assistance, it must also be willing to accept a measure of responsibility for providing the administration with opportunities to pursue such conduct over a period of several years. Before Congress can seriously contemplate filing a resolution of impeachment for presidential misconduct, it must come forward with clean hands, if not with a pure heart.[18]

In the final analysis, Watergate was essentially a domestic scandal—a presidential abuse of power that threatened the constitutional relationship between the governors and the governed. Had the White House plans gone undetected and unchecked, neutral government agencies could have been used as instruments to carry out personal or political vendettas. Citizens' liberties would have been endangered by those claiming allegiance to a higher duty. Wiretaps, mail openings, burglaries, unlawful surveillances, enemies lists, IRS harassment, all might have been rationalized in the name of protecting the national security.

By contrast, the Iran-Contra scandal was perceived as involving a conflict in the constitutional relationship between Congress and the Executive in the formulation of foreign policy and in our dealings with other nations. One could argue that the consequences of the Iran-Contra affair were more far-reaching than those involved in Watergate. And yet, precisely because the sale of weapons to Iran and the diversion of money to the Contras were *perceived* as misguided abuses of process rather than arrogant abuses of power, the central parallel to Watergate failed to take hold. Talk of Watergate or whispers of impeachment were dismissed as the wishful thinking of irresponsible partisans.

By the time the public learned of the scheme to create a self-sustaining covert capability that was to be funded by future arms sales to Iran, those allegedly responsible for the plan—North and Poindexter—had been removed from office. Moreover, it could not be demonstrated that President Reagan had ever known about or authorized the plan that was tantamount to the creation of a secret CIA.

And it was the foreknowledge that no amount of congressional huffing or media puffing was going to blow the White House down that removed the element of high drama from the proceedings.

Show Time

T elevision can be a cruel or a kind eye. Sincerity and verbal skill are indispensable to surviving its unblinking scrutiny, but even these qualities may not be sufficient.

Politicians have long known of the power of television. Indeed, today's campaigns revolve around the use of thirty- or sixty-second advertisements that trumpet the virtues of the incumbent or the challenger. Millions of dollars are raised and spent by consulting firms for the specific purpose of getting "our candidate's message across on television."

The key to a successful use of this pervasive medium is control. In carefully prepared campaign commercials, the candidate's consultants decide the best angle, mood, and message that are to be laminated onto film or videotape, edited and re-edited to project the very best that the candidate has to offer.

Once control passes to network television, however, the same candidate is at the not-so-tender mercies of television cameramen, reporters, and producers. An insightful statement or examination of a witness may fall on the editor's floor. An intense closeup may make an individual's face look like a moonscape. The absence of TelePrompTers or written notes can leave the inarticulate looking incompetent. An inappropriate smile, sneer, or verbal foul-up can spell political disaster.

Given this awareness of the power and pitfalls of television, it is pertinent to ask why the Committee agreed to allow the hearing

to be televised, and whether it considered the possible consequences of doing so to the investigatory process.

The answer to the first question is easy. The Senate Select
Committee on Intelligence and the Tower Board had held weeks
of secret hearings and then filed public reports. The origins of the
arms transfers to Iran seemed clear, but the evidence thereafter
was contradictory and incomplete. Key witnesses had refused to
testify. No evidence had been obtained on the origins or disposition
of the money still secreted in Swiss bank accounts. How had the
money been acquired? How much, if any, was diverted to the
Nicaraguan Contras? How much remained? To whom did it belong?

The American people insist that their elected officials account
for the power and discretion entrusted to them. A whiff of scandal
that the public's trust has been abused traditionally prompts a
demand for full public disclosure, even when it will prove embarrassing to the nation as well as to its officials. In this case, there
was more than the smell of moral grapeshot in the air. Although
the affair admittedly involved sensitive national-security matters,
a secret proceeding would not satisfy the need for answers to the
question of President Reagan's knowledge of or involvement in
the entire affair. Nor would it satisfy doubts about the nature of
the investigation. Had it been thorough? Had the questions been
the right ones? Were logical avenues pursued? Was it biased? Were
the witnesses believable? What was their demeanor?

There is virtually no way in which evidence acquired or testimony presented during closed sessions of such a large Committee
could be contained, even if closed sessions were desirable. Hundreds
of journalists would demand facts and opinions. Selective information would be leaked, or damaging speculative stories would
be written. The President would be buffeted on a daily basis by
partisan whispers, rumors, slanted or distorted stories. Heated
and bitter denials would follow. Rancor and recrimination had
already polluted the political atmosphere. More secrecy would

have turned it poisonous. There really was no realistic or politically desirable alternative to public hearings.

Once the decision was made to hold public hearings, it was not possible to exclude television cameras. Congress is not the legislative equivalent of a court. The public's right to know how and why its government has acted in a given fashion is paramount over other considerations, save national security and the rights of the individual accorded by the Constitution. Television provided the American people with the opportunity to see and judge the testimony of witnesses for themselves.

Did we adequately anticipate the consequences of television's impact upon the hearing process? Quite simply, the answer is no. The Committee and its staff focused on the substance of the investigation and considered only the logistical accommodation of television cameras, rather than the consequences of its coverage. No serious thought was devoted to how Arthur Liman's hair or John Nields's mannerisms would provoke viewers. Nor did we fully appreciate how television would dramatize the exchanges between members and witnesses, catching every nuance of expression and intonation, much of which escaped the participants. Little consideration was given to aesthetics or theatrics.

We delegated to the Architect of the Capitol the problem of how to accommodate twenty-six members of the Committee in the Russell Senate Office Building's majestic Caucus Room. It was obvious that the traditional flat-green baize-covered table used on so many historic occasions would not do. A linear seating arrangement would have stretched from the Caucus Room halfway to the Capitol. The answer was obvious: construct a two-tiered dais, a simple matter of marshaling lumber, carpenters, and money.

The workmanship was excellent. The dais had the appearance and durability of a permanent structure. Each member had an assigned seat from which he could see and be seen. Perfect.

What none of us noticed was that we had transformed the hearing room into a mini-coliseum and that we appeared as the equivalent of Roman potentates turning thumbs up or down on the stoic Christians who would be dragged before us to give testimony.

The American people love to love underdogs—even when those underdogs are not particularly likable. We were to be reminded of this trait on the opening day of the hearings.

There was a vague sense of anticipation on Capitol Hill as Chairman Inouye gaveled the hearings to order. But there was no electricity in the air, no thought of some impending revelation that would doom Ronald Reagan's presidency or send the nation careening into a leaderless void. The Senate Caucus Room, site of the hearings on the sinking of the *Titanic*, the Teapot Dome scandal, the Army-McCarthy hearings, and the Senate Watergate hearings, was stripped of its magnificence and rich luster in the eye-watering blaze of klieg lights. The thick Corinthian columns and classical chandeliers seemed violated by the presence of so many television cameras, cables, wires, and floodlights, like a statue of Athena spray-painted with graffiti and hung with gaudy baubles and bracelets.

Although the tone of Senator Inouye's voice was solemn, the Caucus Room had all the ambience of a crowded train station. Spectators, photographers, journalists, staff were all moving, walking, whispering, nudging, and joking nervously. A low-level cacophony provided a distracting sense of static, imperceptible to those watching on television.

Perhaps those in attendance believed that the story had already been told by the Tower Board or the Senate Intelligence Committee. Ronald Reagan produced all of his files and asked the Committee to tell him the facts. Whether he was being ingenious or disingenuous, the President convinced most people that he had nothing to hide. CIA Director Casey was seriously ill; Donald Regan, Admiral Poindexter, and Lieutenant Colonel North were all out of the White House. There would be no blood on the floor, just a serious search for the facts—hardly the stuff of melodrama.

And yet all of Washington was there. Beneath the smoldering cynicism of the press corps danced a small flame of anticipation that some unknown event or piece of evidence would blow the proceedings into a full-scale fire.

Journalists were looking for stars—or dark holes. Where are the Sam Ervins or the Howard Bakers? Give us a philosopher or a phrasemaker, they importuned during prehearing interviews. A Memorex imitation of John Dean would do. Or the menacing scowl of a G. Gordon Liddy. The lust for good theater would go unsatisfied, at least for several days.

For over two hours during the morning session of the first day, May 5, 1987, Committee members gave opening remarks. Many of the speeches struck redundant themes and were primarily for home-state consumption. Journalists jammed into reserved tables appeared to be stifling large yawns. Let's get on with it, was their message: Enough of the preliminaries; bring on the witnesses.

Actually, the two hours consumed by the members proved helpful in providing some insight into who they were and the manner in which they would perform. We had had a preliminary joint business meeting with the House Commmittee, held for the purpose of discussing the Committee's objectives and timetable, but also designed to establish a bond of fellowship among the members. The time was short, however, and the meeting amounted to little more than a photo-opportunity session in which we exchanged congratulatory backslaps and celebrated our act of statesmanship. The meeting had been adjourned without any of the senators having a real sense about the talents or intentions of the House members, or they about ours.

Senator Inouye revealed that he had reached certain conclusions:

The story is one . . . not of secret diplomacy which Congress has always accepted, but secret policy making which the Constitution has always rejected. It is a tale of working outside the system and of

utilizing irregular channels and private parties accountable to no one
on matters of national security while ignoring the Congress and even
the traditional agencies of the executive foreign policy making. . . . The story is not a pretty one. As it unfolds in these proceedings, the American people will have every right to ask, "How
could this have happened here? It should never have happened at
all."[19]

Senator Rudman, while outlining the spirit in which he believed
the hearings should proceed, charged that there was "sufficient
evidence to establish that this is an inexcusable fiasco of the first
order."

Representative Hamilton could pass for Jimmy Stewart with a
crew cut. Hamilton, a basketball star in high school and college,
had served as chairman of the House Intelligence Committee for
two years. He is a quiet, hardworking moderate who shuns headlines while seeking results. Yet questions had been raised whether
he would be tough enough to lead the investigation. His opening
remarks left little doubt that he had already reached some conclusions about what had occurred and intended to pursue the
hearings with a firm hand.

High officials did not ask the questions they should have asked. Activities were undertaken without authority. Checks and balances were
ignored. Important meetings occurred without adequate preparation.
Established procedures were circumvented. Accurate records were not
kept and legal questions were not addressed.[20]

Representative Cheney, the ranking Republican of the House
Committee, is an intelligent and articulate conservative from Wyoming. Though he is fond of wearing black cowboy boots, he
looks like an Eastern-educated intellectual who enjoys talking about
"the process of decisionmaking" in the White House. His past
service as White House chief of staff under President Ford gives
credibility to his insights. Cheney put the Committee on notice
that Congress also had a measure of blame to accept. "One important question to be asked is to what extent did the lack of a

clear-cut policy by the Congress contribute to the events we will be exploring in the weeks ahead."

Henry Hyde is a man of heroic proportions, with silver hair swept back from a large square face. He enjoys quoting from conservative texts as if from Scripture. Articulate and given to dramatic rhetorical flourishes, Hyde has a doctrinaire conservatism that is softened by his self-deprecating humor, making him a formidable and effective debater. And it was clear from his opening statement that he intended to debate rather than investigate.

Congressman Jim Courter, a conservative protégé of Congressman Jack Kemp, introduced a surprising attack upon the White House—but from the right flank. He boldly asserted that the White House had invited its misfortunes by failing to live up to its first principles: by selling arms to the Iranians and by consistently selling out its convictions to State Department appeasers. This scathing attack left it unclear whether Courter would play the role of White House ally or adversary.

Peter Rodino, the chairman of the House Judiciary Committee, is a small but large-hearted man, who talks as if his voice box is wrapped in strips of dry rawhide. He achieved wide acclaim for the manner in which he conducted the impeachment proceedings against President Nixon. As expected, he demonstrated that he would focus on the issue of the rule of law and the White House's failure to live up to its spirit, if not its letter.

Jack Brooks, chairman of the House Government Operations Committee and also a senior member of the Judiciary Committee, has the reputation of being as mean and tough as a junkyard dog. And he seems to enjoy it. Peering intently over a pair of black reading glasses, Brooks occasionally blows on the ash of his ever-present cigar, as if he were cooling the hot barrel of a six-shooter. There was no ambiguity in his words or intentions. Describing administration officials, he said: "When they couldn't justify their policies publicly, they simply hid their activities from the American people, from the Congress, even from key officials within their own administration. . . . When they couldn't defend their actions with truth, they simply lied—to us and to each other."

We had not conferred on what we would say that morning, but our words struck the same theme:

MITCHELL: These hearings will address important questions for our democracy: the need for high Government officials to respect and obey the law, the need for open and vigorous debate of public policy, the need for vigilant congressional oversight of the way the law is implemented.

In the weeks ahead we will hear of individual and institutional error, of wrongdoing, even of criminal activity. We will be frequently appalled, occasionally amused. Through it all, we should not lose sight of the broader issues.

A democratic nation dependent on the rule of law and respect for that law cannot remain democratic if its Government officials are not accountable to the law. And when the Government abandons open and competitive debate and resorts for inadequate reason to secret decision making by a few the likelihood of error increases.

The Iran-Contra affair is a classic example of that. The law requires the President to notify the Congress in advance of certain covert operations, or if notice cannot be given in advance, then in a timely fashion.

There is little doubt that if the President had notified congressional leaders of his intention to sell arms to Iran and to exchange arms for hostages, they would have warned him not to do it. That was not done.

As a result, a secret policy was pursued that was contrary to our public policy, contrary to what we were telling our allies to do, contrary to our national interest.

In no respect were these actions wise. In every respect they were serious mistakes for the President and the country.

James Madison observed that, "If men were angels, no government would be necessary. In framing a government which is to be administered by men over men, a great difficulty lies in this. You must first enable the government to control the governed, and in the next place oblige it to control itself."

In those few words, Madison captured a central difficulty of government by and for the people. The difficulty was addressed in part by the separation of powers, the system of checks and balances prescribed by and embodied in our Constitution. . . .

Serious wounds have been inflicted [by the Iran-Contra affair]. The reputation of our nation has been damaged. The confidence of the American people in its government has been weakened. Our foreign policies in Central America and the Middle East have been thrown into question.

The Tower Commission criticized a mismanaged White House, casual delegation of important power, the abdication of responsibility by some of our high officials. It answered many questions, but many other questions remain.

What happened to the money? The reports of the Senate Intelligence Committee and the Tower Commission both contain references to millions of dollars raised at home and abroad by Government officials and private citizens. But neither the commission nor the committee had the time or the resources to document the money trail. We will do so.

Who knew about it and who authorized the use of these funds for military assistance to the Contras? Was the President, as he states, unaware of the diversion of funds from the arms sales to Iran and of other money and material assistance to the Contras in violation of the law?

The President is entitled to be believed, entitled to the benefit of the doubt, unless and until there is evidence to the contrary. We will find out if there is such evidence.

And if the President did not know, on whose authority and at whose request were so many elements of our Government mobilized to carry out these unwise and unlawful activities?

These and other questions will be answered in these hearings. We have a solemn responsibility to present all the facts, to bring the full truth to the American people as thoroughly, as fairly, as promptly as possible.[21]

COHEN: Many journalists have been asking the question recently why have these hearings. Will there be any new dramatic revelations?

Is this just another case of Congress trying to tie up Gulliver with trivialities? And finally, won't the American people be bored?

The answer is that our purpose is not to entertain, but to inform; not to electrify the electorate, but to educate our citizens about the importance of our institutions, about the reverence we must have for the rule of law, about the consequences of amputating the checks and balances in our system that guard against arbitrary or illegal action.

Walter Lippmann reminded us that, "The great virtue of democracy—in fact its supreme virtue—is that it supplies a method for dragging realities into the light, of summoning our rulers to declare themselves and to submit to judgment."

These hearings, in my judgment, are not intended to serve as a brass band parade or a funeral march. Mr. Chairman, the Government in this country is based upon the consent of the governed. Consent is meaningless unless it is informed consent. There are times when a President must act covertly to promote our security and to protect our lives. But when major policy is constructed behind closed doors by a few men and carried out by either patriots or profiteers in the shadowy world of covert action, then the American people may belatedly discover that an unwise course of action has been undertaken without their knowledge, without their consent, and against every intuitive sense of propriety.

Moreover, when major policies are not openly debated and formulated, when financing for an undisclosed program comes from private pockets or foreign treasuries, there are promises—expressed or implied—that are made in our name. At some point, at some time, a quid will be called for the quo.

Why should private individuals or foreign countries support the Contras? What is the price of their good will? What measure of compensation will be exacted? Will the cost be affordable or consistent with our ideals or our interests?

The story that has unfolded is not titillating. It is disheartening, in several aspects. First by allowing arms to be included in the effort to obtain American hostages, we engaged in an act of folly and hypocrisy. America's back was placed on the cruel rack of extortionists. Everyone knows an extortionist's price is never paid. It will always be another load of weapons for another group of victims.

Moreover, by openly advocating a policy of not dealing with terrorists and their sponsors, and then covertly practicing another, we undermined our ability to lead the free world in building an effective and unified policy to defeat the threat of international terrorism.

With respect to the Contra aid program, it will become clear that so much time was spent on secrecy, so much time wasted on evasion, so much money was misdirected—or remains missing—there was little chance left for competence in providing effective military assistance to the Contras.

It was not only the American taxpayers who were deceived by fraudulent charitable organizations and Congress that was actively misled about the sources of the Contra funding, but the Contras themselves who were filled with false hopes and empty promises. . . .

These hearings will help determine whether the administration's moral zeal obscured its collective judgment and whether the perceived nobility of its purpose led some individuals into the zone of lawlessness.

The laws we pass may not always be wise. But unless they are faithfully followed, we inch closer to despotism or anarchy where the freedom and safety of our citizens is equally at risk.

If public officials are free to ignore the law, to stultify it, to twist or disfigure its meaning in the name of superior motive or righteousness of cause, then we invite our undoing. . . .[22]

The Beginning
Is the Middle

G reek tragedians often began their plays in the middle of an epic story—*in medias res*. This technique was possible and successful because the audience was well versed in the history and bloodlines of, say, Agamemnon, Antigone, or Clytemnestra. The Iran-Contra affair, however, was not the contemporary equivalent of the House of Atreus, and most Americans, notwithstanding all of the attention devoted to the scandal, did not understand the details surrounding the events.

The Senate Intelligence Committee had already conducted hearings on the sale of weapons to Iran, and the Tower Board had focused almost exclusively on the folly and failure of the NSC staff in taking over an operational role in these sales. The Iran-Contra Committee planned to avoid repetition by first focusing on assistance to the Contras, in order to hold the attention of the American people. The public and the press needed something new, not summer reruns of winter's travails. Besides, it was argued, from a chronological point of view, the Contra supply network was set up by the NSC staff long before that staff called upon the network to assist it in the Iranian arms sales. So it was only right to begin at the beginning. This decision proved to be a tactical mistake.

First, demonstrating the impropriety of assisting the Contras was considerably more difficult to do in public hearings. Our initial task would be to crack into the secret Swiss bank accounts and follow the trail of money to the Contras. This was a complicated process that would take the viewing audience through a labyrinth of paper transactions and a string of shell corporations that stretched from Geneva to the Cayman Islands.

The public could clearly comprehend something as straightforward as a covert arms sale to Iran, which violated Ronald Reagan's stand-tall-in-the-face-of-terrorists image and rhetoric. But they would have difficulty in concentrating on mind-numbing charts, with multicolored bar graphs declaring what conduct was permissible during several different fiscal years. Moreover, television is a medium better suited to simplifying and summarizing complex issues than to displaying in microscopic detail the origins and transformations of secret bank accounts.

Second, the American people, while concerned that the President not be allowed to flout the law, were not particularly exercised over the fact that the President's men had been actively engaged in raising funds for the "freedom fighters." The law was complex and had been changed several times. The President had said on many public occasions that he, too, was a "Contra" and encouraged people to support them. Besides, Congress not only specifically authorized the solicitation of funds for humanitarian purposes for the Contras at one point, but also, in the most recent congressional authorization, allowed for full military support. The public was not rushing to condemn the President over an issue in which the Congress was so divided and inconsistent.

Third, and perhaps most important, House Republicans looked at the decision to focus on financial and military aid to the Contras with a jaundiced and suspicious eye. Duplication and chronology be damned: the Democrats were up to no good.

A preliminary memorandum prepared for the Committee suggested that the Contra-aid program, conducted in violation of the various Boland Amendments, may have become the force that drove the sale of weapons to Iran. The Contras' cause and needs created a current within the White House that led some of Ronald Reagan's advisers to recommend the program of selling weapons to Iran at markup prices, so the profit could be used for and diverted to the Contras—as well as line the pockets of the intermediaries.

For the Republicans, the problem with this theory was that it insinuated that President Reagan either knew of the fund-raising efforts in behalf of the Contras and the sale of weapons at a substantial markup or was totally ignorant of both and was being cynically manipulated by his closest advisers. Either way, the President would lose: if he knew of the transactions, he would have to admit that he either lied or forgot. If he didn't know, he was reduced to the equivalent of an absentee landlord who was unaware that his tenants were smashing the furniture and breaking windows.

If the Democrats were going to go after Reagan, then it was the duty of Republicans to defend him.

As a result, the hearings began on a strong partisan note, with House Republicans chiding Democrats over giving away freedom in our hemisphere, while passing amendments crippling to our heritage and national-security interests. It may have been wishful thinking to believe that the Committee could have begun its proceedings by focusing on an issue on which all members were united—outrage over the sale of weapons to revolutionary Iran. But in turning to the covert assistance to the Contras in the first days of the hearings, we lost the chance to do so.

The Committee had given some thought to calling a panel of so-called Wise Men as the first witnesses—people such as Brent Scowcroft, a retired Air Force brigadier general who served as National Security Adviser under President Gerald Ford, and Admiral Bobby Inman, the former Director of the National Security Agency and Deputy Director of the CIA.

The Wise Men would have described the established process by which a president initiates a covert action—by which the United States can use secrecy to achieve foreign-policy objectives without forfeiting scrutiny and accountability. Based upon their vast experience in government, the Wise Men could have provided a primer on why covert actions may be necessary; when they should be utilized; why Congress should be notified of covert actions; whether or not congressional leaders were in fact worthy of trust in such matters; whether notice to Congress should be withheld by the Executive when individual lives are at stake and, if so, whether such lack of notification should be subject to any time limitation.

This sort of testimony would have provided the American people with some standards against which they could have measured North's charges that the sale of weapons to Iran had to be carried out without notice to Congress because Congress can never be trusted when lives are at stake, or that, since covert actions involve lies, it is permissible to lie to Congress to preserve their secrecy.

But some members opposed calling the Wise Men as the first witnesses, because they would be too dull; they argued that if we didn't capture the attention of the press and public at the outset we never would. Disagreements also arose over who would be included on such a panel. Would the participants help the President or hurt him? And some of the those under consideration to give such testimony were reluctant to do so.

Any plans for the Wise Men panel ceased, however, when Secord agreed to be the first witness. House Majority Counsel John Nields had been negotiating with Secord's counsel, Tom Green, for several weeks. He and Arthur Liman persuaded Secord to forgo invoking his Fifth Amendment privilege against self-incrimination without a grant of immunity. This was considered a major coup. The inducement for Secord was the opportunity to be the first witness.

The proposal to lead off with Secord was not without controversy. Phil Bobbitt, legal counsel to the Committee, argued that a description of the institutional process of covert action should precede any factual testimony by key participants in the scandal. Liman, Nields, and Paul Barbadoro, the Senate Committee's deputy chief counsel, argued that Secord would prove an important witness, whose testimony we would not otherwise get without granting him immunity. This was persuasive. Secord was an important participant. Liman strongly opposed immunity for Secord.

Some members harbored doubts about the wisdom of the decision. It was obvious that Secord agreed to testify first because he would be in a position to describe his activities on his terms, knowing that crucial documents that could be used to contradict or impeach his testimony were not yet available to the Committee. Second, by focusing on the factual witnesses without discussing the institutional mechanisms ensuring that covert activities be conducted within certain rules of accountability, the Committee would be drawn into measuring the strength or weakness of personalities instead of the breakdown of government process and perhaps law. The hearings would then become a contest of the Committee against the witness, a zero-sum game in which, if the witness remained strong, the Committee would look weak.

Nonetheless, the importance of Secord's testimony and the opportunity to obtain it without granting him immunity overrode other considerations.

Ideally, once we were faced with the necessity of beginning with Secord, it would have been better to divide his testimony into two distinct parts, concentrating first on the sale of weapons to Iran, about which most of the Committee members and the American people were truly angry, and then on the Contra-aid operations carried on in violation of the Boland Amendments, over which the public was confused and the Committee members were divided. But events do not always permit us to follow the ideal. Secord was an active participant in both activities, in some instances moving money from one program to bolster the other. There was little chance that he would cooperate by allowing the Committee to focus initially on his role in the arms sales to Iran and diversion of the profits (at least $3.8 million out of $12.2 million) to the Contras without describing the origins of his involvement with the Contras. Moreover, if he did not attempt to raise the cause of the Contras as a beneficiary of the attempt to obtain the release of our hostages in Lebanon, there were many Committee members who would.

The practical result of linking the two programs from the inception of Secord's testimony, however, was to blur the edges of each, merging the offensiveness of trading with Ayatollah Khomeini with the complexity involved in explaining the application of a law that changed from year to year.

The hearings, therefore, opened with an aggressive, combative witness whose testimony, in some respects, could not be effectively challenged at the time, because crucial evidence was still being held up by Swiss authorities and others. As a result, the public was left with the feeling that the Committee had started a complicated and confusing story in the middle. Lacking adequate background to place the testimony in context, the viewing public responded by focusing on the personalities of the witnesses, the counsels, and members of the Committee, instead of the substance of what had been done.

Judging from the mail and telephone calls Committee members received in the wake of Secord's testimony, it was not an auspicious beginning.

Good Copp/Bad Copp?

R ichard V. Secord, a retired Air Force general, stepped before the Committee, raised his right hand, and swore to tell the truth. A short, stocky man with aviator glasses, he looks like a manager of a Mercedes dealership instead of the veteran of hundreds of combat missions over Vietnam and a covert-operations specialist.

Secord, a West Point graduate, had by 1978 risen to the rank of major general and headed the Pentagon's foreign military sales program before becoming Deputy Assistant Secretary of Defense for the Middle East. He reportedly was on a fast track to become the Air Force chief of staff when his name became associated with Edwin Wilson, an ex–CIA agent who supplied explosives to Libya's Muammar Qaddafi. Then he was linked indirectly to the EATSCO case, which involved a company that entered a guilty plea to overcharging the Pentagon by some $8 million for the shipment of weapons to Egypt. No charges were brought against Secord, but it was clear that his career was no longer streaking toward the sun.

He retired from the Air Force in 1983 and became a partner of Albert Hakim in Stanford Technology Trading Group International. It was not long before his talents were called upon by North, who provided him with the code name of "Copp."

Humility was a trait that Secord did not seem to possess in great abundance. He was an intelligent witness, often exhibiting a coolness that slipped into flashes of caustic arrogance. He was clearly angry.

The administration, in his view, had used him in what he believed to be legitimate covert operations, and then, upon their disclosure, left him vulnerable and alone. He was particularly outraged with Attorney General Meese, whom he regarded as a hair-triggered coward who ran prematurely into the arms of the national press corps without giving him, Secord, an opportunity to explain fully what was involved. As a result, Secord was actively under investigation by the independent counsel. And he did not like it—not at all.

John Nields spent nearly two days taking Secord slowly over his professional background and the circumstances of his involvement, along with that of his partner, Albert Hakim, in the supply of weapons to the Contras, then to the Iranians.

It was a classic example of what lawyers call direct examination: lots of soft, leading questions that allow the witness to tell (or withhold) as much of the story as he cares to.

Nields did not challenge or confront Secord on any ambiguities or holes in his testimony. He had spent hours with Secord prior to the hearing, exploring during unsworn interviews Secord's intimate knowledge of and participation in the National Security Council staff's operations. The task of forcing Secord to defend his deeds and words would fall to Liman. We watched Nields use velvet gloves in his interrogation. Liman, we knew, would have to wear brass knuckles.

On the second day of the hearings, Senator Inouye informed the Committee that William Casey had died during the night. Whatever faint hopes existed that Casey might recover from brain surgery so that he could one day tell the whole story had vanished. During the morning coffee break, some members openly speculated on how much blame would now be shoveled into Casey's grave.

For the remainder of the second day, Committee members sat in silence as General Secord spun his tale of woe.

Liman had warned us that Secord would be a difficult witness for the Committee to handle. Secord was smart and possessed a forceful personality. We were told that greed lurked behind his patriotic protestations, but that it would take some tough examination to expose it. John Nields's gentle, deferential approach to Secord during his long, direct examination caught most of us by surprise. Secord had seized control of the hearings, portraying himself as a righteous patriot who had been betrayed by his government. He was unexpectedly aided by revelations of the Gary Hart and Donna Rice affair, which was dominating the headlines. He did not miss the opportunity to point out that his travels did not include Bimini.[23]

Secord had a good run in the hands of John Nields. He had demonstrated excellent recall of dates, facts, and dollars. He had remained calm, confident, and forceful—an innocent man who had been hounded by his government. The press reports and public reaction had been favorable.

The mood in the anteroom was one of gloom. How long was Secord going to proceed without being challenged? Where was the evidence of profiteering we had heard so much about in our private sessions? Where was the sleaze factor? According to Secord, the problem was that we had not sold Iran enough workable HAWK missiles, that McFarlane had left Teheran prematurely and should have agreed to Iranian demands,[24] and that the diversion of profits to the Contras from the sale of weapons to Iran was little more than a charitable donation by Albert Hakim!

Secord allegedly was one of the principal characters in a network of profiteers. If his testimony held up after all of the prehearing publicity, the Committee's investigation would be reduced to a charade. Liman was going to have to be very tough indeed.

Ronald Reagan was on our minds as we listened to Richard Secord testify. But we were surprised to be asked by the White House to come down to see the President. We were even more surprised when told why.

The Penobscot River in Maine is a famed spawning site for Atlantic salmon. Since 1912 it has been traditional for the first salmon of the spring caught on the Penobscot to be presented to the president of the United States. By coincidence, the event was set for Thursday, May 7, the very day on which we expected to be questioning Secord. We had not planned to attend the salmon presentation. The Governor of Maine was coming down for the event, which consists largely of a picture-taking session with the President.

But the Governor's plane was grounded in Boston, and the White House image-makers wanted some public officials from Maine in the picture. So they called, asking—urging—us to come down to the White House. It struck us both as humorous and ironic. But, once we made sure that we could question Secord when we got back, we agreed and rode down to the White House.

The President was, as always, amiable. We joined George E. Fletcher, the eighty-seven-year-old fisherman from Strong, Maine, who had caught it, in presenting a fifteen-pound salmon to the President. We exchanged pleasantries and fish stories. One year the President had been too busy to accept it personally, so the Vice President had done so. Blood had dripped on the rug in the Vice President's office, to the dismay of all who were there. This time, to make sure no blood would drip on the President's rug, someone had brought a Styrofoam container. We gamely held the container under the fish and joined the President in smiling for the cameras.

Neither he nor we betrayed any recognition of the symbolism of our handing the President a dead fish as the Iran-Contra hearings began.

Like all good trial lawyers, Arthur Liman has a prodigious memory for detail and a love for intellectual combat. He is a student of the human heart, knowledgeable about its best and worst instincts.

It was clear from his private conversations with us that Liman did not like what he saw in General Secord. In his view, Secord was shamelessly wrapping himself in the American flag while lining his pockets at the expense of both the Contras and the American people.

Although he produced no "smoking guns," Liman had substantial evidence to show a venal side of General Secord lying beneath his protestations of innocence. Unfortunately, Liman was not prepared for the public reaction to his brand of cross-examination.

Liman began his examination on a civil note: "Good morning, Mr. Secord." These were the last pleasant words Liman would extend. He turned quickly to business, dragging Secord through the minutiae of corporate financial transactions, Swiss bank accounts, profit markups of weapons sold to the Contras and to the Iranians, unrepaid interest-free loans, an attempt to gouge the CIA and the U.S. government by renting and selling to it equipment that had been purchased with the assistance of the government in the first instance.

Secord was shaken. He periodically removed his glasses and gripped the witness table. His voice took on a caustic edge. He used the words "overhead" and "surplus" instead of "profit," because he had been accused by Committee members and the press of being a profiteer, and clearly resented it. Once he responded to a Liman question about charging a profit markup on weapons by saying, "We billed just like lawyers did. We billed for a fee." Liman refused to relent. "Would it shock you to learn that lawyers bill for profit?"

At another point, Secord tried to shift the line of examination: "Let's get off the subject." "You're making the rules?" Liman retorted.

Secord's lawyer, Tom Green, a burly man who wore his reading glasses precariously at the end of his nose, became more animated than his client. He was like a tag-team wrestler, eager to get inside the ring to rescue his partner. His objections to Liman's questions and manner were overruled.

The story extracted by Liman (and later by Committee members) from General Secord under cross-examination was stunning:

• Secord had been asked by North to approach representatives of foreign governments to contribute money to the Contras, and North had indicated that President Reagan would be most grateful for such contributions. Secord regarded such solicitations as "unseemly."

• He had been invited to the Situation Room in the White House to discuss a presidential finding authorizing a covert action in which he and his business partner, Albert Hakim, were to be "commercial cutouts" in the sale of weapons to Iran.

• A plan had been formulated to employ Drug Enforcement Administration agents to pay ransom for hostages in Lebanon. Secord was not aware that a portion of the ransom money had been contributed by Adolfo Calero, one of the major Contra leaders.

• Once the covert action became public, Secord shredded financial documents and phone logs of Stanford Technology Trading Group International.

• He and his partner, Hakim, negotiated with Iranians for the release of American hostages. The Committee subsequently learned that these negotiations included promising to help secure the release of seventeen Da'Wa terrorists held in Kuwaiti jails;[25] helping to depose Iraq's President Saddam Hussein; and exchanging five hundred TOW missiles for one and a half hostages.

• In February 1986, the United States had supplied to Iran certain photographic and intelligence information pertaining to the Iraqi military.

• Secord charged a profit on the sale of weapons to the Contras, but claimed to have refused any share in the profit on sales of weapons to Iran.[26]

• He wanted to return to government service, perhaps as deputy director of operations in the CIA, in order to repair the "stitches" from the wound inflicted to his career by his association with Edwin Wilson.

• While charging a substantial price markup on weapons sold to Iran at the very time the United States was trying to enhance the credibility and influence of a new channel to Iranian moderates, the United States allowed Israel to switch the newer missiles for older ones, even after Iran had voiced strong complaints about the quality of weapons they were receiving from the United States.

• North had arranged for Secord to receive a sophisticated portable encryption device from the National Security Agency so that the Enterprise could send and receive secret messages.

• Eight million dollars remained frozen in a Swiss bank account, money that Secord insisted belonged to the Enterprise.

• The Enterprise had been floating on a slush fund generated by profits from the Iranian arms sales and contributions of third parties—portions of which were to go to the Contras, and the balance for future unspecified activities.

• Funds had been raised for the Contras through tax-deductible charitable gifts and from foreign governments.

The American people should have been outraged by many of those disclosures, which were a clear subversion of our constitutional processes. Government authority and accountability had been delegated to private individuals whose private gain was America's loss. Unfortunately, the medium obscured the message.

While the good-cop/bad-cop method of interrogation may be used successfully in detective work, it did not prove to be a public-relations triumph for the Committee. First, Secord did not look or sound like a criminal. Although parts of his testimony seemed implausible, it generally had the ring of truth. Second, Secord's military bearing had greater public appeal than did Arthur Liman's courtroom manner.

Television is unkind to Liman. He has dark, penetrating eyes and a habit of tucking his chin to his chest as he lowers his head with visible scorn for a witness. His thinning hair is curly and unmanageable. And then there is his aggressiveness and accent—stereotypically New York.

Less than a week into the hearings, thousands of letters, tele-grams, and phone calls started flooding our offices. They com-plained about Liman's hair, abrasiveness, and religion. Secord was a patriotic Anglo-American. Liman was a nasty New York lawyer—translate as "New York Jew."

Committee members, no matter how artful or photogenic, did not fare much better than had Arthur Liman. David Boren is a happy-hearted man whose face is rarely without a smile. He seemed unusually agitated with General Secord, offering him a stern lec-ture about the privatization of our foreign policy:

> We are in the Bicentennial year of the Constitution. Do you think it's appropriate that important foreign policy decisions should be made by Mr. Richard Secord, private citizen, instead of by the Congress of the United States, the Secretary of State and the President of the United States?[27]

Paul Trible (R-Virginia), with the blond hair and youthful looks of a choirboy or a college student, proved to be surprisingly tough in his questions. Trible represented a conservative state with a large community of retired military personnel. Many of his con-stituents (and fellow Committee members) expected him to play a docile gentleman to this retired officer. However, though min-imally respectful, Trible offered no praising chorales. He contin-ued a theme outlined in his opening remarks, that Secord's professed patriotism was tarnished by his pursuit of profits.

But perhaps no member was more critical in his questioning than the Senate's vice chairman. There is always a sense about Rudman that he is about to enter combat. His throat thickens visibly, and he barks questions in a fashion that instructs a witness not to play word games. It was clear that Rudman did not like Secord's activities or his attitude. He particularly wanted Secord to admit that the windfall profits generated by the sale of weapons to the Iranians belonged to the United States taxpayers. Secord refused, maintaining that the money belonged to the Enter-prise.

Secord's attorney had no doubt made it clear to his client that, if he conceded that the funds were legally the property of the United States, such a concession might be tantamount to an admission that he had committed a crime, a fraudulent conversion of United States property. Secord had earlier revealed his anxiety in response to a challenge from Liman. "I've got a special prosecutor over here across the street trying to throw all of us in jail for performing our duty as we saw it. I haven't focused on some technical issues like you're bringing up here. This is crazy."

On the third day of his testimony, Secord said he would make an effort to persuade his business partner, Hakim, to turn over the $8 million still frozen in a Swiss account (after outstanding obligations were paid) to establish a fund in the name of William Casey to aid the Nicaraguan freedom fighters.

Rudman thought it was a laudable sentiment but said: "I must tell you that in my view, you or no one else has a right to send that money anywhere. That money belongs to the people of the United States, and I will assure you that the Justice Department will make that claim."[28] Later, during a press interview, Rudman stated that he was tired of people who "wrapped themselves in the flag and go around spitting on the Constitution."

The Senate offices of Boren, Trible, and Rudman were flooded with angry letters, telegrams, and phone calls, berating them for joining forces with "that New York lawyer."

WSC: *I received hundreds of letters, many of them containing passions similar to that reflected in the following: "The term is disgusting to me, a Republican lady citizen, but it is the only thing that properly describes you. You —! [A most unladylike obscenity.]*

By contrast, Henry Hyde (R-Illinois) praised Secord, saying that he was a patriot who was called upon to do the nation's dirty work and then left to twist slowly in the wind—an image immortalized by John Ehrlichman during Watergate—while everyone else ran for cover. Hyde became an instant hero; many compared him to Everett Dirksen, the late Senate Minority Leader known for his gravelly voice and grandiloquence.

Secord's gamble had paid off. The Committee as a whole had been perceived as hostile, belligerent, pompous, patronizing, or unpatriotic. Because the Committee had not obtained the financial records still in the hands of Albert Hakim and Swiss banks, we were unable to elicit information that would seriously undermine Secord's credibility. The impression would not hold for long, but Secord at the time emerged as the good Copp. And those members who criticized him were seen as the bad.

A Crowd of Sorrows

R obert C. McFarlane, the former National Security Adviser, was the second witness scheduled to testify before the Committee. Though a key witness, he generated little excitement or controversy.

McFarlane had already testified in secret before the House and Senate Intelligence Committees and the Tower Board. Much of the same information given in private was disclosed publicly when he appeared before the House Foreign Affairs Committee. As a result, he could be expected to add little to what already was known by the Committee.

McFarlane would testify:

• That one or two days after the President met with the head of a Middle Eastern country (Country Two), that country agreed to double the amount of money it was sending the Contras. He confirmed that the President was told of this and "expressed gratitude and satisfaction, not surprise." He did not believe that there was any direct solicitation, but the President or his staff had made it clear that contributions would be welcomed by the United States. McFarlane also testified that at the time he did not tell Secretary of State Shultz of the contributions.

• That on one occasion in 1985, the President had called the president of a Central American country to persuade him to release a shipment for the Contras that was being held up. McFarlane could not be certain that the President knew the shipment contained arms.

• That the President had repeatedly made clear that he did not intend to break faith with the Contras even after official assistance had been terminated. He told McFarlane that the administration should assure the Contras of its support in holding them together "body and soul." But McFarlane said the President was not aware of, and did not condone, any illegal support.

• That he had repeatedly made clear to the NSC staff that it was bound by the Boland Amendments prohibiting assistance to the Contras. He told them they were not to "solicit, encourage, coerce, or otherwise broker financial contributions to the contras."

• That, concerning the origins of the Iran arms sales, in early July 1985 President Reagan gave McFarlane the go-ahead to explore the United States' willingness to talk to Iranians concerning hostages. Adolph ("Al") Schwimmer, a private Israeli arms dealer, reported to an NSC consultant, Michael Ledeen, who in turn reported to McFarlane, that Iranians wanted TOW missiles in exchange. McFarlane conveyed this information to the President at Bethesda Naval Hospital; President Reagan rejected the idea of the United States' selling weapons directly, but left open the possibility of an Israeli sale. Various discussions occurred at the White House, culminating with a meeting of Cabinet officials on August 6, 1985. The President decided one or two days later to approve an Israeli sale, and McFarlane conveyed this to David Kimche, director general of the Israeli Foreign Ministry.

• That the administration had expected all the hostages to be released after the Israeli arms shipments in August-September 1985, but that instead only one was released. McFarlane was put in the position of choosing one.

• That both the President and the Attorney General had in 1985 approved the plan to use DEA agents to ransom two American hostages in Lebanon for $2 million.

• That McFarlane came to realize that North had frequent contact with, and was taking instructions from, Director of Central Intelligence Casey.

• That he learned of the diversion of funds to the Contras from North on the return trip from Teheran in May 1986. He assumed the President was aware of the plan, although he never followed up the discussions with anyone.

• That North had advised him, in a conversation on the afternoon of November 21, 1986, that there was "going to be a shredding party" at the White House. But McFarlane did not do anything to stop it. Nor did he advise the Attorney General of this when Meese interviewed him the following Monday. McFarlane testified that when he saw North two days later and asked what had happened, North told him, "I missed one."

• That, when confronted with the version of the chronologies that he worked on—which said the United States did not acquiesce in the August-September 1985 Israeli shipments and contained only a bare mention of the November 1985 HAWK shipment—he continued to maintain these were not deliberate efforts to mislead. He also denied a deliberate effort to mislead Congress with respect to North's activities in support of the Contras, although he stated he had not given as full an account as he might have.[29]

The atmosphere in the hearing room was of one of ghoulish curiosity as McFarlane stood, raised his right hand, and took the oath. In February 1987, McFarlane had attempted to commit suicide by swallowing an unspecified number of Valium pills. Obviously he had been overwhelmed with guilt or grief over events for which he felt, in large part, responsible.

As he began to testify, the question was not what he would say but, rather, how well he would hold up. Was he stable enough to bear the strain of public scrutiny? How does a man who has tried to accelerate his mortality climb back through the ropes into the center ring of Washington politics? Would counsel or Committee members hold back their tough questions? Would he apologize, express remorse, or crack—temporarily shutting down the hearings?

Many of the Committee members were sympathetic to McFarlane, not because of the attempted suicide but because he was considered a decent man who in the past had carried little of the ideological fervor that seemed so prevalent in the White House. McFarlane was born in Washington, D.C., graduated from the U.S. Naval Academy, received an M.S. degree from the Graduate Institute of International Studies in Geneva, Switzerland, and served in the U.S. Marine Corps from 1959 to 1979, retiring with the rank of lieutenant colonel. He had two tours in Vietnam and was awarded the distinguished-service medal and the bronze star. He was the military assistant to National Security Adviser Henry Kissinger from 1973 to 1975, and served as a military analyst with the Senate Armed Services Committee in 1979–81. He left the Committee to serve as a counselor at the Department of State in 1981–82 and then became the Deputy National Security Adviser to William Clark in 1982. When Clark resigned in 1983, President Reagan picked McFarlane to fill the position.

McFarlane was not viewed as the conscience of the conservatives, as was Richard Allen; nor as the personal confidant of President Reagan, as was Clark. Although he had served on the National Security Council staff under Henry Kissinger, he was not regarded as (nor did he purport to be) a man of Kissinger's scope or calculation, or as scholarly as Zbigniew Brzezinski. McFarlane seemed content to lower the profile and function of the NSC and return it to the more pedestrian role of coordinating defense and foreign-policy initiatives, resolving competing analyses of the intelligence community, and helping to shape and articulate a coherence in our national-security interests and objectives. He was viewed as an intelligent, hardworking apparatchik.

McFarlane's inclination to seek accommodation with Congress on issues pertaining to national security was often greeted with disdain by the Patrick Buchanan school of confrontational politics. (Buchanan was a speech writer for Richard Nixon and hard-right guru for Ronald Reagan.) In the Reagan White House, a person of McFarlane's moderate instincts and reputation was worth watching over—for possible signs of philosophical treason or defection. Those not regarded as a part of the team suffered a thousand slights, not always of a subtle variety. When a member of the President's inner circle of confidants expressed anything but total commitment to the President's agenda, his loyalty was questioned from that point forward.

Although conservative, McFarlane resisted the absolutism of some of his White House associates. He believed that an arms-control agreement could and should be negotiated with the Soviets. In an effort to build congressional support for aid to the Contras, he argued for changes in the Contra leadership and methods of operation. It was not out of character for him to explore the possibility of changing the nature of our relationship with Iran and in the process obtaining a release of U.S. hostages. Indeed, he seemed intent on achieving a diplomatic breakthrough during his tenure, something that would identify him as a statesman.[30]

McFarlane has a long, oval-shaped face that looked shiny and puffy under the television lights. He is a taciturn man who rarely exhibits emotion in public. His smile is always controlled, and could just as easily pass for a grimace. Throughout the course of his testimony, he frequently took long draughts from his water glass. It had been speculated that he was still on medication.

McFarlane chose his words carefully and offered them up with the formality of a soldier turned bureaucrat.

> I believe what I said, was that I thought it would be imprudent to assert, as a legal precedent, that the President has exclusive authority to conduct foreign affairs, especially if he were to behave in a way that indicated he is not accountable to anyone. So, it was a hypothetical construct, but I believe that to take the case in point, to assert that the President does have the authority to create entities that function without oversight of—not only the Congress, but not even oversight within the Executive branch—is in direct contradiction of the notion

of accountability in any sense. And that, that would weaken any effort to establish this larger principle, that he is relatively uninhibited in the general conduct of foreign affairs.[31]

More frustrating than the stiffness of McFarlane's vocabulary and syntax was the grudging manner in which he delivered his words. In a flat, low monotone, McFarlane yielded them one by one, as if he were giving birth to each.

In questioning McFarlane, Liman reversed roles with House Counsel John Nields and became the friendly interrogator. McFarlane's testimony, involving the arms sales to Iran, had been well documented in the Tower Board report. Liman chose to focus initially on McFarlane's role in assisting the Nicaraguan Contras.

McFarlane cited the mining of the Nicaraguan harbors in the spring of 1984 as the turning point in congressional support for the Contras. That incident doomed plans to ask for additional appropriations. According to McFarlane, the administration explored options that included asking other countries to undertake operational training and funding of the Contras. The President's Cabinet decided that it was not politically desirable or feasible to subcontract the responsibility for the Contras to another country, but that the President's credibility would be seriously impaired if the Contras were abandoned. Plans were hatched to seek financial support from other countries. The President made it clear that his support for the Contras' cause was an article of faith that he did not want broken.

> He [President Reagan] directed that we make continued efforts to bring the movement into the good graces of Congress and the American people and that we assure the Contras of continuing administration support—to help them hold body and soul together—until the time when Congress would again agree to support them.[32]

McFarlane's insistence that neither the President, nor his Cabinet, nor the NSC staff engaged in any technical solicitation of money from third countries seemed tortured and farfetched. Formal requests, according to McFarlane, were not made to third countries; mere expressions of concern about the future and the fate of the Contras were conveyed. Few on the Committee accepted the explanation. We were told that at least eight countries, far removed from our hemisphere, were eager to rush to the assistance of the Contras. How many foreign nations could be made to dance on the head of this particular pin? we wondered. The cracks in the credibility of the story began to widen.

Most significant, however, was the picture of President Reagan that was beginning to evolve. According to the Tower Board report, the President emerged as a "hands-off" manager who delegated too much responsibility to subordinates and retained too little interest in important details and developments. McFarlane's testimony showed a president more deeply involved with and worried about securing sufficient funds from private and foreign sources for the Contras.

This personal involvement carried over to the sale of weapons to Iran. In fact, McFarlane testified that it was President Reagan's personal concern for the safety and return of the hostages in Lebanon that made him overrule the advice of his top advisers not to sell weapons to the Iranians.

There were poignant moments in the testimony that evoked sympathy for a man who alone among the witnesses expressed any remorse. We learned that in September 1985, after the Israelis had delivered TOW missiles to Iran, the Iranians maintained that not all the hostages could be released, only one. McFarlane was asked, in his words, "to play God," to choose. His request for William Buckley, the CIA station chief in Lebanon, was rejected. Buckley had been tortured to death, although this was not known to the administration at the time. Instead, the Reverend Benjamin Weir was released.

Then, in December 1985, when McFarlane traveled to London to meet with the much-touted middleman Manucher Ghorbanifar (known to the CIA as "an irredeemable liar"), he came away thoroughly disgusted. Ghorbanifar had stripped away all the pretense that the transaction was to be a precursor to a new dawn in foreign policy with Iran. Ghorbanifar reduced everything to a straight trade of weapons for hostages.

McFarlane subsequently joined forces with Secretaries Shultz and Weinberger in urging President Reagan to discontinue the initiative. It was too late. McFarlane had resigned his position as National Security Adviser, and Reagan had appointed Admiral Poindexter to succeed him. North, once treated "like a son" by McFarlane, argued that discontinuing the program would be tantamount to signing the death warrant of the hostages. A meeting between President Reagan and the families of the hostages shortly before Christmas solidified the voices of those who wanted the sales to continue. On January 6, 1986, President Reagan made the decision to proceed.

In the spring of 1986, the President recalled McFarlane from his consulting position with the Georgetown Center for Strategic and International Studies and asked him to undertake a secret mission to Teheran to secure the release of the hostages. Weapons were again to be the barter. His instructions were clear: all the hostages or no weapons.

Once more, McFarlane found himself dealing with fast-fingered merchants schooled in steamy street bazaars instead of genteel, university-educated diplomats.

The Iranians demanded that the United States: pay the upkeep of the hostages; force Israel to return the Golan Heights to Syria; stay out of the Persian Gulf; and arrange for the release of the Da'Wa terrorists being held in Kuwait. Finally, they insisted that McFarlane exchange the weapons for only two hostages. One load of weapons had arrived with McFarlane, North, and the rest of the American delegation.

McFarlane refused, walked out of the meeting, and returned to his quarters to rest. That was at 5:00 P.M. While McFarlane slept, North continued to negotiate with the Iranians for the release of the hostages. McFarlane had advised the Iranians, with respect to the Da'Wa prisoners, "our position is derived from our policy which respects all nations' judicial policies. We cannot ignore their process. I am sad to report all of this. I respect what you said. I'll report it to my President, but I cannot be optimistic."[33]

At nine-thirty on that same evening, North made a different representation:

> The United States will make every effort through and with international organizations, private individuals, religious organizations and any other third parties in a humanitarian effort to achieve the release and just and fair treatment for the Shiites held in confinement as soon as possible.[34]

In addition, North authorized the second planeload of weapons to continue to Teheran. (It had been in a holding pattern, pending the outcome of the meeting.) McFarlane, when advised of this, canceled the order. Then North, on the tarmac of an Israeli airstrip, revealed to McFarlane for the first time that all had not been lost—that money from the initial sales of weapons to the Iranians had been diverted to the freedom fighters in Nicaragua.

It was clear from the beginning of the hearings that North was a central figure in the Iran-Contra affair. His activities had been reported by the Intelligence Committees and the Tower Board. McFarlane's testimony added details to the portrait of a man he described as a can-do, action-oriented officer.

But even McFarlane appeared distressed over the extent of North's high energy level. Two weeks after the report of the Iranian arms sales appeared in a Lebanese newspaper, McFarlane was called by Poindexter and asked to help reconstruct a chronology of events surrounding the arms sale. While they were alone in McFarlane's car, North advised McFarlane that there would be a "shredding party." A Marine colonel who shredded official documents in anticipation of a Justice Department or congressional investigation did not, in our judgment, quite measure up to the heroic dimensions described by President Reagan.

And McFarlane revealed that North may have worn more than one hat while serving on the NSC staff. When asked whether McFarlane had come to believe that North was taking instructions from William Casey, McFarlane, after a long pause, answered, "Yes, sir . . . I think so."

Some of us had joked that Oliver North was the first five-star lieutenant colonel in military history. There were, in fact, few reasonable explanations for North's real or perceived power. He had directed a CIA station chief in a Central American country to report to him. In addition, John H. Kelly, the U.S. Ambassador to Lebanon, bypassed the Secretary of State and instead reported to North. McFarlane agreed that North could not have operated in this fashion without the backing of Director Casey.

When John Nields took over the cross-examination, McFarlane's stoic equanimity began to weaken. The tone of the hearings changed almost immediately. For several hours Nields pressed McFarlane on his specific actions, instead of accepting his blanket assumption of responsibility for events. Nields wanted to know why McFarlane had changed the chronology being prepared for President Reagan to reflect that oil-drilling equipment, not HAWK missile parts, had been shipped to Iran in November 1985. McFarlane offered the press of other business as the reason: "I was almost completely absorbed with preparation for the Geneva Summit . . . absorbed in arms control negotiation, a U.N. meeting, a Moscow presummit session, and what about *Achille Lauro* to occupy your free time?"[35]

Memory can suffer a power outage when overloaded with an inordinate surge of national-security affairs. But there were too many other instances where error appeared less than innocent or inadvertent. McFarlane had offered to key members of Congress absolute denials of improper activities by NSC staff and provided less than complete testimony to the Intelligence Committees. On September 5, 1985, McFarlane sent the first of his responses to Congress. He wrote to Representative Hamilton: "I can state with deep personal conviction that at no time did I or any other member of the National Security Council staff violate the letter or spirit of Congressional restrictions on aid to the Contras. . . ." This letter, drafted by McFarlane himself, served as the model for five additional letters prepared by North, signed by McFarlane, and sent in September and October in response to congressional inquiries.[36] McFarlane would concede only that perhaps he had been "too categorical" in his statements or would "accept the proposition" offered by Nields while refusing to confirm the accuracy of Nields's characterizations.

It was clear that McFarlane was trying to be cooperative without being confessional. He had neither sought nor received immunity for his testimony, although he was under active investigation by Independent Counsel Walsh.

McFarlane's exterior calm was deceiving. Pressure was building internally. After the break for lunch, McFarlane snapped at the Committee, "It was suggested during the lunch hour that I'm a fragile flower that has to be catered to. Nonsense. Shoot your best shot!"

Members accepted the invitation.

GJM: *I asked if he had not "deliberately participated in the falsification of a portion of that [White House] chronology." McFarlane, again with almost rigid self-control, replied sorrowfully that the question was "disappointing for someone who is trying here today to promote the idea of consulting with the Congress and cooperating with it."*

But the line of questioning had lit a slow-burning fuse in McFarlane's mind. Moments later, Senator Rudman pursued an unrelated area of inquiry: a plan to use the Drug Enforcement Agency to bribe individuals in order to secure the release of two Americans being held hostage in Lebanon. The plan, which constituted an "intelligence activity," had been approved by McFarlane and, according to McFarlane, by Attorney General Edwin Meese as well. Such activities required either prior or "timely" notice to be given to the House and Senate Intelligence Committees.

Rudman had asked whether the President had ever signed a finding for this activity and whether congressional committees had been notified. McFarlane answered, "No, sir," to both questions.

Then Rudman posed the next logical question. "Should they have been?"

"No, sir!" McFarlane exploded, spitting the words out as if he were a recruit responding to a drill sergeant at Marine boot camp.

Silence suddenly replaced the hum of monotony in the room. Everyone snapped to attention with anticipation that something unusual was about to occur. Rudman was caught by surprise. He had only been sparring with McFarlane up to that point. Instead of pressing the witness, he backed away and used the reverse technique of lowering his own voice. "Tell me why."

McFarlane erupted. An uncharacteristic kinetic quality infused his words.

> It is more than passing strange to me that we cannot aspire to a policy which is more effective to deal with terrorism. Now it is undeniable that some countries are good at it. And they are good because terrorists know that whenever they commit terrorism against Israel, something, somehow, somewhere is going to happen. Now, it may not always be arms. It may not be preemptive attack. It may be negotiation. It may be bribing. But you can be goddam sure if any Israeli's caught, he's going to have his government going after the people who did it![37]

McFarlane's outburst was a reaction wholly unrelated to the immediate question. Members were put on notice to move more cautiously in framing their questions or run the risk of appearing to torment the witness. Although his outburst was completely spontaneous, through it McFarlane succeeded in muting several tough lines of inquiry concerning inconsistencies in his prior testimony.

The examination dragged on, with occasional sarcasms flashing from McFarlane. At one point, in response to a question about why he remained silent when he learned that North was going to destroy documents, he said bitterly, "That's right, and I deserve responsibility, and I ought to be prosecuted to the full extent of the law and sent away." The words were spoken in anger and frustration.

Most members empathized with McFarlane even as they appeared to criticize his actions. He had helped initiate a program that threatened to unravel the presidency of Ronald Reagan. He had urged its termination. But when called upon to help carry it out, he did not refuse. And when the story broke in the newspapers, he became actively involved in the attempt to construct a false and misleading chronology of events.

It seemed ironic that a man of such broad governmental experience and apparent good intentions could find himself doing things he had warned others against. He had once written a memorandum to Poindexter in which he said, "I lived through Watergate, John. Well-meaning people who were in on the early planning of the communications strategy didn't intend to lie, but ultimately came around to it."

Liman asked McFarlane how someone with his record of proud service, honor, and insight could have participated in preparing a false chronology and the other activities under question. McFarlane responded that "context and perspective" had to be provided to the skein of events and circumstances. It is true that, in the hothouse of presidential power and politics, judgment can be clouded by polemics and the desperate desire to protect the President. But the greatest protection of a president rests in the insistence upon truth, not in the concealment of error.

McFarlane was a tragic example of a decent man who knew the lesson of Watergate yet failed to heed it.

Couriers and Contras

A series of witnesses were called before the Committee in an effort to demonstrate how the White House had improperly or illegally solicited funds from foreign governments and private individuals for the purpose of providing military assistance to the Contras.

The witnesses provided the essential facts the Committee sought, but collectively they proved a point that was more important to the viewing public: they were men who, if flawed, appeared to be neither knaves nor thieves.

Gaston Sigur was the first of these witnesses to testify. An East Asian specialist who had worked on the NSC staff before being assigned to the State Department, Sigur appeared to be a genial and shy naïf. North had asked him to arrange two separate meetings with representatives of certain Asian countries. It was clear to Sigur that North intended to solicit financial assistance for the Contras during these meetings.

Sigur never challenged North's authority to set up the meetings or the propriety of the request itself. He assumed that a request that emanated from the White House must be presumed to be legal.

COURTER: You indicated that when Oliver North asked you to approach another country, you indicated it was for humanitarian aid. He made that point?

SIGUR: Yes.

91

COURTER: And you asked him whether it was legal?

SIGUR: Yes, I asked the question, as I say, it was somewhat pro forma rather than anything else. I never thought it wasn't specifically. . . . It was only because, as I say, of what I had read in the papers and heard about, and of what Congressional action was being taken, and I just wanted to sort of be sure that everybody was, I guess, that he was looking at that.

But I have never doubted it. I never thought for a minute that there was anything wrong with it, illegal about it.[38]

HEFLIN: And at that time was there any discussion that Boland had been adopted a short time previous to that [meeting] between you and, I believe, Colonel North?

SIGUR: There was no specific discussion. As I say . . . I did ask him about whether the conversation that he had had and the things that he had discussed were legal, and he said yes, and . . . clearly, I was referring to actions that had been taken by the Congress.[39]

Sigur, fidgeting at the witness table, did not look as if he had the position or the temperament to challenge a superior. Clearly uncomfortable in such an intense spotlight (his eyes seemed constantly to search for the nearest exit), Sigur was eager to satisfy each Committee member by answering almost every question in the affirmative. Although he was completely candid, he was also careful to characterize a number of errors in North's memoranda as simple mistakes rather than deliberate misrepresentations.

WSC: *At one point, Senator Sam Nunn whispered devilishly to me, "Let's flip a coin to see which one of us asks him: If Colonel North told us that you masterminded the whole operation, would that be a lie or a mistake?"*

Behind Nunn's humor lay a serious question about the nature of a government employee's responsibility to question the authority of his superiors. Sigur had made only a perfunctory inquiry into the propriety of North's requests. North responded with an equally perfunctory assurance that his requests were proper.

Government could not function if every public official felt compelled to question the legality of requests by his colleagues or superiors that carried the Oval Office's stamp of approval. Nevertheless, the Boland Amendments were well known to those in the NSC and the State Department, and a duty to seek something more than pro-forma assurance was called for.

Robert Owen, a tall, slender young man whose earnest face looked as if a razor had yet to touch it, in many ways was a precursor to North—one that we failed to see coming. Obviously well educated, Owen projected a deceptive innocence.

Dubbed "T.C." ("The Courier") by North, he carried out missions as diverse as picking up a roll of cash during Rosh Hashanah at a Chinese delicatessen in Manhattan, running maps, intelligence, and weapons lists to the Contra leaders, and soliciting funds from one foreign country in their behalf. He acknowledged that he and North knew they were walking a legal tightrope and had joked that they might go to prison for their efforts. Sounding what was to become a familiar theme, Owen rationalized his actions: "But I felt that I was working for—or working with—a member of the National Security Council, someone who had access to the President of the United States, and I believed it was the right thing to do."[40]

At one point, during a break in the testimony, Paul Sarbanes (D-Maryland), a veteran of the Nixon impeachment hearings held by the House Judiciary Committee, expressed his exasperation: "This kid is unbelievable. He doesn't understand. He thinks this is all a big joke, that it's some kind of a game, or a movie that he's playing a role in. . . ."

Owen never conceded the existence of error or misjudgment. He remained convinced that the cause of stopping communism in Central America was greater than any concern about what he considered to be vague and ambiguous laws passed by a shortsighted Congress. He was not quite as ingenuous as he had tried to portray himself, or as some had mistakenly concluded.

North had pressured the State Department to employ Owen (through a nonprofit organization which Owen had set up) to work for the Nicaraguan Humanitarian Assistance Office (NHAO). Although the law and his contract with NHAO specifically restricted assistance to the Contras to humanitarian aid, Owen was covertly helping North provide advice and assistance of a military nature. He claimed he had done so on his own time.

Owen had previously served as a Senate staff member and was obviously knowledgeable about congressional resistance to promoting the overthrow of a Nicaraguan regime to which we had extended diplomatic recognition. While working for Adolfo Calero in February 1985, Owen wrote a memorandum recommending that none of the Contra groups publicly admit that their goal was the overthrow of the Sandinistas or they would lose congressional support. He had urged deception and had practiced it.

Owen's advice to practice deception was not much different from that offered later by his idol, North (alias "Steelhammer," and "Blood and Guts"). In a memo to Calero, North advised:

> Next week, a sum of $20 million will be deposited in the usual account. While this must be husbanded carefully, it should allow us to bridge the gap between now and when the vote is taken and the funds are turned on again. . . . Please do *not* in any way make *anyone* aware of the deposit. Too much is becoming known by too many people. We need to make sure that this new financing does *not* become known. The Congress must believe that there continues to be an urgent need for funding.[41]

Owen, contrary to the impression he tried to create, did understand the gravity of his activity; it was the Committee that failed to address the implications of his testimony publicly. Owen's proud account of his dealings with the Contras and his confident demeanor were due not to his innocence, but to his arrogance. He was emboldened, no doubt, by having been given immunity from prosecution by both the independent counsel and the Committee.

At the end of his testimony, Owen asked for permission to read a statement. He quoted what he called "a poem" written by John Hull, a U.S. citizen living in Costa Rica who had actively been assisting the Contras:

> Today on the fertile plains of Central America, cattle graze peacefully on the wooded hills and green valleys, monkeys play, parrots fly by, and song birds send forth their music that echoes over a troubled land. . . . We have stood by the charred remains. . . .[42]

It was not merely bad poetry, but a pathetic paean. Yet, though a few members rolled their eyes, all remained passive, conveying a collective paternal tolerance.

Owen should have received a stern rebuke and a reminder that the activities he had just described to the Committee and to the television audience may have been illegal and that he was fortunate not to be burdened with the prospect of criminal prosecution for what he had done. Instead, he left the hearing room professing that the fault lay not in his deeds, but in the confusion and cowardice of lawmakers.

Adolfo Calero, one of the leaders of the Nicaraguan Democratic Force (FDN)—the principal Contra military and political organization—was called because of his knowledge of the administration's supply of money and weapons to the resistance. He had been in direct contact with North, Owen, and Generals Singlaub and Secord. He would verify that the Contras had received more than $33 million ($32 million from one foreign source) and used most of the money to purchase weapons. He would also establish that very little cash came to the Contras from the diversion of the profits from the sale of weapons to Iran.

Calero created a surprisingly positive impression as a witness. In reading the deposition he gave prior to the hearing, we anticipated that he might prove difficult to handle. The written record suggested that he was an impatient and brusque man who responded to questions he did not like with sarcasm.

Owen's extensive memoranda to North portrayed Calero as a "strong man" who had surrounded himself with greedy, power-motivated liars who treated the resistance to the Sandinistas as a business. Owen had characterized their attitude as calculated exploitation. "There is still a belief the Marines are going to have to invade, so let's get set so we will automatically be the ones put into power."

Owen had also outlined how Calero had resisted U.S. efforts to strengthen the other Contra leaders—Alfonso Robelo and Arturo Cruz—and warned that the United States government was mistaken if it thought it could control Calero. "The question should be asked, does Calero manipulate the U.S.G.? On several occasions, the answer is yes."

An entirely different personality emerged in the public hearings. A tall and solidly built man, Calero projected a sense of power and purpose while appearing relaxed and affable. In his opening remarks he quoted with ease the words of Thomas Jefferson, Benjamin Franklin, Harry Truman, and Will Rogers.

Calero is a graduate of Notre Dame who had returned to his native Nicaragua, where he became a successful businessman. He held top management positions with the W. R. Grace and Coca-Cola companies, while becoming a prominent member of the Conservative Democratic Party, which was opposed to President Somoza's oppressive regime. He had been jailed on at least one occasion by Somoza.

But Calero had become disenchanted with the Sandinistas after their shift away from the revolution's promise of political pluralism and a mixed economy. While he was out of Nicaragua in December 1982, the Sandinistas confiscated his property. In January 1983 he joined the resistance, and became one of the FDN's leaders a month later.

Some Committee members had anticipated that Calero had come to distrust North, as one of Robert Owen's memos indicated. They were disappointed. Calero expressed unqualified gratitude for North's efforts in behalf of the resistance. He did not inquire whether the money came from Country Two or Country Three. Frankly, he did not care, as long as it continued to come. And he was more than willing to reciprocate the generosity being extended to the cause of the Contras. North had requested that he provide money to help retrieve our hostages in Lebanon. Eager to respond, Calero had provided North with approximately $90,000 in blank traveler's checks that could be endorsed by the bearer. This was a significant revelation to most members. It was a reverse diversion: Contra money going to the Iran program. It revealed that North was treating the programs as mutually supportive and reinforcing. Calero explained it in simple terms: "I gave the money for a worthy effort which I considered was one and the same with our own effort."

When asked whether he had complained that Secord had been charging too high a price for weapons, Calero deflected the problem to his brother, Mario, a "great conversationalist," who was more "expressive" than he. Laughter flooded the room. His quick humor proved disarming. Everyone knew about talkative brothers. The Committee did not get an answer to the question.

Did he know that North had used part of the money to make a $1,000 wedding gift to Owen? No, was his answer. But he would not have objected: he would have considered it "a payment, a compensation."

Calero's attention was then directed to large cardboard-backed charts that contained a partial list of traveler's checks that North had cashed. The exhibit showed that dozens of checks had been cashed for what appeared to be personal purposes: dry cleaning at Farragut Valet; items from Appalachian Outfitters; groceries from Giant Food Stores; unmentionables from a hosiery store; snow tires from a garage. . . .

Calero was not shaken by these revelations. He conceded to Senator Rudman that it did not snow in Nicaragua, but he was sure that North could explain the expenditures.

The Committee had taken a calculated risk in using Calero as a vehicle to introduce evidence of what appeared to be petty avarice. However, the attempt to reduce North's heroic proportions with such testimony was short-lived since we did not know (and would not know) whether North had ever replenished these funds spent for personal purposes.

Those who supported Contra aid were justifiably elated by Calero's testimony. For the first time the American people had an opportunity to witness a leader of the cause some of them supported. Calero came off as an educated man with American values, pleading for assistance in the struggle against communism.

Some members of the press corps, however, began to grumble about the Committee's timidity. Why had no one challenged the conduct and atrocities of the Contras? Who would speak up for Benjamin Linder, the young American shot by the Contras while he was living with peasant farmers in a remote village?

A majority of Committee members saw the issue of Contra support as a trap to be avoided. Succumbing to the temptation to argue the merits or morality of the Contra cause would reduce the Committee to debating the Contra-aid program while ignoring the means used by North and others to support it.

Baksheesh—
Coin of the Realm

Whe Albert Hakim, an Iranian-born American businessman, entered the Caucus Room, a curious sense of excitement followed him like a burning fuse. In the preceding weeks we had heard much about "profiteers" and the "privatization of our foreign policy." Now, for the first time, we would have the chance to enter the world of international arms dealers and learn something of their markups and methods of operation. We would walk through a twisting lane of paper corporations, stapled together to confound the unskilled eye. Finally, we would comprehend the consequences of our government's turning to private individuals to conduct the public's diplomacy.

Hakim was Richard Secord's premier financier—a man who could scan a balance sheet and determine immediately whether a venture was (or could be) profitable. He knew how to open Swiss bank accounts and move money among shell corporations with a magician's sleight of hand.

Hakim was dressed immaculately in a dark-blue suit and starched white shirt. He wore his entrepreneurial success with pride and without apology. What was most striking about Hakim's appearance were his large eyes, dark brown, almost black—and cold. Hakim never flinched or looked away from his interrogators. Using measured, precise language, he was like a mason who knew that any misalignment in the cornerstones of his testimony would warp the entire edifice.

Hakim's opening statement reflected his discontent with prehearing publicity, which he characterized as distorted and rife with "veiled ethnic slurs": we were on notice to refrain from references about Persian rug-merchants. He also offered the Committee a beguiling frankness about his reasons for becoming involved with both the Iranians and the Contras. Later we would recognize that frankness as hubris.

> As will become clear during my testimony, my participation in this matter was a result of a variety of motives. Not only was I presented with an opportunity to help my country, the United States, and my native land, Iran, but at the same time I had the opportunity to profit financially as a businessman. I never pretended to undertake the tasks I was asked to perform for philanthropic purposes and I made that clear to all of those with whom I was involved—including General Secord, Lieutenant Colonel North, the CIA, and the Iranians.[43]

From the beginning of Hakim's testimony, conflicts in the evidence surrounding the Enterprise emerged. Secord had testified that he had foresworn all profits generated by the sale of weapons to the Contras and to the Iranians. Hakim, however, testified that in August 1986:

> One-third was put into [his own] account for [his own] benefit. The second one-third, Korel [another Swiss account], were assets for General Secord, and one-third to the C.TEA account that represents Tom Clines' account, and the ten per cent went to SCITECH, which, if you look at the complete name of SCITECH, it is SCITECH Training Group, and if you separate SCI from TECH, you will notice that the abbreviation will form again STTGI, and this was chosen by design to reflect the offshore company of STTGI. That was my design and my idea.
>
> NIELDS: Were these divisions of profits?
> HAKIM: Yes, sir.
> NIELDS: Were they divisions of profits on the procurement of arms for the contras?
> HAKIM: That is correct.[44]

Secord testified that he wanted to return to government service to repair his reputation—perhaps as director of operations in the CIA—and did not want the issue of profit-making to jeopardize that opportunity. When he testified, we were not persuaded by his argument that the President or the CIA would be offended by the notion that he had made a profit out of a plan that had been approved by the President himself. This claim seemed even less persuasive since, after he had allegedly foresworn his profit from arms sales, he and Hakim had formed a company (Tri-American Arms) to manufacture weapons to be sold on the international market. According to Secord's logic, profits from a government-sponsored arms-sale plan might taint the opportunity for future government service, whereas profits from a private arms-sale venture would be disregarded.

Hakim's testimony made Secord's distinction between sources of profit less credible. Hakim had continued to make deposits to Secord's account (supposedly without Secord's knowledge), because he did not believe that Secord would ever be offered a government position. If we accepted Hakim's testimony, his partner, Secord, was the unwitting and unwilling beneficiary of a covert account maintained on his behalf. This arrangement was an IRS agent's bad dream. Profits foresworn by Secord should have been taxable as either a gift or income to Hakim, but Hakim set the profits aside in a Swiss account that remained secret to Secord and the IRS.[45]

Moreover, Secord maintained that his purchases of an airplane ($74,600), a Porsche ($31,825), and a health-center visit ($3,075) were paid for with loans from STTGI, not from a distribution of profits from the Enterprise.[46]

Something was not quite right. The bricks were not level; the plumb line was off. Hakim, by his own testimony, was simply a bottom-line man. Yet we were supposed to believe that he disregarded the express wishes of Secord in order to provide and protect the latter's financial interests.

Even more out of character for a self-described "bottom-line man" like Hakim was his startling revelation that he had set aside $200,000 in a "Button" account (short for "Belly Button") for the benefit of North. Actually, Hakim had wanted to set aside $500,000; only after Secord objected that it was too much money, that Hakim did not comprehend a military officer's standard of living, did Hakim propose the $200,000.

Although Hakim claimed that North had not been notified specifically about this account, Hakim had mentioned to North that he need not fear for the well-being of his family. Hakim contacted his attorney/banker in Switzerland, Willard Zucker, to find a way to funnel to North profits from the arms sale. Hakim said he wanted to find a way to "pluck the eyebrow without blinding the eye." Zucker first considered a distribution of the funds through North's family members. Then he explored the possibility of having Mrs. North paid by earning commissions from phony real-estate transactions. In fact, Mrs. North traveled to Philadelphia to meet with Zucker, but no satisfactory way to transfer money to North or his family was ever devised or implemented. The money remained in the Swiss account, the eyebrow unplucked.

During his examination of Hakim, Liman displayed the razor's edge of his legal talents. The Iranian practice of "baksheesh" has a special aroma, and Liman could smell a "kickback" in any language. Although Hakim acknowledged that he had engaged in baksheesh when he was in business in Iran prior to the Khomeini revolution, he referred to the practice as providing government officials with an "entitlement," not a "kickback."

How was it that Hakim wanted to provide $500,000 (then $200,000) for North after having met him on only one occasion? Hakim explained he had come to "love" the man. Liman expressed puzzlement. Was it a case of "love at first sight"?

HAKIM: I came to learn about the man even during this February meeting in Frankfurt—that he works around the clock, he doesn't care about when he eats or he does eat or doesn't. I saw a man dissipating [sic] so much love for his country and his associates that the radiation of that love—it really immediately penetrated through my system. I saw so much sincerity, so—I was acclimated, Mr. Liman, for this encounter. So, when I saw what I saw, it fell quite in line with what I heard.

LIMAN: Mr. Hakim, do you normally set up accounts for workaholics?

HAKIM: I set up accounts for anyone that falls within my financial and commercial network, and if it's necessary to set up such accounts.

LIMAN: Did you consider Colonel North to be within your financial and commercial network and necessary to set up such accounts?

HAKIM: I considered being asked to structure such an organization. I understand that basically that was my mission, to create the structure that would satisfy a commercial covert activity.[47]

Mr. Hakim was obviously generous to his business associates. It may be that he felt a kinship for and was truly concerned about the welfare of North's family, even though he had never met them. But a disturbing pattern appeared in his dealings with government officials. North, Hakim, and Secord had been disenchanted with dealing with Manucher Ghorbanifar, the Iranian middleman who had difficulty in persuading people—and polygraph machines—of his bona fides. Hakim set up a line of communication to what he called "Iranian moderates" through a Second Channel—an Iranian with a distinguished war record who was related to a leading Iranian government official. Cutting out Ghorbanifar had the additional benefit of increasing the Enterprise's profits, or, to use Mr. Hakim's word, making the operation more "efficient." Hakim was impressed with the repeated acts of courage that "the relative" had demonstrated. As a token of his admiration, Hakim purchased jeans and shirts for the man's children. "The relative" rejected Hakim's act of generosity and stuffed a $100 bill in Hakim's jacket as payment for the gifts.

Hakim's gesture—even if it was a sincere act of good will—revealed a propensity for providing gratuities to individuals with access to high government officials who might generate millions of dollars in profits to his business ventures.

Hakim's testimony contributed to the perception that North's reputation was being tarnished by his association with private international arms dealers. Cashing traveler's checks for several thousands of dollars might be explained or even discounted. But being the beneficiary of a $200,000 secret Swiss account and allowing his wife to meet with a Swiss banker in Philadelphia made more credible the charge that North's patriotism had been compromised by personal gain.

It is not easy to draw the line that separates confidence from arrogance, but it easy to recognize when an individual has crossed it. Secord made little effort to hide his contempt for what he believed to be the incompetence of the CIA. Hakim displayed a similar attitude. When the United States initiated negotiations directly with the Iranians in Frankfurt, Germany, Hakim donned a wig and served as an interpreter because the United States government could not come up with an agent or an official who spoke Farsi. Apparently, neither Secord nor Hakim considered the State Department a trustworthy or competent source for such a specialist. George Cave, a retired CIA agent who spoke fluent Farsi, was subsequently hired to assist in the negotiating process. In October 1986, Cave, Secord, North, and Hakim met in Frankfurt with certain high-ranking Iranians. The negotiations at one point threatened to break down, and North delegated to Hakim the responsibility to carry on bargaining with the Iranians. A nine-point proposal, labeled the "Hakim Accords" by Congressman Ed Jenkins (D-Georgia), emerged from the negotiations. This led to an exchange of five hundred TOW missiles for the release of one hostage held in Lebanon, David P. Jacobsen.[48]

Earlier, North had made at least two other agreements, in the name of the United States government, that were contrary to United States policy: (1) that the United States would fight Russians in Iran in case of invasion, with or without the government of Iran's assistance;[49] (2) that the United States officials would "cooperate to depose" Iraqi President Saddam Hussein.[50]

North later testified that he "would have promised them free tickets to Disney World or a trip on the Space Shuttle if it would have gotten American [hostages] home."[51] There was, in fact, a clownish and dangerously amateurish aspect to our attempt to bargain with the Iranians and to deceive them. The United States might or might not go to war with the Soviets should the latter attempt to seize Iran militarily, but a decision to do so could never be tied to the release of one or two American hostages. Moreover, the likelihood is obviously remote that Congress or the President would be called upon to honor such a false promise made by a retired general, a lieutenant colonel, and a CIA annuitant. But if a false promise to help depose Saddam Hussein were exposed, it might jeopardize the lives of those already held hostage and serve as an open invitation to take more Americans as hostages in the future.

A third promise, one of Hakim's nine points, that struck us as being outrageous and dangerous was a pledge to help secure the release of seventeen Da'Wa terrorists being held in Kuwaiti jails. These were Muslim extremists who had bombed the U.S. Embassy and attempted to assassinate our embassy personnel in Kuwait in December 1983. In 1985 members of the same group hijacked a TWA jet in Beirut and executed two Americans. Chairman Inouye expressed the outrage we felt about Hakim's pledge: "You are telling me that a patriotic general was willing to swap seventeen terrorists, who were guilty of killing American personnel, in return for . . . hostages, who are innocent of any criminal deed?"[52]

Hakim remained unperturbed by the moral implications of such a proposal or the difficulties posed for the American hostages in the event that the United States failed to secure the release of the terrorists. Earlier, in response to Arthur Liman, he exhibited a similar indifference to the niceties or complexities of diplomacy.

LIMAN: Did you feel like you had been the Secretary of State for a day?

HAKIM: I would not accept that position for any money in the world, sir.

LIMAN: Well, you had it better than the Secretary of State in some sense. You didn't have to get confirmed; correct?

HAKIM: I still believe that I have it better than the Secretary.

LIMAN: And—

HAKIM: I can achieve more, too.[53]

It was clear that, for Hakim, baksheesh remained the coin of the realm.

Out on a Limb

Elliott Abrams was the first major administration witness to testify before the Committee.

Earlier in the year, a *Washington Post* article on the life and lore of the Assistant Secretary of State for Latin American Affairs portrayed Abrams as a bright, ambitious young man who bore a combative zest for stopping the cancer of communism. In the mid-1970s he served as a special counsel to the late Senator Henry Jackson, a Democrat whose name was synonymous with a hard line in dealing with the Soviet Union. Senator Daniel P. Moynihan, the intellectual heir of the "Jackson Democrats," employed Abrams as his chief of staff until 1979. Whether Abrams left the Democratic Party or it left him, he began a political odyssey that carried him to the Reagan campaign. In 1981 he switched to the Republican Party and became an Assistant Secretary of State at the age of thirty-three.

Abrams is a thin, narrow-featured man who comes at you with the sharpness and velocity of an arrow. He carries his convictions without apology or diplomacy, lashing out with equal intensity at journalists or congressmen critical of the Contra cause.

According to *The Washington Post*, Abrams was fond of quoting a French proverb to describe himself: "This animal is very wicked. When you attack it, it defends itself."

107

As if to remind the Committee that he regarded the hearing room as an arena for battle, Abrams arrived ten minutes late, his first sword-thrust to the psyche of his opponents.

He spent much of his time during the direct and cross-examination by counsel explaining the confusion and contradictions in the evidence pertaining to the administration's activities in support of the Contras.

He had been preceded at the witness table by Ambassador Lewis Tambs, a white-haired, blunt-spoken professor at Arizona State University who had served as ambassador to Costa Rica from 1985 to 1987. Tambs testified that North had instructed him to "open a southern front" to Nicaragua. The strangeness of the military directive to a diplomat was compounded only by its source—a staff member of the NSC. The State Department is supposed to be Tambs's boss. Tambs testified that he had discussed with Abrams the establishment of a southern front in September 1985, adding that they'd had the conversation in a corridor. "It was obvious to me, at least as I understood it, that he knew as much about it as I did." Tambs also said that a RIG (restricted interagency group) consisting of Abrams, the CIA Chief of the Central America Task Force, and North directed him to assist the Contras. This small group was part of a larger group of interagency personnel.

Abrams categorically denied that he had ever discussed opening a southern front with Ambassador Tambs. He considered it "bizarre" for the Committee to give credence to a remark that allegedly was made in a corridor. "I don't think we discussed any such thing in the corridor or anywhere else." Abrams attacked Tambs's credibility by stating that the RIG consisted of twenty people—not three, as Tambs had suggested—and that "he [Tambs] doesn't know what he's talking about and never attended a RIG meeting." Contradiction in the recollection of events does not prove that someone is lying: a mistake is as possible as a false statement. But there were other contradictions and conflicts in the evidence that served to bring into focus the pervasive practice of deception among some of the members of the administration.

John K. Singlaub, a retired major general in the United States Army, a global crusader for freedom fighters, testified that, shortly before he had traveled to Asia to solicit funds for the Contras, he had met with Abrams to request that a message be sent signifying that his request was legitimate; Abrams agreed to be the person to "give the signal." Singlaub added that while in Asia he received a telephone call from Abrams and was told not to make the request.

Abrams denied having met with Singlaub prior to his departure and denied that any decision was ever made that he would signal administration approval of Singlaub's solicitations.

However, a State Department memo dated May 14, 1986, indicated that "the earlier decision to pass the message had been reconsidered. . . . Tell him the timing was not right. . . ." Another memo, dated May 22, stated that Singlaub wanted to hear from Abrams as to why his solicitation of the Asian countries was untimely.

Abrams angrily denounced any implication that he had initially agreed to signal the administration's approval of Singlaub's activities. He said that the real meaning of the State Department's memos (as opposed to their literal meaning) was that Singlaub was a well-meaning compatriot whose fund-raising activities might jeopardize the strategy of persuading Congress that the Contras were impoverished and in desperate need of funds. In other words, Singlaub was being "strung along" by the State Department so that his enthusiasm and commitment to the Contra cause would not be diminished by an outright rejection of his solicitation activities.

One of the more exquisite ironies in this was that Secretary of State Shultz had also considered the possibility of approaching the same Asian countries for contributions to the Contras but decided against doing so because those countries would demand too high a price in return for their generosity. Yet North, with the assistance of Sigur, solicited $2 million from one of the countries without the knowledge of Shultz or Abrams.

The disarray within the administration was not confined to fund-raising activities. Singlaub traveled to Nicaragua and carried on negotiations with Eden Pastora, the charismatic leader of the Contras based on the southern border of Nicaragua. North and the CIA believed that Pastora, popularly known as "Commandante Zero," was a weak and ineffective leader who was undermining the overall Contra effort. Singlaub and Abrams disagreed. North and the CIA were trying to force Pastora out of the Contra leadership, while Singlaub and Abrams were trying to keep him in.

It was clear that the dangerous conflicts in policy were the direct result of a deliberate effort on the part of certain key officials to conceal their activities from other members of the administration—and a corresponding willingness on the part of those others to remain uninformed.

For example, Shultz considered North to be a "loose cannon" and instructed Abrams to "monitor Ollie." Given some of the stories revealed during the course of the hearings, Shultz's wariness was justified. North had proposed that the Contras seize territory on the Atlantic coast of Nicaragua and then fight the Sandinistas in an Alamo-like last stand. In North's scheme, the American people would be so taken by the courage of the Contras that they would rally to their cause. The Department of Defense and the CIA considered the proposal crazy. North had also suggested to an NSC colleague that the United States capture an Iranian ambassador and hold him hostage until the Lebanese terrorists released the American hostages. On another occasion, North wrote a memorandum to Poindexter stating that he had telephoned Costa Rica's President Oscar Arias and threatened that the United States would terminate economic assistance to Costa Rica if Arias held a scheduled press conference and disclosed the existence of a secret airstrip that was being used to supply the Contras. North was told by Poindexter that he had done the "right thing" but should not talk about it. The Committee discovered that North in fact never made the call. His claim to have done so was one of his many exaggerations.

Abrams, however, did not share Shultz's negative opinion of

North and confined his monitoring activities to asking North on several occasions whether everything North was doing was legal. When an article appeared in the *Miami Herald* on April 30, 1986, alleging that North was actively engaged in fund-raising activities in behalf of the Contras, Abrams did not call North to inquire about the accuracy of the story, but instead complained to Morton Abramowitz, the Assistant Secretary of State for Intelligence and Research, about leaks coming out of his office.

It is not at all clear whether an inquiry by Abrams to North would have produced any information, since North seemed determined to screen his activities from other administration officials. On June 10, 1986, North wrote a memo to Poindexter:

Elliott has talked to Shultz and had prepared a paper re going to [Country Two and Country Three] for contributions. Elliott called me and asked "where to send the money." . . . At this point I need your help. As you know, I have the accounts and the means by which this thing needs to be accomplished. I have no idea what Shultz knows or doesn't know, but he could prove to be very unhappy if he learns of these other countries' aid that has been given in the past from someone other than you. Did RCM [McFarlane] ever tell Shultz? . . . At this point I'm not sure who on our side knows what.[54]

Abrams testified that he was never told about the contributions from Countries Two and Three but was simply advised to "keep quiet" until North talked to Poindexter.

Abrams's ignorance of North's activities was disturbing to the Committee; still more so were his past assurances to the Congress and to the press that were either untrue or misleading.

For example, after Eugene Hasenfus's plane crashed and he was taken captive, Abrams talked with Lieutenant Colonel Robert Earl, an associate of North's at the National Security Council, and the CIA Chief of the Central American Task Force (C/CATF). Both men assured Abrams that there was no U.S. involvement in the flight. At a minimum, C/CATF knew that Tomas Castillo (Joseph Fernandez, CIA station chief in Costa Rica) had been providing assistance to the Contra resupply operation. Testifying before the Senate Intelligence Committee on the Hasenfus crash, Abrams gave a categorical denial of any U.S. government involvement.

Abrams also had appeared on "Evans and Novak," a syndicated television program hosted by two conservative journalists who are strong supporters of the Contra cause. Again, he was confident and aggressive in his responses to questions about the Hasenfus crash.

NOVAK: All right, now, just on Friday the San Francisco *Examiner*, . . . quoting intelligence sources, said there was no CIA connection, but there was connection, of all places, from Vice President Bush's office. That Vice President Bush's security aide, Mr. Don Gregg, had hired this Max Gomez, who Mr. Hasenfus described as a CIA agent. Do you know anything about that?

ABRAMS: Not a lot. I first heard about it on Friday morning as well. I can say first of all that there's no Max Gomez. Whoever that gentleman is, he certainly isn't named Max Gomez. So we need, first of all, to find out who he is. Secondly, I know nothing about any connection to the Vice President's office whatsoever. And thirdly, in his capacity down there in Central America helping whoever he is, he is not on the U.S. government payroll in any way.

NOVAK: Now, when you say gave categorical assurance, we're not playing word games that are so common in Washington. You're not talking about the NSC, or something else?

ABRAMS: I am not playing games.

NOVAK: National Security Council?

ABRAMS: No government agencies, none . . .

NOVAK: We have just under 30 seconds left, Assistant Secretary Abrams. Just looking at this from the broad picture, do you think all this publicity, this hype, do you think this could yet turn around the question in Congress where the—although it's passed both houses— the hundred million dollars in aid would be denied to the contras?

ABRAMS: No. People will try to do that, but the Intelligence Committees who know the facts know that there was no U.S. government role in this.

EVANS: . . . Who's supplying that money?

ABRAMS: I can tell you only one thing about that, and that is that there is no one source, as near as I can make out, nor is there any one organization. There are a whole bunch of them. I don't know who they are. . . .

EVANS: Saudi Arabian money?

ABRAMS: I have heard that again . . . and as far as I am aware, it is just plain false. . . .

EVANS: I can't believe you don't know where that money is coming from.

ABRAMS: I do not know where that money is coming from.[55]

Evans and Novak were convinced. Their final commentary reflected that any doubts or skepticism they may have harbored had been brushed away by the man who, as Assistant Secretary of State for Inter-American Affairs, was in a position to know.

EVANS: Bob, I don't know whether the Assistant Secretary of State for Latin America [sic] has taken lessons on how to be cool under fire, couth under fire, but I gave him the worst pummeling I could. I really tried to get in there. Of course, you were rather aggressive yourself. We didn't get anywhere in bending him out of his position that the U.S. government in no way, shape or form had nothing, in any way, guidance, organizational, orders, et cetera, to do with this unfortunate, this tragic case.

NOVAK: You know, I've seen a lot of cover-ups in this town, Rowland, and we both may end up with egg on our face before this is over, and this is all an elaborate lie, but this doesn't look like a cover-up, and it doesn't because there is no equivocation. He says it didn't come from a U.S. military base. He says that these companies are not CIA companies. The so-called Max Gomez, the CIA operative, supposedly hired by the CIA or Vice President Bush, doesn't even exist. No, no, no, he says.

Unfortunately, the journalists did end up with egg on their faces, as did Congress and Elliott Abrams. By stating categorically that there was no Max Gomez, Abrams implied that the man ("whoever he was") was some imposter who had no connection to the U.S. government. In fact, Max Gomez was an alias used by Felix Rodriguez, who had been recruited by North to work with the Salvadoran counterterrorist program but who was covertly assisting the Contras.

Abrams cited the House and Senate Intelligence Committees as independent support for his position that there was no United States government involvement in the Hasenfus affair or in the resupply of the Contras. Who gave the Intelligence Committees their information? Abrams. He was using their acceptance of his testimony to corroborate it.

Finally, Abrams's statements about not knowing the source of money for the Contras was, at least in part, disingenuous. According to the evidence, Abrams did not know about the contributions by one Middle Eastern country and the solicitations by North from another in Asia. But Abrams had personally recommended that Shultz consider soliciting humanitarian assistance from the country of Brunei. Using an alias, "Mr. Kenilworth," Abrams himself requested funds from a Brunei official during a meeting in London. Because of a typographical error in the numbers of a Swiss bank account, the $10-million contribution Brunei made in response was never received by the Hakim-Secord Enterprise. It ended up in the account of an unsuspecting Swiss businessman.

Engaging in evasive action against two probing journalists may be justified under some circumstances. But evasion must be distinguished from deception. Refusing to answer a question is almost always more appropriate than offering a response that can either mislead or be misconstrued. Deliberately creating a false impression not only undermines a public official's credibility, but also sows seeds of cynicism and distrust among the American people toward their government when the truth finally emerges.

Abrams not only misled the press, he misled Congress. Before a Senate Foreign Relations Committee hearing held on October 10, 1986, Abrams responded to a question about the existence of foreign support to the Contras by saying: "I think I can say that while I have been Assistant Secretary, which is about 15 months, we have not received a dime from a foreign government, not a dime, from any foreign government."[56]

Abrams repeated the denial of foreign assistance four days later before the House Intelligence Committee. His explanation was that he had no knowledge that Countries Two and Three had contributed to the Contras, and that, even though he had personally solicited a contribution from a Brunei official, that contribution had not been received at the time he testified. Therefore, in a technical sense, he had been truthful.

Abrams used his verbal skills to obscure and deceive. At a November 25, 1986, hearing before the Senate Intelligence Committee, Abrams appeared with the C/CATF. Senator Bill Bradley (D-New Jersey) asked whether either of them had any knowledge or indication that the Contras were receiving funds from Middle Eastern sources. Both replied, "No." According to Abrams, he had responded truthfully because Brunei was not a Middle Eastern country.

At the same Senate hearing, he was asked whether he had ever discussed the problems of fund-raising by the Contras with members of the NSC staff. Abrams replied, "No. I can't remember," adding, "We're not—you know—we're not in the fund-raising business."[57]

Once again, before our Committee, Abrams maintained that he had been technically accurate, because he had been asked about "fund-raising *by* the Contras" and he, in soliciting Brunei, had engaged in fund-raising *for* the Contras.

When Abrams later corrected his misstatement to the Senate Intelligence Committee, he explained that he had not been authorized to reveal this solicitation. This led Congressman Brooks to ask, "Do you have to be authorized to tell the truth?"

Even if Abrams considered a pledge of secrecy to a foreign government more important than honesty to our own, Abrams could have simply said, "I'm sorry, I'm not authorized to discuss this question. I will either get authority or suggest that you call upon those who do possess it." There can be no justification for

Executive Branch officials' engaging in deliberate efforts to deceive members of Congress.

Senator Tom Eagleton (D-Missouri) reminded Abrams of this point.

> EAGLETON: Were you then in the fund raising business?
>
> ABRAMS: I would say we were in the fund raising business. I take your point.
>
> EAGLETON: Take my point? Under oath, my friend, that's perjury. Had you been under oath, that's perjury.
>
> ABRAMS: Well, I don't agree with that.
>
> EAGLETON: That's slammer time.
>
> ABRAMS: I don't agree with that, Senator.
>
> EAGLETON: Oh, Elliott, you're too damn smart not to know . . . You were in the fund raising business, you and Ollie. You were opening accounts, you had account cards, you had two accounts and didn't know which account they were going to put it into.
>
> ABRAMS: You've heard my testimony.
>
> EAGLETON: I've heard it, and I want to puke.[58]

Not every member of the Senate Intelligence Committee or of the joint Iran-Contra Committee shared the intensity of Eagleton's visceral reaction to Abrams's deception. But we were all angry. Several Democrats on the Committee flatly told Abrams he had squandered the most important asset any witness can possess— credibility. Representative Brooks said:

> Now, I believe you would have been a lot better informed if you had been reading the daily newspapers, listening to TV, listening to the radio, and I can only conclude after this that you are either extremely incompetent or that you are still, as I say, deceiving us with semantics, or, three, maybe the administration has intentionally kept you in the dark on all these matters so then you can come down and blatantly mislead us, the Secretary of State, and the American people on all of these issues that we have been discussing. I am deeply troubled by it and wonder if you can survive as an Assistant Secretary of State.[59]

Abrams shot back:

Fortunately, I guess I have to say I don't work for you, I work for George Shultz and he seems to be pretty satisfied with the job I have done for him. That makes me very happy and very proud.[60]

Both Brooks and Abrams were right. Abrams enjoyed the confidence of Secretary Shultz and would remain at the helm of the Contra-aid program. Brooks expressed publicly what many others privately concluded: credibility is not easily established and, once lost, is not easily regained.

In venting our anger at Elliott Abrams, Committee members passed over the embarrassment and sense of betrayal experienced by Abrams at the hands of his friends.

Abrams had a deserved reputation as an intelligent and dedicated public servant with limitless opportunities in the future. He was consistently successful in his advocacy of administration policies. No member of Congress had ever had cause to doubt his word or representations. In fact, it was Abrams's very credibility that others permitted him to trade away, so that the veil of deceit might remain draped over the facts. At best they gained a few weeks to dig deeper holes in which to bury the truth. And at what price? He was allowed and encouraged to become the vocal and visible point man for the administration. North, Poindexter, the C/CATF, and others knew that his categorical denials to Congress and the press were false, and they remained silent, leaving him to twist in the gathering wind.

The Perfect Spy

A basic tenet of spycraft is that a spy must look like anything but a spy. Wide-brimmed hats, trench coats, dark glasses, and furtive movements are the stuff of low-grade fiction. Glenn A. Robinette, a sixty-six-year-old white-haired man with sparkling blue eyes, could easily pass for a family physician, lawyer, pastor, or grandfather whose lap was constantly occupied by children. In fact, he is a security consultant who worked for twenty years in the technical-services division of the CIA—a department that specializes in creating forged documents, disguises, and exotic technical devices for intelligence agents.

Robinette testified that in March 1986 Secord hired him to gather derogatory information about several individuals, including Tony Avirgan and Martha Honey, two American free-lance journalists living in Nicaragua, who had filed a lawsuit against Secord and others who were involved in assisting the Nicaraguan Contras. Secord paid Robinette $4,000 a month plus expenses. On April 29, 1986, Secord told Robinette that North was concerned about threats to his home and family, such as the shining of lights into the house, sand poured in the gas tank of his automobile, threatening phone calls, flattened tires, and suspicious packages in the mail.

Robinette went to North's home the next day and met with his wife to determine the type of security system that might be compatible with a household of young children and family animals. Shortly thereafter, Robinette met North at the National Security

Council suite in the Old Executive Office Building, explained the nature of the security system he recommended, and estimated the cost to be in the neighborhood of $8,000 to $8,500. North indicated his approval and urged Robinette to hold the cost down, because "I am a poor lieutenant colonel."

Robinette advanced $6,000 toward the payment of the system, which ultimately cost approximately $13,800. Secord reimbursed Robinette $7,000 in cash ($1,000 for expenses) from the supply he kept in his office. Later, in August, Secord gave Robinette a cashier's check for $9,000. Robinette had no contact or conversation with North after their first meeting in May 1986 until he received a phone call from North sometime after North had been dismissed from the NSC, between November and Christmas of that year. In a friendly tone of voice, North said, "Hey, you have not sent me a bill for the security work." Robinette never expected North to pay for the system and had already been paid by Secord. But he knew what the call meant.

Robinette was aware that federal law prohibits government officials from accepting gratuities for or because of any official act. An official who violates this statute can be imprisoned for up to two years and fined as much as $10,000. Those providing the gifts can also be fined and imprisoned. Robinette also knew that, at the time of the call, North had been removed from the staff of the NSC, had hired an attorney, and was being investigated by the FBI and possibly other agencies. He assumed North was trying to cover himself.

Robinette needed no further direction from North or Secord. He prepared two bills, the first dated July 2, 1986, the second dated September 22, and mailed them in one envelope to North, through North's attorney, Brendan Sullivan. Both bills were phony. The bill dated July 2 listed the cost of the system as $8,000, and the "second notice," dated September 22, indicated that the delay in sending the bill was "due to paperwork."

Within a week of receiving the Robinette letters North prepared and sent Robinette two separate letters, the first dated May 18,

1986, and the second dated October 1, 1986. Robinette had not received or seen these letters before December 1986. The first letter was very formal in tone, addressed to "Mr. Robinette" and signed "Sincerely, Lt. Col. Oliver North." In this letter, North suggested that the security system might be paid for by making "our home available for commercial endorsement of your firm." The second letter was informal and chatty. North addressed Robinette as "Glenn" and signed the letter "with warm regards, Ollie." In addition, the letters "E," "G," and "U" were only partly formed, as though the keys were damaged on the typewriter. In fact, North had added a postscript to the October 1986 letter apologizing for the quality of the type, saying, "Please forgive the type, I literally dropped the ball." It was clear that North had attempted to create the impression that the two letters had been typed at different times. The Committee later obtained expert advice that the letter "E" could not have been damaged in the fashion that it was by the type ball's being dropped and that it had probably been "filed down."

Although Robinette initially claimed that he had acted with his heart instead of his head in attempting to help North out of his difficulties, he conceded that he also wanted to remain on good terms with Secord, who had been providing him with his principal source of income.

Considered a "minor witness" by the Committee, Robinette nevertheless had a major impact upon the administration's most ardent defenders. The cumulative evidence was corroding North's image as a hero. First, Adolfo Calero revealed that he had provided North with $90,000 in traveler's checks, some of which North had cashed for apparently personal purposes. Perhaps these transactions could be explained away, but Hakim's revelations about a $200,000 insurance policy for North's family and the attempts to funnel money to Mrs. North through relatives or fraudulent real-estate payments were more disturbing. Now Robinette was making a powerful case that North had engaged in an improper if not an illegal act, and had tried to cover it up with fraudulent documentation.

Senator Orrin Hatch (R-Utah), during his remarks to Robinette, said, "I find it a little difficult to avoid the feeling of being let down because of what you've told me here today." Representative Hyde was quoted as saying, "I think it's very harmful, very damaging. . . . I think it's sad, it's sleazy."

Senator Trible reacted in even stronger terms:

The evidence here establishes that a government official received a substantial gratuity to which he was not entitled. The gratuity was paid, at least in part, from funds generated by the sale of arms to Iran. That you and Col. North and General Secord endeavored to mislead and to cover your tracks . . .

What we see here, it seems, is a confusion of the public interests and the private interest. And all this demonstrates once again the corrosive and corrupting effect of generating operations without checks and balances.[61]

The Law Men

The Committee members were divided on the advisability of calling Bretton Sciaroni, a thirty-five-year-old lawyer and the sole professional staff member of the President's three-member Intelligence Oversight Board. The Board's responsibility is to report to the President on possible illegal activities conducted by intelligence agencies. Administration supporters on the Committee, who wanted a spokesman on the application of the Boland Amendments to the NSC, prevailed in the decision to have Sciaroni appear as a witness. In August 1985, after press accounts surfaced that North was engaging in possibly illegal activities, Sciaroni, on his own initiative, prepared a legal opinion concluding that the Boland Amendments did not apply to the NSC. Several Republicans viewed that opinion as an important factor in judging the conduct of NSC officials who had assisted the Contras during the proscribed period.

Sciaroni's reasoning was simple and, in our view, wrong. He concluded that the two-year ban on aid to the Contras, which took effect in October 1984, specifically prohibited the use of CIA or Department of Defense funds to assist the Contras; it also prohibited such use of funds from "any other agency or entity of the United States involved in intelligence activities"; but since the NSC, Sciaroni reasoned, was not part of the "intelligence community," the ban did not apply to it.

Historically, it is true that the NSC is not considered to be a part of the intelligence community or involved in intelligence operations. It was created to serve as an advisory body, collating and synthesizing intelligence information collected by others, and assisting the President in formulating his national-security policies. It is because of this advisory and nonoperational role that the National Security Adviser has not been subjected to Senate confirmation or required to testify before Congress.

Moreover, prior to the passage of the Boland Amendments, the only agencies involved in assisting the Contras were the CIA and the Departments of State and Defense. It was clear that Congress intended to bar those who were actively engaged in assisting the Contras from continuing their activities. The key objective of the legislation was to prohibit not just those agencies that were "part of the intelligence community," as Sciaroni maintained, but, rather, those who engaged in "intelligence activities." According to Sciaroni's reasoning, the President could have detailed Defense or CIA operatives to the Department of Agriculture to carry on the Contra-aid program. Since the Department of Agriculture is not part of the intelligence community, it would follow that this would be a perfectly legal way for the President to continue aid to the Contras. It is precisely this twist in logic that permitted Poindexter to testify later that the NSC had acted in full compliance with the Boland Amendments while not revealing that in his judgment this was because the law did not apply to the NSC.

Like the sale of weapons to Iran and the continuation of financial and military assistance to the Contras, the White House view that the Boland Amendments did not cover the NSC was kept covert. In fact, Sciaroni's legal opinion was stamped "classified." Mr. Sciaroni conceded that "It would seem to be the implication that if Congress found out about the legal opinion, it would move to prevent NSC officials from acting."

The skepticism that greeted Mr. Sciaroni's legal analysis deepened almost immediately with the disclosures concerning his background and the circumstances under which he had conducted his review.

He had failed bar examinations twice in California and twice in the District of Columbia before passing an exam in Pennsylvania. Sciaroni's encounter in August 1985 with North about his alleged improper activities lasted only five minutes, during which time North issued a flat denial that he had provided any military advice or financial assistance to the Contras. Sciaroni conducted a forty-minute interview with NSC Counsel Paul Thompson. North's office was overflowing with documents, but Thompson referred to them as North's "working papers," which Sciaroni could not see. Instead he provided Sciaroni with a sheaf of documents about an inch thick.

Based on these documents and his brief interviews with North and Thompson, Sciaroni wrote an analysis, which he conceded was his very first legal memorandum. It is doubtful that he or the White House expected it to receive such a wide audience.

In spite of the embarrassing revelations concerning the preparation of the memorandum, several House members, including Michael DeWine and Henry Hyde, continued to wave the document in the air as evidence that the Boland Amendments were ambiguous in wording and uncertain in reach. But most Committee members publicly questioned the justification of the NSC's operational role in aiding the Contras on the basis of such a cursory investigation and analysis.

A different kind of skepticism toward the White House's interpretation of the law greeted the appearance and testimony of Assistant Attorney General Charles Cooper. Cooper had never been requested to render an opinion on the legality of the Iran or Contra operations, even though he directed the Office of Legal Counsel, which specifically has the responsibility for rendering such advice to the Executive Branch.

No one challenged Cooper's capabilities. Indeed, he is a young and gifted lawyer who once served as a law clerk for now Chief Justice William H. Rehnquist. His responsibilities as an assistant attorney general involved principally civil-law matters. At the time when Attorney General Meese had asked Cooper to analyze the legal issues involved in the sale of weapons to Iran (November 7, 1986), Cooper had had no experience in investigating criminal matters. Although at the outset there was no apparent evidence of possible criminal activity, within a matter of two and a half weeks an assistant attorney general discovered the diversion memorandum. A more formal investigation was warranted. It became clear during Cooper's testimony that top officials were able to carry out a plan of deceit and destruction of evidence that skilled investigators might well have prevented.

Speaking with a soft Alabama drawl, Cooper provided the Committee with dramatic evidence of deception and dishonesty practiced by key administration officials in an attempt to cover up the Iran/Contra programs:

• On November 7, 1986, several days after the sale of weapons to Iran was disclosed, Meese appointed Cooper to examine the legal issues involved in the sale and, specifically, to undertake a legal analysis of the presidential finding of January 1986 that authorized the sale.

• On November 17 Cooper received a chronology prepared by the NSC that covered the transactions during 1985–86, including Israel's shipments of TOW missiles and HAWK missiles to Iran that had been authorized by the United States.

• On November 20 Cooper attended a meeting with North, Poindexter, Casey, Deputy CIA Director Robert Gates, National Security Council Attorney Paul Thompson, and Meese. The purpose of the meeting was to discuss preparation of the forthcoming testimony of Casey before the House and Senate Intelligence Committees. North falsely stated that no one in the U.S. government had any knowledge that the Israelis had shipped HAWK missiles to Iran in November 1985. But, in fact, many U.S. officials knew at the time that the Israelis had delivered HAWK missiles to Iran.

Although he did not attend this meeting, Abraham Sofaer, a

former federal judge and the State Department's legal adviser, protested about the false and misleading testimony being prepared for Casey (that the United States was unaware of the shipments). Sofaer told Cooper and White House Counsel Peter Wallison that Shultz had notes of a conversation Shultz had with McFarlane in November 1985 about the shipment of HAWK missiles. According to his sworn deposition, Sofaer stated that he would leave government if Casey did not modify his proposed testimony, and Cooper responded that he, too, would leave. In the face of Sofaer's threat, the false statements were removed from Casey's testimony.

On November 21 Casey nonetheless told the House Intelligence Committee that the Israelis had informed the crew of the CIA's proprietary aircraft that the plane was carrying oil-drilling equipment. Actually, CIA documents indicated that the pilot understood that he was carrying missiles. Casey also testified that the Israelis had transferred weapons to the Iranians before the United States got involved. The CIA's own chronology stated that the United States approved the shipment of weapons in September and November 1985.

• On November 21, 1986, McFarlane told Meese that he had first learned of the HAWK shipment during his briefing before departing for Teheran in May 1986. McFarlane testified to the Committee that he was aware of the shipment in November 1985.

• On the morning of November 22, 1986, Assistant Attorney General William Bradford Reynolds discovered the so-called diversion memo in North's office. Shortly thereafter Reynolds attended a luncheon meeting with Meese and Cooper. When Reynolds disclosed the existence of the memo, Meese replied, "Oh, shit." Although everyone understood the memo's significance, no action was taken to formalize the investigation or protect evidence, at the very least by sealing North's office.

• On November 23, 1986, Meese and members of his staff met with North. North told them that the Israelis had advised him that they were shipping oil-drilling equipment to Iran in November 1985. North later said that he, in fact, doubted that the shipment consisted of oil-drilling equipment, but added that he could probably pass a lie-detector test to the effect that it *was* oil-drilling equipment. This seemed a curious comment, evidence either of North's confidence in his persuasive powers or of a subtle probe to determine whether Cooper wanted him to stick with a phony cover story.

Meese inquired about the diversion of profits from the sale of weapons. According to Cooper, North "was visibly surprised" by the question. When shown the diversion memo, North indicated that he did not think the President had seen it. North then asked if the memo included a cover sheet. After Reynolds said it did not, Meese asked, "Should we have found one?" North responded, "No, I just wondered," and then volunteered to search his files for a cover letter, "if there was one."

Later that evening Cooper spoke with Sofaer, who said, "It's just a real mess." Sofaer had checked the price list for the TOW missiles and concluded that excess profits must have been realized from the sales. He discovered that Southern Air Transport, an airline known because of the Hasenfus crash to be involved in aiding the Contras, had also transported weapons to Iran. This raised a red flag in Sofaer's mind and suggested a connection between the two programs. Cooper, however, did not disclose to Sofaer the existence of the diversion memo.

• Meese continued informal and private interviews with Poindexter, McFarlane, and Casey. He took no notes.

• On November 28, 1986, the FBI went to the NSC to seal North's office and search for evidence. The previous day, the *Los Angeles Times* had reported that NSC officials had been shredding important documents.

Unanimous anger greeted Cooper's testimony. Even though he sought to praise Meese's conduct in the investigation, Cooper could not erase the doubts raised about the professionalism and integrity with which the Attorney General had handled the entire matter. Admittedly, the Justice Department was lied to and misled by North, but the informal nature of the investigation facilitated the falsehoods and evasions. But how could the President deny on November 19, 1986, in a nationally televised press conference, that any third country had assisted in the arms sales, only to have his press spokesman retract the denial? Why, once the diversion memo had been discovered, did the Attorney General proceed so casually, allowing North to delay his interview for twenty-four hours and permitting North access to his files for three days after he had been fired? Why did the Attorney General not make a record of his interviews with Casey and Poindexter? Was it customary to provide the subject of an official inquiry with advance notice of the investigation while he had access to potentially incriminating documents? Did anyone understand that, when North asked about a cover letter to the diversion memo, Meese and his team were telegraphing exactly what evidence they had—and, conceivably, what North should destroy?

Warren Rudman fumed that the entire investigation reflected professional incompetence. Other Committee members implied, however, that the selection of Cooper and Reynolds represented a deliberate effort to provide North with enough time and opportunity to complete a search-and-destroy mission for incriminating evidence.

House Republicans turned their fire on those who had misled Meese. Bill McCollum (R-Florida) offered scathing criticism of North for his false statements to Meese.

Representative Louis Stokes extracted the most damning response from Cooper concerning North's credibility. Cooper testified that when he interviewed North in November of 1986 he found him to be "entirely believable."[62]

But Stokes wanted Cooper's current assessment of North's credibility and what weight the Committee should give to his testimony.

STOKES: Based upon everything you know about Colonel North as a result of your contact with him and your interview of him, let me ask this: would you believe him under oath?

COOPER: Congressman, I would not, but I personally don't believe an oath in any way enhances the obligation of truthfulness.[63]

Most of the Committee believed that, with that statement, Charles Cooper had dropped North's veracity into a shredder.

Beauty and the Beasts

Washington, generally a serious-minded city, experiences moments of adolescent giddiness. A twenty-seven-year-old part-time model turned secretary filled the nation's capital with helium and sent it soaring.

Fawn Hall has a name worthy of a Hollywood starlet and golden hair cascading about a fine-boned face. She projected a casual stylishness, reminiscent of actress Farrah Fawcett. In fact, it was rumored that the actress had expressed a desire to play the role in the Fawn Hall story.

Exactly what story was to grace the marquees of America? Was it that of an innocent woman led astray by a swashbuckling Marine? Had Fawn Hall placed loyalty to a cause above the law? What would she say about the man who had become the focus of the Committee's attention? Would she tell all? Exactly how did she smuggle those documents out of the Executive Office Building? . . .

As Hall moved down the marble corridors of the Rayburn House Office Building, a gaggle of photographers followed, their cameras a chorus of metallic crickets. Fawn arrived at the witness table, Botticelli's Venus yielded from a foaming sea. She raised her right hand, swore to tell the truth.

Hall's starlet status infected members of the Committee. Jokes about asking her for her phone number belied real concern about what the Committee members would actually ask. Most were familiar with the story that emerged from her deposition: A loyal, hardworking, and dedicated secretary, Hall altered a number of classified documents, shredded others, and smuggled out of the Executive Office Building those that she was unable to shred. The alteration of documents came at North's request; much of the shredding was a joint effort; the smuggling, a spontaneous act of her own.

Hall's motivation was not complicated by self-doubt. A moral imperative to protect the "initiative" compelled her to engage in these obstructive, nonsecretarial duties.

While inquiring about the inner workings of North's office, we would focus upon a narrow band of time—November 3 to November 28, 1986. Hall would be asked to identify specific documents, specific alterations, specific actions taken in destroying and smuggling documents, specific conversations held with North, his then attorney, Tom Green, and his NSC staff associate Lieutenant Colonel Robert Earl.

Members were concerned about their manner in questioning Hall. Notwithstanding the substantial progress made in recent years to extend equality of rights to women, a double standard still exists in our society's expectations about, and treatment of, women. We all wanted to avoid causing Hall to falter or break emotionally before the millions who would be watching.

Most Committee members were lawyers by education; many, trial attorneys by experience. One of the ten commandments of litigation is: Never make a woman cry under examination, or allow her to persuade a jury that you made her cry. The penalty of violating the rule is sometimes the loss of the case itself.

It was obvious that Hall had been well prepared by her attorney. With her handsome family lining the front row of the visitors' seats, she responded to questions with clipped, almost military precision: "Yes, sir." "No, sir." "Correct." "That is true." She avoided volunteering any information beyond what was specifically asked of her.

Judge Walsh, the independent counsel, had granted Hall immunity for her testimony before a grand jury. Walsh had obviously concluded that her testimony would provide a link in the chain of evidence of any criminal misconduct by her superiors. She was a functionary rather than a conspirator, following instructions rather than initiating actions. He was not interested in trying to slam an iron door on her.

The Committee followed the same reasoning in granting Hall immunity for her testimony. She was not a target for prosecution, and since Walsh was not pursuing criminal proceedings against her, there was no danger of complicating his investigation by granting her immunity.

It behooved Hall to be as miserly as possible with her answers. Volunteering information or providing elaborate responses to questions only expands the opportunity for a more effective exploration of evidentiary conflict and ambiguity.

Hall had a trial run during her deposition. She could anticipate, with the assistance of counsel, those areas that would be explored. She had watched the prior witnesses on television. She knew which Committee members would be sympathetic and supportive, which skeptical and hostile.

She also knew that the Committee would be on the defensive. Senator Heflin, in a television interview prior to the hearing, had stated that Hall had smuggled documents from the Executive Office Building by stuffing them into her brassiere. Hall immediately issued a statement labeling Heflin a "sexist." Her swift rebuttal had its intended effect—Heflin was put on the defensive, even though Hall had in fact smuggled documents out by tucking them under her shirt and in her boots. She needed only to keep her answers short, her head cool, her demeanor respectful, and the Committee would be on trial.

For the first day Hall followed her instructions perfectly. Her opening statement was short and forceful, consisting of two and a half typewritten pages. One sentence was typed in bold capital letters: "**I CAN TYPE.**"

Mark Belnick, conducting the direct examination of Hall, fired questions in a neutral and nonjudgmental voice. Her responses were crisp and revealing. She disclosed, among other things:

• That President Reagan, to her knowledge, had never called North prior to his dismissal.
• That she had shredded the logs of phone calls to North along with electronic interoffice memos as a belated "spring cleaning."
• That, because of the overload, the shredder broke down and had to be repaired.
• That North kept notes in a spiral-bound notebook that she recalled seeing in North's attorney Brendan Sullivan's office.
• That she did not know whether North kept large amounts of cash in his office but believed that rumors to that effect were true.
• That she had borrowed $60 from North in traveler's checks drawn upon a Central American bank, to use for a weekend at the beach. North told her to repay the money, since it was not his, and she did so.
• That she had misled the White House counsel about her shredding activities.
• That, after smuggling documents out of the Executive Office Building in her boots and the back of her dress, she was asked by Tom Green, then North's attorney, what she would say if asked about the shredding. She responded that she would say, "We shred every day." Green responded, "Good."
• That she did not remember specifically having received $16,000 in cash from Secord's secretary to be given to North, but did not deny receiving it.
• That, when she learned that the President had dismissed North from his position, she became emotional and started to cry.

On several occasions during the afternoon session, Hall's eyes misted up and her hands trembled slightly. Committee members exchanged silent glances, as if to acknowledge that an explosive device was about to be detonated by the weight of a serious question.

The Fawn Hall that emerged on day one was fragile and vulnerable—sympathetic to Committee members and viewers alike.

But something happened overnight. Perhaps the Committee's passivity emboldened her. Whatever the reason, day two brought forth a different Fawn Hall. There was a sharp edge to her voice. Disdain was no longer contained or camouflaged. Each answer was concluded with an obligatory "sir," which sounded more like an expression of contempt than of respect.

During the course of her deposition and the first day of her testimony, Hall had attempted to characterize herself as little more than a human typewriter, a mindless conduit for the transfer of oral or written instructions. The role didn't quite fit. Her alteration of documents displayed a precise understanding and appreciation of what was to be achieved by the modifications. Her eager shredding of North's phone logs and electronic messages was more than an act of spring cleaning.

On the second day, she described herself as a member of the NSC team, who "panicked" while in a "protective mode " "Just what were you trying to protect?" Senator Rudman asked.

HALL: I was protecting the initiative.

RUDMAN: From whom?

HALL: From everyone because I felt that I knew we were trying to get back the hostages and I knew we were dealing with Iranian moderates and if this is exposed, there would be people whose lives would be lost. And I also felt that it divulged—if this breaks out we are sitting up here talking about all kinds of things, we are revealing sources and revealing everything. In my opinion I don't think this is proper. . . . A lot of damage would be done if a lot of top secret, sensitive, classified material was exposed in public, so that the Soviets and everyone else could read it. That is how I felt.

RUDMAN: Ms. Hall, did you know that it was the White House personnel that was standing in the office barring people from leaving? You did know that.

HALL: I knew it was an NSC official, yes.

RUDMAN: It wasn't the KGB that was coming, Ms. Hall, it was the FBI.[64]

Senator Nunn wanted to know if Hall had any regrets other than those expressed previously about failing to shred all of the documents.

HALL: Sir, I wished a lot of things could have been done differently. I wish that Congress had voted money for the contras so that this wouldn't have had to happen.

NUNN: In other words, you wouldn't have had to shred the documents if Congress had gone on and done its job and voted aid?

HALL: I believe that—sir, I have no comment.[65]

It was clear that she realized she was becoming an advocate rather than an impartial secretary.

She grew agitated when a debate ensued among Committee members as to whether North was "entitled" to be granted immunity so that he could tell his story to the American people. She could no longer resist and jumped into the fray.

HALL: Sir, I would like to comment on your comment regarding Colonel North and his grant of immunity. I think that Colonel North is first a U.S. citizen and he has the same rights that you yourself do, sir. . . . If the idea is to complete the investigation, then why not grant Colonel North immunity?[66]

WSC: *When I suggested that no person is* entitled *to immunity and that, if North had not engaged in any wrongdoing, the question of immunity would not be an issue, Hall glared and responded acerbically,* "We have our separate opinions, sir."[67]

The plastic veneer had been scratched. Underneath was solid wood. Fragility had been replaced with feistiness and flashes of temper.

It's been written that "The art of cross examination . . . is not the art of examining crossly. It's the art of leading the witness through a line of propositions he agrees to until he is forced to agree to the one *fatal question*."[68]

Thomas Foley (D-Washington), the House Majority Leader, is a large man with an expansive mind. His manner is brusque and brooks no nonsense. He pressed Hall on whether she understood the consequences of altering official documents.

> FOLEY: Without any reference to possible obstruction of justice, which is not the purpose of this committee to determine, did you not know that alteration of existing documents in a major, fundamental way was a violation of the responsibility of those who possess those documents?[69]

The discipline Hall had maintained during the previous day started to dissolve. The mask of the secretarial mannequin who reflexively followed instructions fell away:

> HALL: I agree with you, sir, and at the time, as I stated before, I felt uneasy but sometimes, like I said before, I believed in Colonel North and there was a very solid and very valid reason he must have been doing this for and sometimes you have to go above the written law, I believe.[70]

Hall knew immediately she had made a mistake and tried to call the words back. Too late. She had written the next day's headlines. The words—and message—would be forever associated with her name.

Her statement should not have been so shocking. After all, Hall had merely articulated what appeared to be the credo of those engaged in the affair, that the good of the goal justified the means used to achieve it.

Rather than pose questions to Hall, Chairman Hamilton decided to sum up the evidence as we were concluding Phase One of the hearings.

> For the past six weeks these committees have been meeting to try to find out what went wrong in the processes of the American Government

and why. . . . Surely it seems to me these committees have heard some of the most extraordinary testimony ever given to the United States Congress. Let me mention a few things that stand out in my mind.

An elaborate private network was set up to carry out the foreign policy of the United States.

Private citizens, many with divided loyalties and profit motives, sold arms and negotiated for the release of American hostages.

Private citizens were given top secret codes and encryption devices and had access to Swiss bank accounts used for United States covert actions and operations.

The President was involved in private and third country fund raising for the contras.

Wealthy private contributors were courted at the White House, solicited in coordination with government officials, and given what they were told was secret information.

American policy became dependent on the contributions of private individuals and third countries.

The President approved the payment of . . . funds . . . to terrorists to secure the release of hostages.

Senior officials did not know and chose not to know important facts about policy.

A National Security Advisor and an Assistant Secretary of State withheld information and did not tell the Congress the truth concerning U.S. involvement in the contra supply operation and the solicitation of funds from third countries.

When official involvement with the contras was prohibited, officials of the National Security Council raised money, helped procure arms, and set up a private network to ship arms to the contras.

A United States Ambassador negotiated an agreement with Costa Rica for a secret airstrip.

The CIA agent facilitated supply flights.

An official designated by the Secretary of State as a loose cannon carried out highly sensitive negotiations to obtain the release of American hostages. He gave the approval of the White House to a plan to depose Saddam Husayn and to go to war with the Soviet Union in defense of Iran.

This same official participated with others in an effort to rewrite chronologies, altered critical documents, and organized a shredding party to destroy those documents.

This money from the sale of U.S. arms to Iran was diverted to the contras and for the use of several private individuals.

Money raised for the contras was used to finance a DEA operation to seek release of hostages.

Contra funds were also provided to Colonel North, perhaps even—although this is not proven—for personal use.

What these committees have heard is a depressing story. It is a story of not telling the truth to the Congress and to the American people.

It is a story about remarkable confusion in the processes of government. Those involved, whether public officials or private citizens, had no doubt they were acting on the authority of the President of the United States.[71]

At the conclusion of Hamilton's observations, Hall departed, wafted by floodlights to celebrityhood. She had come, was seen, and had conquered. The mail literally poured into our offices, much of it profane and abusive toward individual Committee members. The public's reaction provided an interesting insight into our society's values. Virtually all of the negative mail and phone calls came from men who resented the tone of questions posed to a woman who was, after all, just doing her job. By contrast, the positive mail came mostly from women who were grateful to those members who had treated Hall as a person instead of a sex goddess.

As for Hall, her beauty and composure assured her more than Andy Warhol's fifteen minutes of fame. She was destined to appear with Barbara Walters on ABC's "20/20" television program and receive numerous requests to be guest of honor at banquets and association dinners. She signed with Hollywood superagent Norman Brokaw of the William Morris Agency, and landed a television contract—proving that the formula for celebrity is not always predictable.

Time Out

After five weeks of testimony, the Committee called time out. Our staffs had been working long days, most nights as well. They needed time to sift through the voluminous testimony, reflect upon its meaning, and then prepare for the remaining witnesses.

Committee members were also in need of relief. It was as though we had been swimming under water too long. We craved air, needed to see some landmark, a point to fix our progress. Had we, in fact, made any progress? It was difficult to tell.

Our other congressional assignments had necessarily been slighted. Although the two of us managed to return to Maine almost every weekend during the hearings, it was difficult to give adequate attention to legislative proposals on which we had to pass judgment. An avalanche of correspondence, demands, and requests had thundered into our offices. After each long day at the hearings, we had to spend hours in the evening preparing for the next day's testimony.

Then there were the unrelenting requests for interviews by members of the press who were looking for interpretations of evidence, explanations of contradictions in testimony. We both received extensive coverage from the print and television media, local as well as national. We ordinarily are called upon to articulate our views as part of the political process. But during this investigation, the pressure to do so was magnified a hundredfold. Obviously we were flattered that our opinions were being sought out by the major networks and newspapers. But the requests stretched our days from six in the morning until midnight. In addition, during the periodic breaks taken in the morning and afternoon sessions, the television networks, National Public Radio, and others pulled and tugged us and other members into the circle of their Capitol Hill "hookups" outside the hearing rooms. They did not meet much resistance. Fatigue was overcome by the renewed flow of adrenaline. Throughout the long, tiring days we were conscious of the need to remain alert and cautious. One verbal slip, one unintended revelation, and a headline would be born— one that would immediately be challenged. "Caution" was a word we repeated like a mantra.

The power of the press, particularly that of television, is enormous. Decisions by the networks on the extent of their coverage were having a major impact upon the public's attitude toward the hearings. The three major networks broadcast live Richard Secord's and Robert McFarlane's testimony, leaving to CNN and C-SPAN the responsibility for live coverage of other witnesses. This real scandal could not compete with fictional scandals on the popular soap operas. Albert Hakim was no match for "The Young and the Restless." Not until Fawn Hall did the networks return to live coverage. She offered glamour and romance—the girl next door who was close to the man who was the central figure in the scandal. The potential for melodrama was irresistible. The soaps could wait.

Many Americans do not have cable television service. Because they saw primarily sympathetic witnesses and only highlights of the other testimony, a disjointed and fragmentary portrait of our investigation emerged. Reducing a complex story to thirty-second "sound bites" was the equivalent of taking snapshots from a moving train. Much of the landscape was missed.

The presence of the witnesses' family members had a subtle influence on the members of the Committee. Robert McFarlane's wife, Jonda, sat with a stoic elegance behind her husband. Rachel Abrams was more intense and energetically involved. Frequently she shook her head at a question. Her facial expressions and head movements reflected her assessment of the fairness or inappropriateness of a line of inquiry. Fawn Hall's handsome family sat with their hands linked together as she testified, as if in prayer. We later saw a quiet, demure Betsy North and Linda Poindexter, an ordained Episcopal priest. Initially we did not realize that Mrs. Poindexter was dressed in clerical collar. The cross she wore on a long chain finally caught our attention. She often leaned forward, conveying intense interest in the questions posed to her husband, lending to the witness her loyalty and love. This posed a dilemma for us. It is more difficult to press a witness with hard questions while looking into the faces of parents, spouses, and children, who suffer the blows of every question. We tried to block them out of our line of vision, but the camera always caught their anguish and silent testimony.

The most frustrating aspect of serving on the Committee was the necessary surrender of control over the investigation to a professional staff. They reviewed the thousands of documents, conducted the research, took the deposition of witnesses. Their work was contained in our briefing books, but these were usually available only a short time before a witness was scheduled to testify. Often we would see relevant documents for the first time as the witness testified during the public hearings. Little could be done to avoid this situation. Once the hearings began, we were on a fast track. Few of us had the time to become involved in such detailed preparation.

We were also constantly interrupted by roll-call votes that required us to leave the hearing room and go to the Senate floor to vote. When the Committee met in the Senate Caucus Room, we could rush over the Senate floor, vote, and return in ten or fifteen minutes. When, on alternate weeks, the hearings were held in the Rayburn House Office Building, Capitol police officers lined up their vehicles, caravan style, and drove us to the Senate to vote— a process that usually took about thirty minutes. A similar problem confronted House members. The hearings proceeded in our absence. Upon our return, our staffs would busily recount what the witness had said, but lost for us were the spontaneity and a sense of continuity, the ability to follow carefully a line of questioning.

Because many of the Committee members were trained, experienced litigators, we knew that the key to a successful search for the truth lies in the knowledge of detail. One must listen to every word a witness utters, detect hesitation, voice inflection, and nuance. It is critical to observe witnesses as they testify, because their movements—particularly their eyes—often reveal more than their words. As Louis Nizer, one of America's pre-eminent trial lawyers, has written:

> There is an imponderable overall test of a witness's honesty. Does he look and sound truthful? It is a kind of summation of all the emanations which make him believable. It is his face, voice, directness, and above all, his sincerity. That is why credibility has no relationship to education or culture. An illiterate cleaning woman may be impressively honest. A refined executive may appear shifty. Character is a letter of credit written on the face.[72]

As a result of our absences from the hearings during roll-call votes, we were often forced to fall back on questions our staffs had prepared, some of which may have been covered previously by another member. And we had to keep one eye always focused on the clock, which confined us (unless we were designated hitters) to five or ten minutes. Reporters would berate us, "Why didn't anyone ask . . . ?" We usually passed off the questions with a smile or a shrug rather than offer the lame excuse that we had missed the point because we were off voting.

WSC: *I recall telling Adam Pertman, an intelligent and aggressive reporter for the* Boston Globe, *in a joking why-don't-you-go-to-hell tone, "Adam, why don't you just go to . . . law school!"*

We tried to mask our frustration with levity. In truth, there were times when we felt that members of the national press corps were more knowledgeable than we were and had raised pertinent follow-up questions that we had missed. But the discontinuity and interrogation gaps went with the territory of a twenty-six-member Committee. Moreover, we could not expect other members of the House and Senate to defer their legislative responsibilities just to accommodate our investigation.

Nevertheless, in spite of these limitations and the attempts by those who wanted to turn the investigation into a forum to debate the merits of the administration's Contra-aid program, we believed the Committee was succeeding in achieving the goals of Phase One.

Although Secord made a forceful defense of his activities, subsequent testimony indicated that he had not fully abandoned thoughts of profit-making from the Enterprise. The more comic aspects of Robert Owen's courier activities had long since faded. McFarlane's pain in explaining his role in recommending the Iranian initiative, and his inability to shut it off, muted somewhat the criticism of his subsequent activities in trying to "gild" the President's record. Arthur Liman had cracked into Albert Hakim's colony of hollow corporations and traced the flow of money into and out of the Enterprise. Elliott Abrams's experience in soliciting funds from Brunei left little doubt that other nations were ever moved by charitable motives when they helped the Contras. Moreover, Abrams demonstrated how his excess in the advocacy of a cause resulted in misleading Congress and impaired the credibility he had worked so hard to establish.

Through McFarlane, Gaston Sigur, Abrams, and Sciaroni, the Committee discerned the administration's contempt for, and intent to circumvent, the Boland Amendments. Fawn Hall demonstrated poise and loyalty and a determination to help in a cause even if it carried her beyond the written law. The words "privatizing a foreign policy" were given substance with the revelations of Hakim's practice of baksheesh and his negotiation of a nine-point plan to obtain the release of American hostages. Finally, through the disclosure of insurance funds, security fences, and traveler's checks, a cloud of corruption was starting to gather across the monument that had been erected to Oliver North. Or so we thought.

PART II

If ever the constitutional democracy of The United States is overthrown, we now have a better idea of how that is likely to be done.

—Theodore Draper

Top Gun

In June, as the lawyers began final preparation for the deposition of North, the Committee was jolted by the demand from North's lawyer, Brendan Sullivan, that North be permitted to testify in public without first testifying in private. That demand was detailed in a twenty-seven-page letter from Sullivan to Senators Inouye and Rudman delivered on June 17. Sullivan argued that the Committee had agreed with the independent counsel to defer taking North's testimony until North would no longer get any benefit from use immunity, since the independent counsel by then had built a strong case against North. He complained that North would no longer receive any benefit from immunity and yet would be forced to disclose his defense and thus lose the element of surprise, which is important to every defense attorney.

On the following day Sullivan met with Liman and Nields to make several additional demands:

• North would testify only if he could do so in the immediate future, the very next week if possible.

• His testimony would have to be limited to three consecutive days in sessions of ten hours a day, without interruption during his testimony for the calling of other witnesses.

• North could not later be recalled as a witness.

• If for any reason the Committee declined to have him testify on the agreed-upon date, then he would not have to testify at all.

• If North had any documents that fell within the Committee's subpoena, he would turn them over to the Committee three days before he testified.

• He would produce documents only for the specific time period from January 1, 1984, to November 26, 1986.

• Sullivan would certify compliance with the subpoena, and his certification would be final and not open to question or challenge. In other words, the Committee would have to accept the word of North's attorney that North had complied with the subpoena; the Committee would be unable to check the accuracy or veracity of his word.

On Friday, June 19, the Senate Committee met late into the evening to consider Sullivan's demands.

Although the first round of comment was uniformly one of indignation and anger, it soon became clear that several members of the Committee were ready to accede. They argued that, if we did not agree to Sullivan's demands, there would be a lengthy court process in which the Committee would try to have North found in contempt of Congress and punished; in the meantime, the extended October 30 deadline for completion of the Committee's work would come and go without the American people's knowing what happened, and the matter would hang unfairly over the President's head for the rest of his term. In this view, unless the Committee bowed to North, it could not accomplish its objective.

Other senators were bitterly opposed to any concessions. They argued that North should be treated the same as every other witness, and that to give in to him would create a precedent that would haunt future congressional committees.

It was clear that the Committee was divided and on the verge of splitting apart. So a motion to reject Sullivan's demands was made but was never called up for a vote. Instead, the Committee accepted Liman's recommendation that our chairmen and vice chairmen and those who would be North's designated questioners meet with Sullivan to try to resolve the matter through negotiation. The members of the Committee were influenced by Liman's assertion that North could be effectively questioned, even under the proposed constraints.

For the next week, there was a swirl of negotiations, meetings, exchanges of letters and documents. Almost daily a new agreement was reached, only to be reopened as Sullivan returned with a new demand. Finally, the Committee's lawyers sent Sullivan a "letter of intent" expressing the Committee's intentions regarding North's testimony. Although the letter included some conditional language, insisted upon by members who were opposed to any concessions, it was a victory for Sullivan. Oliver North and the Committee had gone eyeball to eyeball, and the Committee had blinked. It was the prologue of what was to come.

The Committee's letter of intent was a fig leaf to cover the embarrassment of what had happened.[73] The Committee had caved in. To get North to testify, we had let him set the time and terms of his testimony. This was the single most important decision made by the Committee. Several senators expressed strong concern that the decision was a mistake, but there were persuasive arguments to the contrary. There is no question that the investigation would have been incomplete without North's testimony. Would he have testified in the absence of the Committee's concessions? The Committee decided not to take the risk. We believe so, but cannot know for sure.

North won the sympathy of many Americans and put the Committee on the defensive. But did the public gain something from his testimony? Surely his description of the off-the-shelf covert-action capacity, his intimate knowledge of the negotiations with the Iranians, his detailed recitation of aid to the Contras at a time when it was prohibited by the Boland Amendment, his chilling admissions of lies and destruction of documents—all this and more informed the public.

A more fundamental question is whether Congress can effectively confront a military hero who has engaged in misconduct. Congress does well confronting members of the Mafia, drug dealers, and inside traders, or questioning bankers, administration officials, and defense procurement consultants. But it frequently backs off before a war hero who wraps himself in patriotism. This is not new. Douglas MacArthur, who was fired for insubordination to his commander in chief, received a standing ovation from Congress. Given the force of his personality, Oliver North might well have swept the nation even if he had testified privately in advance of his public testimony.

GJM: *The first thing I noticed was the uniform. Then the medals: a chest full of them. His handshake was tight, even hard, as though he was trying to make a point. His eyes were clear, his gaze was firm, his smile quick. Before he said a word, I knew Oliver North would be a very tough witness.*

We met in private, in a small corner room in the basement of the Rayburn House Office Building. Under the agreement between the Committee's lawyers and Sullivan, North was to testify in private only on the question of the President's knowledge of the diversion. Present were the House and Senate chairmen and vice chairmen, the other designated questioners of North (Senator Trible, Representatives Cheney and Jenkins), and the Committee counsel.

The session was brief, almost perfunctory. North, reading from typewritten notes, testified (as he would in public a week later) that the President had not known of the diversion. What he said was predictable, even anticipated. My main purpose in attending was to size up the man who was the central figure in the affair and whom I would have to question for an hour in the public hearing.

I had been strongly opposed to any concessions to North. When the Senate Committee met privately to discuss the issue, I made the formal motion to reject all of Sullivan's demands. But after a lengthy discussion, at the request of Senators Inouye and Rudman, I did not press my motion to a vote. While I made clear my opposition to any concessions (as did Senators Sarbanes and Heflin), I recognized that Inouye and Rudman had worked hard, and successfully, to forge a bipartisan attitude on the Committee. A vote on my motion would be close, I thought, possibly splitting the Committee along party lines. If that happened, and if the Committee were forced to go through a lengthy contempt process in court, the investigation might have fizzled to an inconclusive end before anyone had heard from North. I believed that Sullivan was bluffing and that he very much wanted North to testify publicly as long as he had immunity. It seemed to me that North's best hope of avoiding criminal conviction was to testify and then to get the criminal charges dismissed on the ground that the prosecution of those charges had been compromised by his testimony before the Committee. But I obviously couldn't be sure. So I yielded to the Committee leadership, and will forever wonder what would have happened if I had insisted on a vote on a motion.

Now, as I watched and listened to North for the first time, I felt a resurgence of doubt about the Committee's decision to accede to his demands. This man would be an effective witness, I thought, with his military bearing, his apparent sincerity, his almost boyish charm. I was aware that, during the negotiations over North's appearance, Sullivan had asked that the public questioning of North begin with the security system around North's home, which was paid for by Secord and Hakim, and regarding which North had later falsified records. That seemed like one of the most damning incidents in which North had participated. Although he wasn't questioned about the security system until the second day, if his lawyer had wanted to begin there in public it was obvious that North had an effective response ready. Little did I realize just how effective the response would be!

Tuesday, July 7, 1987, a Washington summer day, dawned clear and hot. As the day passed, it grew hotter. But it was nothing in comparison with the political temperature in the Senate Caucus Room. There, in one week, Oliver North leaped from obscurity to fame.

An aggressive lawyer, Brendan Sullivan believes in creating advantages for his clients, and in exploiting those advantages to the limit. Having once cowed the Committee, he was clearly determined to do so again and again.

The Committee's rules provided that any witness wanting to

make an opening statement had to notify the Committee of his wish and deliver copies of the statement to the Committee staff forty-eight hours in advance. There were sound reasons for the Committee's rule. It allowed the members and staff time to determine the truth or falsity of any factual claims made in the statement and to prepare rebuttal evidence if necessary. More important, however, a witness who had been granted limited use immunity might include statements designed to expand his protection against subsequent criminal prosecution. Criminal lawyers call this technique "taking an immunity bath." The Committee did not want to provide an opportunity for such an immersion and later be blamed for having scuttled the efforts of the independent counsel.

At 9:30 P.M. on July 6, eleven and a half hours before North was scheduled to testify (the time and date having been dictated by Sullivan), Sullivan delivered to the Committee a letter announcing that "Lt. Col. North would like to give an opening statement *in the event* he testifies tomorrow morning" (emphasis added), and asking that the Committee's rules be waived for North. The opening statement was not included with the letter, but was delivered to the Committee at eight-fifteen the following morning, forty-five minutes before North's testimony was to begin. A debate involving several Committee members occurred in the anteroom adjacent to the Russell Caucus Room. Some argued, "We should chastise North for flouting our rules and then let him read his statement." Others protested, asking, "How many times do we have to run up the white flag to this man?"

North's request was too much, even for the agreeable chairmen of the Committee. Inouye and Hamilton, who had reluctantly agreed to Sullivan's terms for North's testimony, refused. As the public hearings opened, Inouye told North he could deliver his opening statement forty-eight hours later, in accordance with the Committee's rules.

Sullivan protested. He described the hearings as "the most extraordinary proceeding . . . in our 200 years." He portrayed North as the innocent victim of a coordinated effort by the Committee and the independent counsel to "defeat" North's rights under "the immunity statute."

To make his point that North was David to the Committee's Goliath, he complained about the unfairness of North's having had *only* seven days to review the large number of documents:

> On June 30, when those records were delivered, we were so stunned by the volume of them and the lateness of their arrival that we actually tried to humor ourselves a little bit by piling the documents end on end and taking a photograph of them so we could demonstrate how serious our problem was. The documents piled together exceed the height of Colonel North and cannot possibly be read, studied in a week.[74]

As he spoke, Sullivan dramatically produced a photograph of North standing next to a pile of documents that reached over his head. Unaware at that time of the impact on the television audience, no one on the Committee bothered to point out the truth.

The Committee had earlier issued a subpoena to North ordering him to produce certain documents in his possession. On June 18 Sullivan told Liman and Nields that, if North had any documents covered by the subpoena (which he then refused to admit or deny), he would produce them three days before North testified. Sullivan had long before demanded that the Committee turn over to North any documents it had that might be used in questioning him. He wanted to receive the Committee's documents weeks in advance of the hearing. Later he proposed that the Committee get North's documents three days in advance. His request was so absurdly unfair that it was dismissed. All documents would be exchanged on the same day. The only question was how far in advance of North's testimony the exchange would occur.

Liman and Nields, eager for more time to review North's documents, insisted that the exchange occur earlier than the three days proposed by Sullivan. A compromise was reached under which the documents were exchanged seven days before North testified.

The Committee's lawyers and some Committee members were aware of these facts; the viewing public was not. All they heard was Sullivan complaining about the lack of time given to his client to review an enormous stack of documents.

Was this a trick? Crafty words by a cunning lawyer? Perhaps, perhaps not. But there can be no doubt that it worked. Before North had given a word of testimony, Sullivan had succeeded at what he set out to do: to create public sympathy for North and hostility toward the Committee.

They were unlikely adversaries. Both short and erect. Both decorated war heroes. Both deeply devoted to their country.

But as Oliver North stood straight in his Marine officer's uniform, and raised his right hand, he was taking the oath from a man who, for all their similarities, had a very different view of America.

When Daniel Inouye said to North, "Raise your right hand," Inouye raised his left hand. His right arm had been torn off in Italy by a German grenade during World War II.

The irony was obvious, the drama palpable, and it continued at high pitch for a week. In that time, "Olliemania" swept the nation. The hearings, described a few weeks earlier by President Reagan as boring, suddenly were the focus of national attention.

The pattern was quickly set in North's testimony. John Nields began the questioning aggressively. Within minutes he drew from North admissions that he had participated in telling lies to the Iranians during the negotiations with them, and to the American people when the secret Contra-resupply effort was exposed. But North immediately counterattacked with what would become his standard, and highly effective, line:

I think it is very important for the American people to understand that this is a dangerous world; that we live at risk and that this nation is at risk in a dangerous world. And that they ought not to be led to believe, as a consequence of these hearings, that this nation cannot or should not conduct covert operations. By their very nature, covert operations or special activities are a lie. There is great deceit, deception practiced in the conduct of covert operations. They are at essence a lie.[75]

Of course, no member of the Committee had suggested that the world is a safe place, and no member ever said that this nation should cease covert operations. Nor would any member. To justify his own lies, North described all covert operations as "at essence a lie." Because some lies must be told in covert operations, according to North, all lies told in furtherance of such operations are justified.

If one reads them later, in the cold reality of a printed transcript, North's words lack logic and are unpersuasive. But as delivered, with North's conviction, emotion, and charisma, they *seemed* logical to many and were immensely compelling.

In his very next response to Nields, North moved to what would be the mainstay of his defense throughout his testimony: He was just a good Marine, following orders:

> Throughout the conduct of my entire tenure at the National Security Council, I assumed that the President was aware of what I was doing and had, through my superiors, approved it. I sought approval of my superiors for every one of my actions and it is well-documented. I assumed when I had approval to proceed from either Judge Clark, Bud McFarlane or Admiral Poindexter, that they had indeed solicited and obtained the approval of the President.[76]

For two days Nields hammered at North, only to be hammered harder in return. Did North shred documents? Yes, of course he did. Did North lie to the Iranians? Of course, he'd tell them anything to get the hostages out. Did North lie to the CIA? To the Congress? Yes. Yes. But this is a dangerous world, Congress can't keep a secret, and I had to choose between lies and lives.

As skilled as Nields is as a lawyer, as overwhelming as the case against North looked on paper, with each exchange North gained in sympathy, strength, and confidence.

North had accepted as a gift from Secord and Hakim, who stood to make millions of dollars from the deals in which North engaged them, a $13,800 security system to protect his home. When it appeared that the gift might become public, North falsified documents and fabricated a cover story to conceal that he had not paid for the system.

The question by Nields was a simple one that could have been answered yes or no: "Were you aware that the security system was paid for by General Secord?"

But North didn't answer yes or no. For nearly fifteen minutes he gave an emotional response that dramatized the danger to his life, and the lives of his family.

> The issue of the security system was first broached immediately after a threat on my life by Abu Nidal. Abu Nidal is, as I'm sure you and the intelligence committees know, the principal, foremost assassin in the world today. He is a brutal murderer.

If his words weren't clear enough, North referred to a grisly photograph:

> We have an exhibit that we can provide for you that shows what Abu Nidal did in the Christmas massacres. One of the people killed in the Christmas massacre, and I do not wish to overdramatize this, but the Abu Nidal terrorist in Rome who blasted the eleven year old American Natasha Simpson to her knees, deliberately zeroed in and fired an extra burst at her head, just in case. Gentlemen, I have an eleven year old daughter, not perhaps a whole lot different than Natasha Simpson. . . . [77]

It was now clear why Sullivan had tried to get the public questioning to begin with the subject of the fence. North's response sealed his triumph. Nields tried to interrupt to get an answer to his question, but North brushed him aside. From that moment,

Nields's interrogation faltered while North and Sullivan gained force.

North also gained public attention and support. The July 9 edition of *The Washington Post* contained twenty-three pictures of North. Twenty-three pictures of one person in a single edition of a daily newspaper! North stories were featured in other newspapers around the country. In addition to carrying all of North's testimony live, the three networks provided extensive coverage in their nightly news shows. He dominated radio talk shows across the country.

Soon the telegrams started to come, first in the hundreds, then in the thousands, then the tens of thousands. Always alert to opportunity, sensing that the members of the Committee were increasingly intimidated, Sullivan began to place ever-larger stacks of telegrams on the table in front of North.

Just in case any member of the Committee missed the point, Sullivan finally drove it home with brutal directness:

Why don't you listen to the American people and what they have said as a result of the last week. There are 2,000 telegrams in our room outside the corridor here that came in this morning. The American people have spoken. . . . [78]

Sullivan, strengthened by the reaction, became even more militant, saying to Liman, who had just asked North a question, "That is none of your business. . . . Get off his back."[79]

The effect on the members of the Committee was immediate and, in some cases, overwhelming. All America was watching. And all America liked Ollie, or so it seemed. Careers hung in the balance. Committee members began to worry about how many constituents would remember their feelings of antagonism toward their representative on the next election day.

Two days into North's testimony, no one seemed to remember the testimony of Charles J. Cooper, the handsome young Assistant Attorney General for the Office of Legal Counsel, one of the highest-ranking officials in the Department of Justice. When Attorney General Edwin Meese began his preliminary inquiry in November 1986, into the then breaking story, Cooper was one of a handful of close aides to whom he turned.

With obvious pain, the conservative attorney had explained how in November North had falsified a statement they and others were preparing for delivery to Congress to explain and contain the scandal. When asked if he would believe North under oath, Cooper said he would not.

As Representative Bill McCollum said on June 25:

We had a group of people, at least three and possibly four—Colonel North, Admiral Poindexter, Mr. McFarlane and probably Director Casey, who were deliberately deceiving and lying to the Attorney General of the United States. . . . I must say in all candor that I am deeply disappointed in those gentlemen. . . . So we have a whole series running from November 1985 through November 1986 where [in] at least three or four specific instances the Attorney General of the United States, our top legal officer . . . was being misled and was not being fully informed and yet was being called upon to make judgments and decisions.

I think that that in itself may well be a crime. If it is not a crime, it is certainly one of the highest acts of insubordination and one of the most treacherous things that has ever occurred to a President, it seems to me, in our history.[80]

But after listening to North, and reading his mail, McCollum changed his tune. On July 14 he told North:

Colonel North, you've served your country admirably. You have been a dedicated, patriotic soldier, and there's no question you've gone above and beyond—on many occasions—the call of duty. For that, I personally [am], and I know the country is grateful, and will remember forever, regardless of anything else. Thank you very much.[81]

Although no other member of the Committee underwent so complete and obvious a transformation, all felt the effects of Olliemania.

1. On February 26, 1987, John Tower handed a copy of the Tower Commission Report to President Reagan. The report criticized a mis-managed White House, casual delegation of important power, and the abdication of responsibility by some high officials. It answered many questions, but many more remained.

2. Ten weeks later, when the Iran-Contra Committee began its public hearings, the Senate Caucus Room had been redesigned to accommodate the twenty-six members of the joint Committee and vast numbers of staff and press. What none of us noticed was that we had transformed the hearing room into a mini-coliseum in which we resembled Roman potentates, turning thumbs up or down on the stoic Christians dragged before us to give testimony.

3. Chairman Daniel Inouye's designation of Warren Rudman (left) as vice chairman conveyed to the Republican members a signal that they would be full partners in the Committee's operations. Representative Lee Hamilton (right) was chairman of the House Committee.

4. Arthur Liman fit the role of Senate counsel perfectly. As *The Washington Post* said, he is "perhaps the top trial lawyer in New York—and one of the best securities and white-collar-crime lawyers in the country." But no one ever paused to consider how Liman might project on television or how the American public would react to an aggressive New York lawyer.

5. When, in his examination of North, John Nields asked, "You put some value, don't you, in the truth?" his manner provoked many television viewers, who flooded the Committee with critical telegrams.

6. Since 1912, the first salmon caught on Maine's Penobscot River has been presented to the president of the United States. Neither Reagan nor we (Senator Mitchell, far right; Senator Cohen, second from left) betrayed any recognition of the symbolism of our handing the President a dead fish as the Iran-Contra hearings began.

7. Lawrence Walsh was appointed independent counsel for the purpose of determining whether members of the Reagan administration had violated criminal statutes in the selling of weapons to Iran and the raising of funds for the Contras. The tensions between the roles of the independent counsel and the Committee became evident almost immediately.

8. In his opening remarks on the first day of the hearings, Representative Dick Cheney shared his prehearing conclusions that "high officials did not ask the questions they should have asked. Activities were undertaken without authority. Checks and balances were ignored." He also put the Committee on notice that Congress had a measure of blame to accept.

9.   "I'm tired of people who wrap themselves in the flag and go around spitting on the Constitution," Rudman said after hearing the testimony of Richard Secord.

10.   We were told that greed lurked behind General Secord's patriotic protestations, but that it would take some tough examination to expose it. Secord took the offensive on the first day of the hearings, portraying himself as a righteous patriot betrayed by his country.

11.   William Casey's death, the night before the public hearings began, convinced many Committee members that the full story of the Agency's activities would never be known. Others doubted that he would have provided information in any case. Even if you did ask Casey the right question, you were never sure that you had received the right answer. It was a common joke that the CIA director had a built-in voice scrambler.

12

12. Robert McFarlane was escorted by Capitol Hill police to a closed-door hearing of the Senate Intelligence Committee. Later, the atmosphere in the hearing room was one of ghoulish curiosity as McFarlane took the oath for his public testimony before the Iran-Contra Committee.

13

13. The administration expected all of the hostages to be released after the Israeli arms shipments in August and September of 1985. Instead only one would be released and McFarlane was put in the position of choosing. He chose William Buckley, but Buckley was dead. The Reverend Benjamin Weir (right) was chosen instead.

14

14. Robert Owen projected a deceptive innocence, but contrary to the impression he tried to create, he did understand the gravity of his actions.

34

34. One of the great stories reported about North was of him sitting with President Reagan and watching three television screens showing the arrival of American students from Grenada. When Jeff Geller deplaned at Charleston Air Force Base in South Carolina, he dropped down and kissed the tarmac. Reagan allegedly turned to him and said, "You see, Ollie, you ought to have more faith in the American people." At the hearings North testified that he'd never had such a meeting with the President.

35

36

35. Representative Henry Hyde waved the document containing the Boland Amendment before television audiences and argued that Congress was responsible for creating confusion and inconsistency in our foreign policy.

36. On his own initiative, Bretton Sciaroni, the sole professional staff member of the President's three-member Intelligence Oversight Board, prepared a legal opinion concluding that the Boland Amendments did not apply to the NSC.

37. Senator William Cohen, confronting the National Security Adviser on his obfuscating language, said: "I find it troubling that you say, 'I withheld information from Congress, but I did not mislead it,' that the United States 'acquiesced in the shipment of weapons to Iran but did not authorize it,' that the administration's support for the Contras was 'secret but not covert.' If the administration wants to gain the support of the American people, it must stop insulting their intelligence and tell them the direct, unvarnished truth."

37

38

38. Poindexter said 184 times that he could not recall the events about which he was questioned, raising doubts about his credibility. The billowing screen of smoke that shrouded his face as he puffed on his pipe produced an unwitting metaphor for his testimony.

39. The presence of the witnesses' family members had a subtle influence on the members of the Committee. Linda Poindexter, an Episcopal priest, attended the hearings wearing her clerical collar.

39

40. George Shultz's appearance before the Committee was as welcome as that of a Saint Bernard at an avalanche. It was Shultz who warned the President against selling arms to Iran and swapping arms for hostages. It was also Shultz who could not bring himself to acknowledge that the President, by intent or inadvertence, contributed to misleading his own Secretary of State.

40

41. Peter Rodino, chairman of the House Judiciary Committee, conducted the impeachment proceedings against President Nixon in 1974. In the Iran-Contra hearings, he focused on the rule of law and the White House failure to live up to its spirit, if not its letter.

42. Edwin Meese III was the Attorney General of the United States because he is, as were many attorneys general before him, a close personal and political friend of the president he served. In politics, loyalty sometimes outweighs other values, and Meese's behavior during the initial investigation of the Iran-Contra affair raised serious and difficult questions.

43. Don Regan seemed to have joined the Committee not for combat but for cocktails. That he did not have much more than a surface understanding of either the Iran operation or the Contra-aid program was itself significant in revealing how White House foreign policy was organized and run.

44. With vast experience in government, Caspar Weinberger always proved to be a formidable witness at congressional hearings, scolding those who attempted to interrupt him as if they were schoolboys caught trespassing in his backyard. During his testimony before the Iran-Contra Committee, he made it clear that he was concerned about the credibility of the United States and the impact that the sale of weapons to Iran might have upon America's allies.

44

45

45. The Committee did not focus on the role of Vice President George Bush, who frequently described himself as "out of the loop." Records show, however, that he attended many briefings during which the arms sale and the hostage issue were discussed. And in his controversial January 25, 1988, interview with Dan Rather, the Vice President stated, "I went along with it [the arms-for-hostages deal]."

46

47

46.   The judgments of the majority report were stated in stark and solemn terms. The responsibility for the Iran-Contra affair was placed directly on President Reagan. His fall led him to reach for a rope with which to pull himself to safety—a successful meeting with the Soviet leader, Mikhail Gorbachev, featuring a nuclear-arms agreement. Seven months to the day after the public hearings began, the President and Gorbachev signed the historic INF treaty.

47.   On March 16, 1988, a federal grand jury returned criminal indictments against Oliver North, John Poindexter, Richard Secord, and Albert Hakim. North quickly announced his resignation from the Marine Corps, stating that his resignation was prompted by the need to subpoena documents and testimony from his superiors, "the highest-ranking officials in the government . . ."

Why? How did a Marine lieutenant colonel capture the nation in a single week, when the events leading up to his testimony had been so damaging to him?

We think it was the confluence of four factors: the person, the place, the conditions of his appearance, and television.

First, the person.

• Ollie North is a man of action. He gets things done. In our complex world, we are increasingly bound by rules. You need a license to drive, a permit to build a garage, permission to leave school or work. Each of us longs for a simpler world, even as we acknowledge the necessity for rules and regulations. But we all think about cutting through red tape, bypassing the bureaucracy, and beating the system. Ollie North does what most people dream about doing.

• Ollie North is a stand-up guy, willing, as he so colorfully put it, to take the spear in his chest to save the President. In fact, North's testimony carefully steered the spear into Admiral Poindexter's chest, but no one seemed to notice.

• Ollie North is a man of commitment, willing to act on his strong convictions. For most of us, life is filled with gray areas and uncertainty, and we often suffer from self-doubt. There are no gray areas in Ollie North's mind. He's right, and anyone who disagrees with him is wrong. Few people are so compelling as those who offer certainty in an uncertain world.

• Ollie North is a genuine war hero. Most of us will never have our courage tested in the horror of war. We rightly admire those who have faced and passed that test.

• Ollie North has the guts to tell Congress off. For two centuries, Americans have been skeptical of politicians. When a lone underdog Marine lieutenant colonel told off twenty-six politicians and their lawyers, it was natural for America to cheer.

The place.

Republican Representative Michael DeWine of Ohio devoted his allotted questioning time to praising North and criticizing the

Committee's processes as unfair to North. He complained about the manner in which the Committee used some exhibits, about the selective presentation of evidence, about the use of hearsay testimony. He even threw in a reference to the Army-McCarthy hearings. His point was clear: Congressional hearings are different from trials in a court of law, and they are different in ways that are unfair to witnesses. Specifically, this congressional hearing was conducted in a way that was unfair to this witness, Oliver North.

No one bothered to refute DeWine, so many Americans accepted his point as correct. But was it? Is a witness really worse off in a congressional hearing than in a court of law? We think not.

There are advantages and disadvantages to both. We think the advantages to a witness of being before a congressional committee, especially a televised congressional hearing, outweigh those of being in a court of law. No witness used those advantages more effectively than Oliver North.

In court, a witness sits alone in the witness box while his lawyer sits across the room at a table reserved for counsel. The witness cannot consult his lawyer before answering a question. Though his lawyer may object to a question, he cannot communicate privately with the witness during questioning.

In a congressional hearing, the witness and his lawyer sit side by side at the witness table. They can consult before answering a question. North and Sullivan consulted so regularly that it led to this exchange with the Senate counsel:

> LIMAN: Colonel, is it fair to say that November 25, 1986, was one of the worst days in your life?
> (Pause while North confers with counsel)
> LIMAN: I wasn't asking whether it was one of the worst days in Mr. Sullivan's life.[82]

On another occasion Liman asked North what he was consulting when he paused to review a tabulated notebook that he kept at the witness table at all times. Sullivan loudly charged that the notebook was the product of his own labors and was protected by the attorney "work product privilege."[83] No trial court in the country would have permitted North to examine material while testifying without permitting the opposing attorney to examine it as well, regardless of its origin. Yet Liman, lacking support from Committee members, dropped his inquiry.

In court, a witness must answer questions directly. Statements not responsive to questions are cut off.

In a congressional hearing, witnesses frequently give lengthy, unresponsive answers that often amount to speeches in their own behalf.

There is no better example of the decisive advantage this practice gives a skilled witness like North than his response to Nields's question about the security system given him by Secord. Nields asked simply whether North knew that General Secord had paid for the system. In a court of law, North would have been allowed a yes-or-no answer. Instead, North gave the emotional, powerful fifteen-minute speech that decisively turned the tide of public opinion in his favor.

In a court of law, the prosecutor and judge have different functions. A congressional committee is trapped in the unattractive dual role of prosecutor and judge.

Finally, a congressional committee rarely speaks with one voice on important questions. Political and regional differences prevail. This was evident in the Iran-Contra hearings. North had many apologists on the Committee.

The conditions of his appearance.

As part of the Committee's negotiations with Sullivan, we had expressed our intention to complete North's testimony within a period of approximately thirty hours. Sullivan insisted upon a time limitation so the Committee would not have the weekend in which to digest the details and full implications of North's testimony and then put him back at the witness table for further interrogation. Although there was no binding agreement to adhere to the time limit, it provided Sullivan a stick with which he constantly beat the Committee.

Several Committee members joined Sullivan in chiding Nields and Liman for taking too long and being too aggressive. Pressure was constantly applied to shorten and soften the examination.

In addition, North's technique of giving long narrative answers—some to questions that were never asked—had the effect of practically nullifying the participation of the "nondesignated hitters" (twenty-two of the twenty-six members). Each member would have at most three or four questions to ask in a period of fifteen minutes. Members were faced with a dilemma. They could try to develop a serious line of inquiry, knowing North would be likely to deflect it; or they could attempt to negate North's testimonials by making speeches themselves. Most chose to make speeches (relieving North of further questioning), and few speeches were as effective as North's.

North and Sullivan were using the time limits effectively, having already ensured—by refusing to testify privately first and holding documents—that the Committee would be inadequately prepared to question him effectively.

Many of North's statements, some of them important, were contradicted by subsequent witnesses, particularly by Poindexter, but by that time the television networks were back to their soap operas, and public attention had largely turned to other things. Had the Committee refused to give North special treatment, the result might have been different.

Finally, television.

We have already commented on the importance of television to this entire affair. Television is a medium that embraces some individuals while scorning others. No amount of cosmetics, practiced elocutions, or entreaties will soften its judgment or turn its heart. High cheekbones, angular features, articulate speech invite its affections. But ultimately it is manner that makes all. With Oliver North television had a torrid love affair.

Those of us who sat on the two-tiered dais could not fully appreciate the magnetism that North generated. From a distance,

North looked attractive in his Marine uniform and rows of medals, but thin and not particularly imposing.

It was not until we slipped into the anteroom to drink coffee and watch the proceedings on the television sets there that we saw the dramatic transformation. His telegenic face filled the entire screen. His clear gray eyes (perpetually moist) reflected sadness, anger, sympathy. His voice was alternately soft and forceful, and it cracked at just the right emotional moment. He sat ramrod-stiff, Clint Eastwood, Audie Murphy, Alan Ladd, and John Wayne all buttoned up in one charismatic persona.

He challenged the terrorist Abu Nidal to go one on one with him any time, any place, any way. He had no fear for himself—only for his wife and family. He made a mistake in accepting a protective security fence for his loved ones. Who would blame him?

We shook our heads in disbelief. That fence might keep out the neighborhood dogs or some anti-Contra activitist who had poured sand in his car's gas tank. But Abu Nidal? Hardly. Still, the theater was far more compelling than our doubts.

What about the $2,440 in traveler's checks cashed at Sugarland Texaco, Giant Food, Drug Fair, and the National Tire Whole-salers? Gentlemen, he said, his voice once again cracking, he had taken money from his monthly paycheck to help the Contras. The traveler's checks were merely reimbursements. Really? Secord and Hakim had $8 million sitting in a Swiss bank account, and North was forced to take food money from the family budget to help the Contras?

Before he was asked about the check cashed at Parklane Hosiery, he chastised Committee members for holding lustful thoughts:

When you put up things like Parklane Hosiery—and you all snicker at it—and you know that I have got a beautiful secretary and the good Lord gave her the gift of beauty, and that people snicker that Ollie North might have been doing a little hanky-panky with his secretary, Ollie North has been loyal to his wife since the day he married her. . . . [84]

No one on the Committee had even hinted that Fawn Hall was romantically involved with North. Most were familiar with the *Washington Post* story that detailed her prior relationship with Arturo Cruz, Jr., the son of one of the Contra leaders. But none of us had to be reminded how such a pledge of marital fidelity was playing in Peoria, when the Gary Hart/Donna Rice and Jim and Tammy Bakker disclosures were still burning up the scandal sheets.

All right, what about the hosiery purchase? His attractive wife, Betsy, who sat stoically just behind him during his testimony, had reminded him: "Of course, you did, you old buffoon, you went there to buy leotards for our two little girls."[85]

Some thought they were witnessing a comedy skit on "Saturday Night Live." But the audience wasn't laughing. They were cheering for North. When the television set showed a split screen with North on one side and House Counsel John Nields on the other, one reason for the applause became clear. Nields, a polished, Ivy League–trained lawyer, his long hair touching the top of his shoulders, could have been one of those who were in the streets demonstrating against the Vietnam War. North, with his Huck Finn looks and Marine bearing, was one of those who were in the trenches doing the fighting. Just who was Nields to be badgering North? It was an unfair image, but one that would not be erased during the remainder of North's appearance.

No sentiment went untapped by North, no role untried. North begged the Committee not to let his transgressions jeopardize America's support for the Contras: "Hang whatever you want around the neck of Ollie North. . . . But for the love of God and the love of this nation, don't hang around Ollie North's neck the cut-off of funds to the Nicaraguan resistance again."[86]

North enraged a number of the Committee members by implicitly branding those who disagreed with him as lacking in a love for either God or country.

Finally, in a demonstration of supreme confidence, North put a friendly arm around the terrierlike Sullivan and told him, "Take it easy, counselor, I can handle it." With that gesture, North told everyone watching that one Marine against twenty-six lawyer-politicians was still an even match. Actually, it wasn't even close. North held a Gatling gun while we sat like ducks in a shooting gallery.

The American people loved it. A real Rambo had come to Washington.

GJM: *By Wednesday night I knew I had a real problem. After two days of testimony Oliver North had become a national hero. My offices, in Maine and in Washington, were swamped with telephone calls, most of them favorable to North.*

And I knew the worst was yet to come. On the following morning North would belatedly deliver his opening statement. I had read it and knew that it was a combative defense of his actions and a powerful indictment of the Committee. It would have been effective if delivered by North at the beginning of his testimony. Delivered two days later, after North had acquired the aura and self-confidence of a national hero, it would be even more impressive.

That would be followed by questioning by the House minority counsel, George Van Cleve. An able, amiable man, he would be trying to make North look even better than he did. I knew he would serve up puffballs for questions, giving North the chance to make as many speeches as he wanted. This is how Van Cleve's questioning began:

VAN CLEVE: Colonel North, in your opening statement, which you just gave, you testified that you graduated from the Naval Academy in 1968. Is that correct?

NORTH: Yes, I did.

VAN CLEVE: And in 1969, did you serve on active combat duty in the Armed Forces of the United States in the Republic of Vietnam?

NORTH: Sixty-nine? Yes, correct.

VAN CLEVE: And is it the case that, during your service there, you were awarded a series of military citations, including two Purple Hearts, the Bronze Star and the Silver Star?

NORTH: I was.

VAN CLEVE: And the Silver Star was awarded for "conspicuous gallantry and intrepidity in battle," is that correct?

NORTH: I believe that's the way the citation reads.[87]

And so it went, for an entire morning. I wasn't critical of Van Cleve. His clients, the House Republicans, wanted him to make North look good. That's what he did.

By noon on Thursday, when Van Cleve finished, North was at his peak, and I had one hope: that somehow my time for questioning him would not come until the following Monday. I needed the weekend to figure out what to do, what to say, what to ask.

I was lucky. Arthur Liman questioned North for a day. Then it was the turn of the Committee members. Before the public hearings began, North had been designated a House witness. Just as the House lawyers, Nields and Van Cleve, preceded the Senate lawyer, Liman, so the House's designated questioners, Representatives Ed Jenkins and Dick Cheney, would precede me and Trible. When Cheney finished, it was nearly five o'clock on Friday afternoon, too late for another questioner to begin. I breathed a deep sigh of relief.

I had already made two decisions. I canceled a series of events in Maine that had been scheduled for Saturday: I needed that day to prepare, to think through my line of questions. I would go to Maine on Sunday, with Bill Cohen, to participate in the launching of a guided-missile cruiser at the Bath Iron Works. If I could get my thoughts down on paper by Saturday night, I could spend the time on the flight to and from Maine reviewing and rethinking them.

I also had decided that I would not just ask North questions. I had tried many cases as a lawyer and was confident of my ability to question witnesses. With unlimited time to question North, I thought I could conduct a satisfactory inquiry. But I didn't have unlimited time. I had one hour. I had just watched North testify for four days. He was a skillful and successful witness. In part that was because, whenever he felt like it, he simply made a speech. Sometimes his speeches were in response to a question, sometimes not. I recognized early in the week that if I wanted to get a point across I had to do it myself, in a speech of my own.

The really important question for me remained: What point did I want to get across? What was the message I had to deliver?

I got a lot of advice. All week I felt a growing pressure. On those occasions when we left the hearing to go to the Senate floor for a vote, I was surrounded by my Democratic colleagues.

"Why are you guys letting him get away with those speeches?"

"You've got to turn this thing around!"

"We're counting on you!"

"Why don't you ask him . . . ?"

Most of the suggested questions had already been asked by one or more of the lawyers. But the senators, most busy with their own hearings or meetings, were unaware of it.

So I finally had to decide, myself.

I recognized early that one important point had to be made. On the first day North said that the American people "ought not to be led to believe, as a consequence of these hearings, that this nation cannot or should not conduct covert operations." For four days he created the impression that the Committee opposed covert operations. And he justified lying to Congress on the now famous ground that he had to choose between lies or lives.

But no member of the Committee favored a prohibition of covert operations. We all recognized that there are some circumstances in which the United States must conduct such operations. The problem is that covert operations, by their very nature, conflict with democratic values. Covert operations require secrecy and deception. Our democratic process places a high value on the opposite characteristics of openness and truth. So the real question, the much more difficult question, is, how can covert operations be conducted in a lawful manner in a democracy in which public officials are accountable for their acts? I wanted to get that point across, that the real question is not whether one is for or against covert operations but how they can be reconciled with democratic values.

For weeks I was troubled by the tone and direction of the hearings.

Some of the Committee members who favored military assistance to the Contras used their allotted time to make speeches in favor of such assistance, rather than ask questions. Or they asked leading questions intended to make the same point.

Those of us who opposed military assistance to the Contras chose not to respond in kind. To the criticism that the hearings were becoming a debate in which only one side was participating, we replied that the investigation was being conducted to find out what had happened in the Iran-Contra affair, not to debate the administration's policy in Central America. Someone had to ask questions. But it was not a satisfactory reply, to us or to the critics.

My concern increased during North's testimony. He was an effective spokesman for Contra aid, and he linked that aid to patriotism. Ollie North's message was direct and powerful: If you love America, you support the Contras. The reverse implication was clear: If you don't support the Contras, you don't love America.

Nationalism has had an emotional and enduring appeal, across the globe and through the ages. It is particularly strong in the United States, one of the least homogeneous of nations. If, in public debate, you can convince enough Americans that someone, something, some idea, is not "American," the debate is over, the issue decided.

North had done that, or so it seemed. Overnight polls showed a sharp upsurge in support for Contra aid. North himself was an instant sensation, a national hero. His person and background made his arguments even more appealing. This is not a man who merely talked of patriotism. He lived it. By all accounts, his military record was one of personal courage and commitment. I admired him for it, as did all Americans.

In the face of North's success, how could I possibly get across another point of view? Where should I begin? Where should I try to do it, in an opening or a closing statement? If I waited to make a closing statement, would I be caught without enough time, in the middle of one of his speeches? My mind was filled with ideas, but nothing had jelled.

By Friday evening I was disheartened, not confident of my ability even to discern the proper message, let alone frame and deliver it. I talked with three aides: Martha Pope, my administrative assistant; Rich Arenberg, my staff liaison on the Committee; and Jamie Kaplan, an associate counsel on the Committee. Their comments helped to focus my thoughts, and I began to prepare a written outline.

Earlier that day I had talked with Bill Cohen. "Take him on on the issues," he said, "but don't attack him personally. If you do, you won't succeed in the attack, and the issues will be drowned out." He knew that I was thinking about trying to question North about his many contradictions and lies, and he warned me not to do it. He also affirmed my own thinking when he said, "If you've got something to say, say it. Don't think you'll get anything across through questions and answers. He'll filibuster you whenever he needs to."

Late Friday evening I called Hal Pachios, a close friend who practices law in Portland. He has been active in politics for years, as deputy press secretary to President Johnson and later as chairman of the Maine Democratic Party. He has good political instincts, and his advice is usually sound.

We discussed the situation. "If you call him a liar, which is what you'll be doing if you directly attack his credibility, that will be the story; nothing else you say will get across," he said. "And what's the point? He's already admitted lying. So stay away from that. Pick one issue and stick with it." When I asked him what that issue should be, his response was immediate. "North said today that you guys should vote aid for the Contras for love of God and country. That's outrageous. It's insulting. You can take that and turn it around. Not only can you do it, you have *to do it."*

In that moment I knew what I would do. I didn't write anything down until the following morning. I let the thoughts percolate in my head overnight. When I sat down at my desk on Saturday morning, the words came without effort:

You have talked here often eloquently about the need for a demo-cratic outcome in Nicaragua. There's no disagreement on that. There is disagreement over how best to achieve that objective. Many Americans agree with the President's policy; many do not. Many patriotic Americans, strongly anti-communist, believe there's a better way to contain the Sandinistas, to bring about a democratic outcome in Nicaragua and to bring peace to Central America.

Many patriotic Americans are concerned that in the pursuit of democracy abroad we not compromise it in any way here at home. You and others have urged consistency in our policies, you have said repeatedly that if we are not consistent our allies and other nations will question our reliability. That is a real concern. But if it's bad to change policies, it's worse to have two different policies at the same time; one public policy and an opposite policy in private. It's difficult to conceive of a greater inconsistency than that. It's hard to imagine anything that would give our allies more cause to consider us unreliable than that we say one thing in public and secretly do the opposite. And that's exactly what was done when arms were sold to Iran and arms were swapped for hostages.

Now, you have talked a lot about patriotism and the love of our country. Most nations derive from a single tribe, a single race; they practice a single religion. Common racial, ethnic, and religious heritages are the glue of nationhood for many. The United States is different; we have all races, all religions, we have a limited common heritage. The glue of nationhood for us is the American ideal of individual liberty and equal justice. The rule of law is critical in our society. It's the great equalizer, because in America everybody is equal before the law. We must never allow the end to justify the means where the law is concerned. However important and noble an objective, and surely democracy abroad is important and is noble, it cannot be achieved at the expense of the rule of law in our country.

You talked about your background and it was really very compelling, and is obviously one of the reasons why the American people are attracted to you.

Let me tell you a story from my background. Before I entered the Senate I had the great honor of serving as a federal judge. In that position I had great power. The one I most enjoyed exercising was the power to make people American citizens. From time to time I presided at what we call naturalization ceremonies; they are citizenship ceremonies. These are people who came from all over the world, risked their lives, sometimes left their families and their fortunes behind to come here. They had gone through the required procedures, and I in the final act administered to them the oath of allegiance to the United States, and I made them American citizens. To this moment, to this moment it was the most exciting thing I have ever done in my life.

The ceremonies were always moving for me because my mother was an immigrant, my father the orphan son of immigrants. Neither of them had any education and they worked at very menial tasks in our society. But because of the openness of America, because of equal justice under law in America, I sit here today a United States Senator. And after every one of these ceremonies I made it a point to speak to these new Americans. I asked them why they came, how they came, and the stories, each of them, was inspiring. I think you would be interested and moved by them given the views that you have expressed on this country.

And when I asked them why they came they said several things, mostly two. The first is they said we came because here in America everybody has a chance, opportunity. And they also said over and over again, particularly people from totalitarian societies, we came here because here in America you can criticize the government without looking over your shoulder. Freedom to disagree with the government.

Now, you have addressed several pleas to this committee, very eloquently. None more eloquent than last Friday when in reponse to a question by Representative Cheney you asked that Congress not cut off aid to the contras for the love of God and for the love of country. I now address a plea to you. Of all the qualities which the American people find compelling about you, none is more impressive than your obvious deep devotion to this country. Please remember that others share that devotion and recognize that it is possible for an American to disagree with you on aid to the contras and still love God and still love this country just as much as you do.

Although He's regularly asked to do so, God does not take sides in American politics. And in America, disagreement with the policies of the government is not evidence of lack of patriotism.

I want to repeat that: In America, disagreement with the policies of the government is not evidence of lack of patriotism.

Indeed, it is the very fact that Americans can criticize their government openly and without fear of reprisal that is the essence of our freedom, and that will keep us free.

I have one final plea. Debate this issue forcefully and vigorously as you have and as you surely will, but, please, do it in a way that respects the patriotism and the motives of those who disagree with you, as you would have them respect yours.[88]

As it turned out, some of what I said was not prepared. It just tumbled out spontaneously, because it seemed to me to be appropriate. And some of what I'd written I didn't use, because it didn't seem necessary. But for the most part I said what I felt needed saying.

The response was immediate and overwhelming. Before I finished speaking, every line in every one of my offices was busy. By the thousands they came in, first the telephone calls, then the telegrams, then the letters. Most were favorable. The unfavorable, although few in number, were intense in their hostility.

I felt at ease. I don't think I dented Ollie North's image a bit. I'm sure the supportive comments to him far outnumber those I received. But at least I got across a different point of view, one worth restating: "Although He's regularly asked to do so, God does not take sides in American politics, and in America, disagreement with the policies of the government is not evidence of lack of patriotism."[89]

WSC: During North's testimony, I felt like an observer rather than a participant in the proceedings. This was partly intentional. I was trying to maintain a certain distance from the hearings at that point, something akin to what Henry Adams might have described as "sitting on a fence and watching the Committee walk by." The psychological separation was in part unavoidable. A full week would pass before I would be able to question North, and then I would be allotted only fifteen minutes! All of the important questions would have been asked, most of the speeches given.

As I listened to North testify, I found my emotions running from admiration to bemusement and anger.

I had serious doubts about a number of North's answers. I found

*it difficult to believe he had to advance money from his monthly pay-
check to the Contras while Hakim and Secord were sitting on millions
of dollars in a secret Swiss account. I did not accept his rationale for
destroying the ledger books that contained an accounting for the money
and traveler's checks he kept in his office safe (lives were at stake, and
Bill Casey told him to destroy them). The Committee could find no
record that North had ever reported receiving a threat from Abu Nidal.
A $13,800 security fence would hardly deter professional terrorists.
North's denial of any knowledge of a $200,000 insurance policy
set up by Albert Hakim strained credulity, particularly in view of Mrs.
North's visit to Philadelphia to meet with Hakim's lawyer.*

*North's boast to Assistant Attorney General Cooper that he could
pass a lie-detector test saying that he believed oil-drilling equipment
and not HAWK missiles had been shipped to Iran in November 1985
revealed not only his self-confidence but a possible willingness to stick
to a phony cover story if Cooper approved. . . .*

*I concluded that I was drifting off course, just as some on the
Committee had done for several weeks. During Phase One, the Committee, through witnesses such as McFarlane, Hakim, Calero, Robinette, and Cooper, disclosed facts that undermined the "hero" status
President Reagan had conferred upon North.*

*Questions about personal gain, evidence of venality, obviously would
be important factors in assessing North's credibility as a witness when
he testified. North undoubtedly was the center of attention and controversy; the Committee had been drawn inexorably into the web of treating
him as the central recipient of responsibility and culpability.*

*North was, in McFarlane's words, an "action-oriented, can-do of-
ficer." He was hired to serve on the NSC staff precisely for these
qualities. His propensity for exaggeration and "creativity" (off-the-
wall proposals) was well known to those with whom he worked. He
had carried out the twin goals of the President by arranging for the
transfer of weapons to the Iranians and funds to the Contras. That he
conceived of the notion of merging the two programs did not and should
not have come as a shock to his superiors (Poindexter thought it was*

*a good idea, and he believed the President would think so as well).
With Lieutenant Colonel North, the administration got exactly what
it wanted.*

*North had engaged in clearly improper—perhaps illegal—activity,
and we had an obligation to elicit evidence of his conduct. But almost
from the moment John Nields began to question him, the proceedings
turned hostile and confrontational. Suddenly it was Nields against
North, North against the Committee, an obvious mismatch. In* King
Henry VI, *Dick the Butcher shouted: "The first thing we do, let's kill
all the lawyers."*[90] *The American people seemed to concur.*

*I thought that Arthur Liman would pull North's testimony back into
focus. His examination was brilliant, but Liman had been thrown off
stride. The night before Liman was scheduled to interrogate North,
ABC's Capitol Hill correspondent Brit Hume predicted on "Nightline"
that Liman's aggressive style of cross-examination would be a public-
relations disaster. During Liman's examination of North, several House
Republicans—the very ones who just days before had publicly referred
to North as a liar and guilty of insubordination of the highest order—
began to shout North's praises. They interrupted Liman, charging that
he was taking too much time or was too prosecutorial.*

*The criticism was unwarranted. In fact, at one point Liman asked
North about notes he had written in November 1986 that listed his
personal priorities. North seemed upset at the prospect of having to
disclose those priorities. Liman charitably did not pursue the question,
and North sent Liman a personal note expressing his gratitude for being
spared an embarrassment.*

*Liman was visibly dispirited by the interruptions and criticisms com-
ing from the Committee members, and by the antics of Brendan Sullivan. I spoke out of turn:*

Mr. Chairman, shortly before we broke for lunch, there was an indication that perhaps our counsel should cut short his questioning of
Col. North. I wanted to point out just for the record that no member
of the Senate interrupted House counsel during their questioning of
Col. North: not one member ever interrupted either Mr. Nields or

Mr. Van Cleve. Number two, there were no time limits imposed upon House counsel. It took two and a half days, and I reject the notion that somehow because the members don't like either Mr. Liman's tone or style, that he should be forced to cut short his questioning. Point number three, is Oliver North has demonstrated he's not only a brave military officer, but he's also a superb witness. And, I think he's had a lot tougher things thrown at him during his lifetime than questions by Arthur Liman and I think he's fully capable of handling those questions without the able assistance of members of Congress.

And, the final point I'd like to make is, perhaps the most serious revelation to have taken place during the course of these proceedings is that of a plan, proposed by or conceived by high-ranking officials, to create a contingency fund for the intended purpose of carrying out other covert operations at some time in the future, with or without presidential findings, with or without notice to Congress. . . . If Members of Congress are not disturbed about that revelation, then I think the American people should be, and if it takes more time to discuss this in depth and other related issues, I am perfectly happy to yield whatever time I have allocated to me so that Mr. Liman might continue. But I strongly object to the notion raised by House members of trying to impose a gag rule upon Mr. Liman.[91]

Arthur sent me an appreciative note that captured his wry humor: "But why does your name have to be Cohen?" The vicious anti-Semitic letters he had received had not been entirely dismissed.

The mail in my office was running heavily in favor of North and against the Committee. Although I was certain that the authors did not have Shakespeare in mind, many of them expressed the desire to hang me along with "that Jew, Liman."

The tide did not turn until members of the Committee began to question North. I thought George Mitchell provided the first real break in North's virtuoso performance. His questions to North were sharp and insightful and his words, reminding North and the American people that patriotism embraces diversity of opinion rather than divinely endorsed unanimity, were the most memorable of the hearings.

Representative Stokes reminded North that he had once worn the same uniform as North and fought in the same trenches. But there was one major difference—Stokes was not allowed to eat in the same mess halls or sleep in the same dormitories. He and millions of other black Americans had to ride in the backs of buses, barred from motels and luncheon counters until such time as they could change the law.

As I listened to Stokes's deep voice, I found my mind playing tricks. I kept hearing the unique and powerful voice of another black person, Barbara Jordan. It was the summer of 1974, and Texas Congresswoman Jordan was delivering her remarks on the subject of impeachment.

Earlier today we heard the beginning of the Preamble to the Constitution of the United States. "We the people . . . " It is a very eloquent beginning. But when that document was completed on the 17th of September in 1787, I was not included in that, "we the people." I felt somehow for many years that George Washington and Alexander Hamilton just left me out by mistake. But through the process of amendment, interpretation and court decision, I have finally been included in "we, the people." Today, I am an inquisitor. My faith in the Constitution is whole, it is complete, it is total. I am not going to sit here and be an idle spectator to the diminution, the subversion, the destruction of the Constitution.[92]

Senator Warren Rudman, who earlier had defended Chairman Inouye against racial attacks, spoke as a combat veteran of the Korean War and a supporter of Contra aid:

Colonel North . . . you said about the Congress, "I suggest to you that it is the Congress which must accept the blame in the Nicaraguan freedom fighting matter, plain and simple. You are to blame because of the fickle, vacillating, unpredictable, on-again/off-again policy toward the resistance."

You are entitled to your view, but I want to share some of my views with you. . . .

Under the latest Harris poll in June, 74 to 22 people in this country oppose aid to the contras. In April of '86 [there] was an astounding poll which I think refutes your idea the American people somehow don't understand what's going on. That indicated that 56 percent of the American people were aware of the threat which Nicaragua poses to its Latin American neighbors, that 50 percent of those polled believe it is in the long-term interest of the United States to eliminate communism from Latin America—so far so good—and then 62 percent of the same polling group say no aid to the contras.

. . . I can tell you myself, Colonel North . . . as one who has with reluctance on occasion but in the final analysis found there was no other solution, voted for that aid to the contras—the people in this country just don't think that's a very good idea. And that is why this Congress has been fickle and vacillating. . . .

. . . I want to point out to you, Colonel North, that the Constitution starts with the words, "We, the people." There is no way you can carry out a consistent policy if we, the people disagree with it, because this Congress represents the people.

The President of the United States, the greatest communicator probably we have seen in the White House in years, has tried for eight years [to gain American support for the Contras] and failed; you have tried, and I think probably failed . . . and this relatively obscure senator from New Hampshire has tried with no success at all. . . .

I guess the last thing I want to say to you, Colonel, is that the American people have the constitutional right to be wrong. And what Ronald Reagan thinks or what Oliver North thinks or what anybody else thinks makes not a w[h]it.

. . . There comes a point when the views of the American people have to be heard.[93]

These and other speeches started to shift the focus away from North's personal behavior to the central question of the meaning of the rule of law in our lives. Britt Snider, Jim Dykstra, and Natalie Bocock, three staff members of the Senate Intelligence Committee, had prepared over twenty pages of possible questions for North. I looked at the stack of papers and smiled. Each of the questions was worth asking. With my allotted fifteen minutes, I would be lucky to pose three or four of them.

I had closely observed North during his direct and cross-examination, looking for areas that needed further exploration. On Thursday, July 9, North testified briefly in a private session about the other covert activities the Enterprise stood ready to execute. The hearing, more of a meeting actually, took place in a small, low-ceilinged room in the

Capitol where the Senate Intelligence Committee had once held its classified briefings and hearings. North sat at a small witness table that faced a horseshoe-shaped table reserved for the members. Witness and interrogators were now on the same level and in close proximity.

We had entered an inner sanctum, an unofficial clubhouse when men could drop their guards. North remained magnetic, but in a different way. His manner was relaxed. He smiled easily. He seductively invited us into his confidence, as if to say, "Look, fellas, now that the cameras aren't here, let me tell you how it really is out on the front lines. . . ." All formality and tension were gone. A storyteller was in our midst, sharing his secrets. North's transformed manner was mirrored by the members. No longer were we adversaries; here we were equals. It was as if some tacit agreement existed between us, one that said that here we would suspend hostilities, declare a momentary truce, before renewing the public contest.

I wondered whether it would have been more productive to have taken all of his testimony in this fashion, behind closed doors, away from the glare of cameras. But then I had to remind myself how often North had resorted to fabrication to influence the opinions or actions of others. How would we know the difference between fact and fiction? Did North himself always know or respect the difference? I found myself anxious to return to the formal proceedings, where everyone's guard was up. . . .

I decided to structure a series of short questions that North could (and, I hoped, would) answer in a single sentence. His relationship with President Reagan had been the subject of a number of articles and a great deal of speculation. First there was the remark he allegedly made to Felix Rodriguez (code name "Max Gomez"). Rodriguez said that once when he was in North's company North looked up at a television program, pointing to members of Congress, and said, "You see those guys. They want to get me. But they are not going to get me. Because the old man loves my ass."

I wanted to know whether the "old man" was Ronald Reagan or Bill Casey. I never got an answer, because North denied that the conversation had ever occurred.

In the July 1987 issue of The Washingtonian *magazine, North was reported to have said that upon occasion he would slip in to see President Reagan privately without recording or "logging in" the meeting. North testified that he had never done so: "I never made any surreptitious visits to the President, sir."*

North was placed in charge of running two separate programs. It is easy to understand why he and Admiral Poindexter might think it a "neat idea" to use profits generated by the sale of weapons to Iran to help support the Nicaraguan Contras. General Secord had been purchasing and, through Southern Air Transport, delivering weapons to the Contras. President Reagan signed a finding authorizing third parties (i.e., commercial cutouts) to be used in selling weapons to Iran. Israel had overcharged the Iranians for weapons from the very first sales. For the sake of logistical efficiency, it made perfect sense to merge both programs, to allow the hated Ayatollah Khomeini unwittingly to contribute to the cause of the Contras. Several Committee members expressed an enthusiastic endorsement of the scheme.

HYDE: Why was this different? Why did you have to lie to Congress, why was this different from other covert actions? You know it's very simple when you have a covert action that everybody agrees with. . . . When you get a controversial one, then you have a whole different problem. . . . The end doesn't justify the means. . . . It's a useful, ethical statement, I suppose, but I'll tell you, that phrase doesn't seem to me to establish the moral context for every tough decision someone in government has to make. . . . The moral choices that you have to face as to keeping faith with people who have relied on you and who are out there with their lives in the mountains of Nicaragua or obeying one of the five versions of a very ambiguous law that is attached to a military appropriation is a very tough, moral choice. But it isn't simple, and many times you end up with having to take the lesser evil. And I think that ought to be realized by people who are so quick to condemn and to give you the phrase the end doesn't justify the means. . . .

Let me give you a quotation that you might carry with you, and I quote, "A strict observance of the written law is doubtless one of the high duties of a good citizen. But it is not the highest. The laws of necessity, of self-preservation, of saving our country when in danger are of higher obligation." And that same person said, "On great occasions every good officer must be ready to risk himself in going beyond the strict line of law when the public preservation requires it." The person who said those things had a little bit to do with the founding of this country. We have a monument to him called the Jefferson Memorial. . . . So the notion of betraying freedom fighters bothers you whether they are at the Bay of Pigs or whether we're taking off from the roof of the Embassy at Saigon on April 25, 1975, or whether leaving them to fend for themselves in the mountains of Nicaragua. So you have got a few more mountains to climb, Colonel North, but remember everybody remembers Billy Mitchell and nobody remembers who his prosecutors were.[94]

HATCH: I don't think that we should have had a diversion of funds here, even though I have to confess I kind of think it is a neat idea, too, to take money from the Ayatollah and send them over to freedom fighters in Nicaragua. What a nice use of those funds, except you have to be—I don't think it was right. I think it points out the difficulties. . . . I think you were right—at least well motivated in your desires to help them, because we weren't helping them like we should up here. We weren't supporting this policy in our own hemisphere. . . .

I don't want you prosecuted. I don't. I don't think many people in America do. And I think there's going to be one lot of hell raised if you are. That doesn't mean they won't. It doesn't mean that sticklers in the law won't pursue the last pound of flesh, but I'll tell you, I don't want you prosecuted.[95]

To my knowledge, however, the use of one covert program to support another violates every tenet of sound intelligence practice. It is unwise and, in my judgment, possibly illegal. Aside from the issues raised about conflict of interest and fraudulent conversion of U.S. assets, the diversion plan created a more practical and dangerous problem.

North repeatedly reminded us that the lives of our hostages were at stake, but Hakim, Secord, and North seemed to me to be increasing, not decreasing, the danger. They believed they had found a more reliable avenue to Iranian moderation—called the "Second Channel." They even gave their contact to the "Second Channel" a discount on the price of arms, to enhance his credibility. North had characterized the Iranians as unsophisticated and angry at having been scammed by the Israelis in November 1985. It could reasonably be anticipated that, when the Iranians discovered the Enterprise's price-gouging scheme, they would be angry. In fact, when they learned of the charges, they complained bitterly. North's response was to produce phony price lists of weapons rather than to reduce the weapons' price. He said that excessive charges to their new friendly channel posed no risk to the hostages. He, Casey, and Poindexter had determined they were charging less than Ghorbanifar; besides, the Iranians were so desperate they would have paid anything. Perhaps. But it was a risk that need never have been run—except that North and others were trying to fund other covert activities. It seemed a strange way to seal this much-discussed bond of good relations with Iranian moderates.

In addition to my alarm over learning of the "stand-alone, off-the-shelf, self-sustaining entity" that was to be funded by the Iranian arms sales and used for other covert activities, I bristled at the repeated declaration that, whenever lives are at stake, the President need not notify congressional leaders of covert activities until he decides that those lives are no longer in danger. There is great irony in this view. The United States Constitution grants to Congress the sole responsibility to declare war against other nations. In the nuclear age this is a power that holds the lives of millions of people in balance. Yet the President and his men argued that in covert actions—some of which might be tantamount to acts of war—the President is not required to confide even in eight leaders of Congress until the activity has been completed. It is a remarkable argument, rendered even more ludicrous in this case when we consider some of the individuals who were entrusted with the knowledge we were denied: Manucher Ghorbanifar, a known fabricator; Adnan Khashoggi, an international financier and arms merchant; Roy Furmark, one of Khashoggi's business associates and legal advisers; two unknown Canadian businessmen who attempted to blackmail Director Bill Casey in order to recover their $10-million loans;

Albert Hakim; Richard Secord; an undisclosed number of Israelis and Iranians; pilots of Southern Air Transport. . . .

There was not time enough to debate this issue with North, only to raise it.

I wanted to conclude my remarks with an important observation made by a distinguished military officer:

Finally, I want to just recall the words of General Singlaub. I know he is somebody that you admire. . . . He retired from the Army because he was upset. He was upset because President Carter had declared a unilateral withdrawal of troops from South Korea.

Now, a number of us were also upset about it. I recall that Senator Nunn, myself and several others, we went to South Korea, met with the troops, met with the leadership of South Korea; we came back, went to the White House, sat down with President Carter and pleaded with him not to carry forward that plan to unilaterally withdraw troops from South Korea.

And in some small measure, perhaps, we were successful, because he withdrew that plan. But General Singlaub didn't have that option. He was faced with the prospect of having criticized the Commander-in-Chief and he couldn't do that and remain in uniform, so he resigned.

After his retirement, he said the following. . . . "This Administration doesn't want to hear anything that is contrary to the decisions they have already made. That is a bad thing. It is the first symptom of a totalitarian regime when you start rejecting any legitimate criticism, any advice from the loyal opposition."

Well, if General Singlaub is right, we have to ask what it means to reject not the voice of the loyal opposition, but the voice of the majority in Congress and the country. . . . Democracy demands not only that the rights of the minority be protected, but that the rules of the majority be respected. That is true even if you and I believe the majority is wrong.

We have to respect the rule of law until we can change the law itself, because otherwise the rule of law will be reduced to the law of rule.[96]

Lives or Lies?

Oliver North lied. He admitted lying to the Congress, to the CIA, to his adversaries, to others. But, he said, he didn't like lying: "It does not leave me with a good taste in my mouth. I want you to know lying does not come easy to me."

He said he had to lie because he "had to weigh in the balance the difference between lives and lies." He was engaged in delicate, secret operations that exposed the participants to risk.

Senator James McClure correctly stated that there are situations in which lying may be a morally justifiable imperative. An American soldier or intelligence officer held captive by hostile forces would be justified in lying about the location of his unit or imminent tactical operational plans. North was not a prisoner of war, however, nor was the Attorney General the moral equivalent of a hostile foreign force.

The law requires that some congressional leaders be notified of covert operations. According to North, the law was not observed in these cases because Congress could not be trusted to keep the operations secret. Thus, when forced to choose, he chose lies to save lives.

But that was not the real choice. The lies were told not to save lives but to conceal an operation so unwise in concept and flawed in execution that those involved knew that if it ever were disclosed, the American people would condemn the operation. The sale of arms to Iran and the exchange of arms for hostages were major mistakes in judgment that seriously damaged the President and the nation.

The real motive for the lies in this case is made clear by the fact that during the Reagan administration there had been other covert operations in which lives were at risk but of which the Congress *was* notified in accordance with the law. Indeed, according to the administration itself, in no other covert operation was notification withheld from Congress. If it were necessary to lie to Congress to save lives, why did the administration notify Congress about every other covert operation in which lives were at risk? The answer, of course, is that the decision against observing the law in this one case, and the decision by North to lie to Congress about it, were calculated to save the architects of the plan from political embarrassment by public disclosure, not to save lives.

There can be no doubt that some members of Congress have acted irresponsibly when in the possession of classified information; there have been leaks by some in Congress. But although the misdeeds of a few may be reason to argue for change in the law, they are not an excuse for violations of the law.

That is especially true since most leaks come from the Executive rather than the Legislative Branch of the federal government. It is, after all, the Executive Branch that determines what is or is not classified, and that possesses the overwhelming majority of classified information.

Ironically, the two instances invoked by North to support his contention that the Congress cannot be trusted with sensitive information proved instead to be examples of Executive Branch responsibility for leaks: the *Achille Lauro* affair and the bombing raid on Libya. According to North:

> There were revelations immediately after the Achille Lauro capture of the terrorists that very seriously compromised our intelligence activities which allowed us to conduct the activity itself. . . . The statements made by a number of Members of Congress . . . seriously

jeopardized that effort and compromised those intelligence-gathering means.[97]

North went on to say:

> In the case of the Libya raid, there was a detailed briefing provided at the White House in the Old Executive Office Building. . . . The President several times in the course of that briefing on what we were planning to do that evening noted the sensitivity and the fact that the lives of Americans were at risk. Nonetheless, when the briefing concluded at about 5:00 or 5:30, two Members of Congress proceeded immediately to waiting microphones and noted that the President was going to make a heretofore unannounced address to the nation on Libya.
>
> I would tell you that the volume of fire over the Libyan capital was immense that evening. Two American airmen died as a consequence of that antiaircraft fire, as best we can determine.[98]

But in both instances the sources of the leaks were administration officials. In the case of the *Achille Lauro,* according to *Newsweek* magazine, it was North himself.

Shortly after North testified, *Newsweek* ran an article headed "Two Leaks, but by Whom? North's charges against Congress have some holes." The article read:

> As Oliver North explained it, he lied to Congress because he thought it could not be trusted with sensitive intelligence. When asked by a congressman last week to provide examples to support that contention, North cited two leaks. Neither bolsters his argument.
>
> North told the committee that shortly before the bombing of Libya last year, two members of Congress left a briefing by the president and told reporters that Reagan was going to speak to the country about Libya later that evening. He strongly implied that the comments provided enough warning to the Libyans to increase their ammunition. "Two American airmen died as a consequence of that antiaircraft fire," North said. But as Daniel Inouye, chairman of the Senate Iran-contra committee, pointed out, in the week preceding the attack there had been more than a dozen press accounts in which administration sources hinted that an attack was imminent and even discussed possible targets.

North's second example was the terrorist seizure of the cruise ship Achille Lauro in 1985, in which an American tourist was murdered. Afterward, in a daring operation, the United States intercepted an Egyptian plane containing the terrorists. North complained last week that after the capture, "a number of members of Congress" made revelations "that very seriously compromised our intelligence activities." But the colonel did not mention that details of the interception, first published in a *Newsweek* cover story, were leaked by none other than North himself. Moreover, David Halevy, a Time magazine correspondent who used North as a source, cowrote an article in the July 1987 issue of The Washingtonian in which North identifies the Israelis as the source of major intelligence during the Achille Lauro affair.[99]

The article in *The Washingtonian* offers further insight into North. This article, entitled "The Ollie We Knew," was written by Halevy and Neil C. Livingstone. According to the authors, in a footnote to the article:

As a military-affairs correspondent for *Time* magazine, covering terrorism, insurgencies, and intelligence matters, David Halevy first met Oliver North in early 1985 when Halevy was preparing a story on the *contras*.

From that first meeting until North's firing in November 1986, Halevy met with him at least once a week, sometimes twice, often at the McDonald's half a block from the Old Executive Office Building at 17th Street and Pennsylvania Avenue, Northwest.

Neil Livingstone, a long-time writer and consultant on terrorism and low-intensity warfare, first met Oliver North in 1983. As he followed the evolution of the Reagan administration's anti-terrorism policies, he became fascinated by the fact that all roads seemed to lead to a little-known lieutenant colonel at the National Security Council.[100]

The article is a dramatic account of North's activities as a member of the National Security Council staff. It is unstinting in its praise for North, lauding his courage, his vision, his loyalty.

Of all the compelling anecdotes in the article, none is more fascinating than North's encounter with the man he revered, President Reagan, during the invasion of Grenada. As Halevy and Livingston tell it:

> On October 25, 1983, less than a week after the murder of Grenada's Marxist leader, Maurice Bishop, by another Marxist faction, the United States invaded the tiny Caribbean island, ostensibly to restore order and to protect some 1,100 Americans living there from being taken hostage. U.S. troops encountered resistance from Cuban soldiers and airport workers, and the final American toll was put at 18 dead and 91 wounded.
>
> North coordinated military and policy-planning groups in preparation for the invasion and fought a losing battle to persuade Pentagon brass to use only Marines in the operation instead of a combined force of Marines, the 82nd Airborne, elements of Delta Force, Navy SEALs, and Army Rangers. He also traveled to Caribbean nations to enlist support and approval of the operation, and put together the regional multinational force that never went ashore. During this period, he slept in his office.
>
> It was North who was dispatched by McFarlane to get President Reagan's signature on the presidential order authorizing the deployment of the 22nd MAU (Marine Amphibious Unit) to Grenada so that invasion could proceed. When "Operation Urgent Fury" was launched on the 25th with a predawn landing by Navy SEALs, North monitored the drama from the White House Situation Room. "I couldn't do anything more," he said later. "At that stage it was up to the invading troops."
>
> A key element to his plan was for transport planes to leave Miami and fly to Grenada, where they would evacuate the Americans residing on the island, including many students attending a medical school in St. George's, the capital. Intelligence briefers were scheduled to go along with the planes and brief the evacuees on the return trip.
>
> To his chagrin, North learned that the Air Force planes had not picked up the intelligence briefers and had gone to Grenada without them. He feared that without an understanding of the administration's motivations and its estimate of the danger they were in, the students would accuse the President and the U.S. government of conducting a needless military operation. He feared that criticism by the students

would play into the hands of members of Congress and the media waiting for Reagan to stumble.

North decided to report the impending disaster at once to his boss, national security adviser Bud McFarlane, and to admit personal responsibility for not adequately supervising that stage of the operation. He ran upstairs from the Situation Room and poked his head into the Oval Office in hope of glimpsing McFarlane. Instead he saw the President who called him into his office.

According to those close to both men, the President's relations with North were informal and warm. Reagan probably saw in the dashing young Marine, his quick mind and easy humor, something he never saw in his own sons.

When North met with Reagan, he often entered the Oval Office through the side door, and his meetings were not logged in.

North reciprocated the President's trust and affection, and more than once told friends he would stand in front of bullets for Reagan. He idolized the man he believed was responsible for making America "stand tall."

"What's the problem, Ollie?" Reagan asked. "You appear to be disturbed by something."

North told the President what had happened and took responsibility for having failed his commander-in-chief.

"Where are the planes now?" asked the President.

"On their way back from Grenada with the students," North responded.

"Come with me," said the President, leading the way into an adjacent room, where there was a TV cabinet with three screens.

"Sit down and let's watch their arrival." Reagan consoled the younger man in a fatherly way. "Everything will be okay. You ought to have faith."

While the battle for Grenada was still under way, the President and North sat opposite the three TV screens and watched the arrival of the American students. When the first student, Jeff Geller, deplaned at Charleston Air Force Base in South Carolina, he dropped down and kissed the tarmac.

Reagan turned to North and said, "You see, Ollie, you ought to have more faith in the American people."[101]

A great story! The only problem is that it is apparently untrue. At the hearings, under oath, North admitted that he had never met with the President alone. The White House confirmed that no such meeting ever took place. The incident deepened our doubts about North's credibility, as did the testimony about his interview by the Attorney General.

That interview is described with precision and power in the Committee's report on the Attorney General's investigation. According to that report:

The Attorney General's investigation continued to build on Sunday, November 23, toward the afternoon interview with North. . . .

. . . North, who had told the Attorney General he was not available for an interview until the afternoon because he wanted to go to church, called McFarlane Sunday morning and asked to meet with him. McFarlane was getting ready to leave for church himself and told North to meet him at his office at noon. North said he would bring his attorney. North arrived alone at McFarlane's office at 12:30 P.M. North told McFarlane everything was on track except for one thing that could be a problem: the diversion. According to McFarlane, he asked North if the diversion had been approved and North replied that he would not do anything that was not approved. North said that the diversion was a matter of record in a memorandum he had written for Poindexter. North did not explain to McFarlane why he thought the diversion could be a problem in light of his belief that all documents relating to the diversion had been destroyed. On the other hand, North testified that he recalls only assuring McFarlane that all diversion documents had been destroyed; he expressly did not recall telling McFarlane that there was a memorandum describing the diversion that might cause a problem.

At that point, attorney Thomas Green arrived at McFarlane's office. Green told McFarlane he had been an Assistant U.S. Attorney and had dealt with problems of this kind before. Green advised McFarlane and North to state the story truthfully and let the chips fall where they may. Not long thereafter, Richard Secord arrived as well, but by that time, McFarlane had to leave for an appointment.

From approximately 12:45 P.M. to 2:00 P.M., Attorney General

Meese, Reynolds, Cooper, and Richardson met to discuss the upcoming interview of North. North arrived, alone, at approximately 2:15 P.M. Meese did most of the questioning. Richardson and Reynolds took notes.

The Attorney General began by telling North he wanted all the facts, and did not want North to cover up to protect himself or the President. He then asked North to explain the arms sales from the beginning. North replied with a combination of fact and fiction. All the while he knew that the Attorney General was acting under orders from the President and that the Attorney General's findings would be reported back to the President.

North said he was unaware of the first shipment of 504 TOWs until after it occurred. Regarding the November 1985 HAWK shipment, North said he received a call from McFarlane in Geneva who told him to contact Israeli Defense Minister Rabin to help Israel move something to Iran. North then claimed that Defense Minister Rabin told him it was oil-related equipment. North sent Secord to help with the shipment. North also called Duane Clarridge at the CIA to get a CIA proprietary to fly the equipment. When Secord saw the shipment in Israel, he told North the cargo was 18 or 19 HAWK missiles. The implication in North's statements—that he was unaware until informed by Secord that the flight was to contain HAWK missiles— was false. As North subsequently admitted in his public hearing testimony, he knew the nature of the cargo from his first involvement in the November shipment.

North also claimed, falsely, that Poindexter knew nothing of the November 1985 HAWK shipment. North stated, again falsely, that when he discovered from Secord that there were HAWKs on the plane he notifed someone at the CIA, possibly Casey.

While lying to the Attorney General about other aspects of the November 1985 HAWK shipment, North admitted that his statements about that shipment in the NSC chronology and at the November 20, 1986, meeting to review Casey's draft testimony were false. As discussed above, North had claimed in the chronology and at the meeting that the United States had to force the Iranians to return the HAWK missiles. In his interview with the Attorney General, North admitted that it was the Iranians who were dissatisfied and demanded their money back.

Attorney General Meese then asked North to describe the money flow. Again, North lied. North said the money passed from the Iranians to the Israelis who in turn paid into a CIA account which reimbursed the Army for the weapons. North made no mention of Secord or the Lake Resources account through which the money had actually passed.

Then the Attorney General showed North the diversion memorandum. The first page referred to U.S. acquiescence in the August 1985 TOW shipment. Meese asked North to explain if this was an arms for hostages deal. North asserted that, although he discussed the strategic opening of Iran with President Reagan, with the President "it always came back to the hostages." North said the President was drawn to the linkage between arms and hostages and it was a terrible mistake to say the President wanted the strategic relationship with Iran, because the President wanted the hostages.

After that exchange, the Attorney General turned to the diversion. He directed North's attention to the section of the memorandum describing how the "residuals" would go to the Nicaraguan Resistance. North appeared to be "visibly surprised." He asked if they had found a "cover memo." Reynolds said that none had been found—without first questioning North as to whether he recalled a cover memo, or to whom it had been directed, or what it said. After Reynolds informed North that no cover memo had been found, the Attorney General asked North if they should have found a cover memo, and North said "no."

The Attorney General asked North if he had discussed the diversion with the President. North replied that Poindexter was the point of contact with the President.

Attorney General Meese pointed out that if the President had approved the diversion, North probably would have a record of it. North agreed and said he did not think it was approved by the President. The Attorney General asked whether other files might contain a document indicating Presidential approval, and North said he would check.

The Attorney General asked North if there was anything more. North said that only the February 1986 shipment and the second shipment had produced residuals to the Contras. North also said that only three people in the Government knew of the diversion—Poindexter, McFarlane, and himself. North said the CIA did not handle the "residuals" and, though some in the CIA may have suspected a diversion, he did not think anyone at the CIA knew. If North's testimony at the public hearings was truthful, then these statements, too, were lies. At the hearings, North testified that Casey knew, approved, and was enthusiastic about the diversion as early as February 1986.

And of course, North was aware when he spoke to the Attorney General that Earl [his own deputy] knew of the diversion.

North claimed that the diversion was an Israeli idea, probably Nir's— another lie refuted by documentary evidence. He said the money went straight from the Israelis into three Swiss bank accounts opened by FDN leader Calero. In fact, the diverted funds were deposited to the Swiss account maintained by Secord and Hakim. North claimed that the October 1986 shipment of TOWs did not produce residual funds because North, over Nir's objection, charged much less for the weapons. He did this, he said, because the Contras had $100 million in U.S. aid and North did not want to create the impression of private profit.

The Attorney General asked North if there were any other items he had not told them about and North responded negatively. However, North volunteered that if the diversion were kept quiet, the only other problem would be the November 1985 HAWK shipment, which someone ought to say was authorized. The Justice Department officials made no reply.

Attorney General Meese then confirmed to North that he had to share this information with the President and determine if he was aware of it. Meese again asked North about other problem areas, including complaints from people who financed the deals and lost money. North responded only that Ghorbanifar had lost money in a "sting."

At this point in the interview, the Attorney General left to pick up his wife at the airport. Cooper continued further questioning North regarding authority for the 1985 shipments. Cooper asked North if he believed at the time that the November shipment contained oil drilling equipment. North replied that he really thought it was munitions, but boasted that he could nevertheless pass a lie detector test on whether he thought it was oil drilling equipment.

North also volunteered that Southern Air Transport (SAT) hauled the 1986 arms shipments and that SAT was being investigated by the Justice Department for its involvement in the Contra resupply operation.

The North interview concluded at 5:55 P.M. as the Attorney General was returning. North was not told what would happen next. Although the Justice Department officials noticed North's surprise that they had a copy of the diversion memorandum North had written, no one asked North if he had shredded or otherwise disposed of documents, nor did the Justice Department officials take any steps to secure North's remaining documents.

Later that night, Sofaer called Cooper to find out the status of the investigation. Cooper asked the basis of Sofaer's earlier concern about the possibility of surplus funds being generated from the Iran arms sales. Sofaer explained that he thought there may have been a difference between the purchase price and cost price. Sofaer also volunteered that he suspected that SAT may have been given excess profits from the Iran arms sales to finance the Contra resupply operation. Cooper did not mention the diversion memorandum or North's interview.

That evening, North called McFarlane and Poindexter. Afterwards, North shredded additional documents at his office until at least 4:30 A.M., when a security guard noticed that North's office had not been secured for the day. North responded to the officer's security report by claiming that when the officer checked the office, North was in the bathroom.[102]

The investigation uncovered other examples of North's tendency to exaggerate and falsify. There is no sadder aspect of the complex tragedy that has come to be known as the Iran-Contra affair than the extent to which Oliver North became entangled in a web of deception in behalf of a president to whom he was so deeply devoted and in the process nearly established an unaccountable government to circumvent the one enshrined in the Constitution.

Beethoven's Fifth

I don't recall."
  "I do not recall it."
  "I don't recall that."
"I simply don't recall it."
"I don't recall doing that."
"I don't recall his doing that."
"I don't remember."
"I don't remember that."
"I did not remember it."
"I simply can't remember that."
"That is a very fuzzy time period for me."
"I am very fuzzy on that."

In 1958 John Poindexter graduated from the U.S. Naval Academy, first in a class of nine hundred. He then obtained a doctorate in nuclear physics at the California Institute of Technology. Over the next three decades he rose swiftly in the Navy, reaching the rank of rear admiral. In 1981 he became the military assistant to Bud McFarlane, the National Security Adviser to the President; in 1985 he moved up to the position of National Security Adviser. In his dealings with Lieutenant Colonel North, Poindexter adopted or was given the code name "Beethoven."

His rapid rise was due largely to the quality and capacity of his mind. In the 1970s his superior officer said of him: "Poindexter has a spectacular mental capacity. He reads and understands every paper or report that comes into the office. Furthermore, he retains

194

fully, recalls accurately, and evaluates with a keen sense of what is important and what isn't."[103]

Yet, during his public testimony before the Committee, Admiral Poindexter said 184 times that he could not recall the events about which he was questioned. His inability to remember reached spectacular proportions when he was asked about a luncheon meeting he had had with former CIA Director William Casey on Saturday, November 22, 1986.

The arms sale to Iran had been disclosed publicly nearly three weeks earlier. The White House had immediately become a scene of frenetic activity. On November 13 the President addressed the nation on television. On November 19 the President held a televised news conference. On both occasions Poindexter briefed the President. On both occasions the President made several statements that were false and others that were misleading.

The activity reached a peak on the weekend before Thanksgiving. Rather than quelling the crisis, as hoped, the President's speech and press conference had fanned its flames by raising more questions than he answered. On Friday, November 21, Attorney General Edwin Meese obtained the President's approval to conduct a fact-finding inquiry to, as Meese put it, "get all the facts in one place."

Poindexter had been at the meeting with the President and the Attorney General, so he knew that Justice Department lawyers, acting on behalf of the Attorney General, were reviewing documents at the NSC. In fact, he had on the same day destroyed the December 5, 1985, presidential finding—the only document that identified the transaction as a straight arms-for-hostage trade—to protect the President from political embarrassment.

On the next day, Saturday, November 22, a crucial day, a sense of crisis enveloped the White House. Poindexter spent over two hours at lunch with Casey, a meeting arranged at Casey's request. Elsewhere in Washington, at lunch in the Old Ebbitt Grill, Meese was learning from his Justice Department lawyers that the diversion memo had been found in North's files.

But, when questioned about it during the hearings, Poindexter said he could recall virtually nothing about the meeting, except that he had a sandwich for lunch.

That inability to recall, and the 183 others like it, raised serious questions about Poindexter's credibility.

And yet Poindexter's testimony on the narrow question of whether the President knew of the diversion of funds to the Contras from the sale of arms to Iran is all we have. If Poindexter was credible on this issue, then, for some congressmen and Americans, no more need be said. The Iran-Contra investigation, the hearings, were over; the report of the Committee written. From the point at which John Poindexter testified that he made "a very deliberate decision not to ask the President" about the diversion to "insulate [the President] from the decision and provide some future deniability for the President if it ever leaked out," they believed the Committee should have packed up its briefcases and turned off the lights. We did not share this view.[104]

Oliver North had boasted melodramatically that he would take a spear in his chest for Ronald Reagan, but he stepped deftly aside as the spear headed toward Poindexter. North had rocked the Committee back on its heels with a passionate defense of his actions. When Poindexter took the witness stand, at nine o'clock on the morning of Wednesday, July 15, the atmosphere was much different from what it had been eight days earlier.

For one thing, the nation had seen how an aggressive lawyer could disrupt the proceedings and gain sympathy for his client. Poindexter's attorney obviously did not want to suffer by comparison with Brendan Sullivan. So, before Poindexter could say a word, his lawyer, Richard Beckler, leaped to the attack. Beckler spoke in a very loud voice, as though he was unaware of the electronic amplification provided by microphones.

The presiding officer was Lee Hamilton, chairman of the House Committee. Hamilton had obviously learned from the events of the preceding week. The constant interruptions, the strident tone, the accusations of unfairness hurled at the Committee by North's lawyer, Sullivan, had been unexpected and had proved difficult to handle. Senator Inouye was caught in a cross fire of criticism between those who thought he was too tough on and unfair to Sullivan and North and those who thought he let them walk all over him and the Committee. Inouye had actually handled a difficult situation well.

With his opening words, Beckler made it clear that he was looking for legal combat. But his transparent effort to out-Sullivan Sullivan was anticipated. With an appealing combination of eloquence and restraint, firmness and soft words, Hamilton turned aside Beckler's bull-like rushes. Beckler was unable to gain for Poindexter the sympathy Sullivan had won for North.

Even if Beckler had done so, it is doubtful that the sympathy would have lasted long. For it soon became clear that as a witness Poindexter was no North. First there was the matter of appearance. Poindexter was bald, trifocaled, and dull in his dark business suit. Though he could have worn medals, as had North, he chose not to. There was no reminder to the public of his military service and courage. His memory was deficient, his manner halting, his answers qualified. North was a sleek warrior, a top-gun Marine. Poindexter appeared to be a stodgy bureaucrat who generated all the warmth of an IRS auditor. Too often he puffed his pipe, sending up a billowing screen of smoke that would shroud his face. The habit unwittingly produced a metaphor for his testimony.

Admiral Poindexter's decision not to wear his military uniform was a matter of some significance. He said that, since he was not acting in a military capacity while serving as the President's National Security Adviser, he believed it inappropriate to wear his uniform when called to testify about those very activities. We treated his decision as a principled one. The absence of a handsome uniform with several rows of ribbons and gold braid on his sleeves deprived him of the special respect accorded North.

Initially, Committee members were relieved and grateful that we would not appear to be engaged in the public degradation of another military officer. Yet Poindexter's rationale for not wearing his uniform raised several perplexing questions. Did it mean that Lieutenant Colonel North was functioning as a military officer while assigned to the NSC? Was Poindexter implying that North was hiding behind his uniform, using it as a shield against congressional scrutiny?

Did Poindexter have a different reason for appearing before the Committee in civilian clothes? Had he considered in advance what the public's reaction would be to a uniformed officer declaring under oath that the "buck stopped with me"? Would the cumulative impact of a Marine lieutenant colonel and a Navy admiral testifying that they had acted without the President's knowledge or approval have justified the charge that a military junta was operating within the White House?

Speculation about Poindexter's appearance evaporated as soon as he began to testify. Though he spoke in a soft voice and an innocuous, matter-of-fact tone, Poindexter's words struck like thunderclaps. He said, for example, that he had withheld information from Congress but not misled it; that the administration's support for the Contras was secret but not a covert action; that the diversion of arms-sales profits to the Contras was a technical implementation of an approved policy, not a substantive decision; and that the United States did not trade arms for hostages, even though he had the President sign an arms-for-hostages finding in December 1985 and Albert Hakim's nine-point plan contained a formula of one and a half hostages for five hundred TOWs.

There was an Orwellian quality to Poindexter's testimony, but even more striking than his use of language was his inconsistent memory. Although Poindexter repeatedly claimed an inability to recall certain events, he testified in great detail about other events in the same time period. The impression was quickly created, and reinforced through his four days of testimony, that his memory lapses were more convenient than real.

Arthur Liman began the questioning of Poindexter. He drove

quickly to the point that Poindexter had destroyed a presidential finding authorizing the sale of arms to Iran in exchange for the release of Americans held hostage in Lebanon.

> LIMAN: But you do recall that whatever you recommended, the President read it and he signed it?
> POINDEXTER: Yes, he did. He did sign it.
> LIMAN: What happened to that finding?
> POINDEXTER: As I said earlier, I destroyed it by tearing it up on the 21st of November, because I thought it was a significant political embarrassment to the President, and I wanted to protect him from possible disclosure of this.[105]

Poindexter was right: the finding was deeply embarrassing to the President. Read and signed by the President on December 5, 1985, this was the first presidential finding authorizing the sale of arms to Iran, and it made clear that the transaction was a straight swap of arms for hostages.

When Poindexter saw the finding again on November 21, 1986, he knew that within the previous week the President had on two occasions stated publicly, on national television, that there had been no exchange of arms for hostages. During his November 13 televised address, reading a speech that Poindexter had been deeply involved in preparing, the President told the American people, "We did not—repeat—did not trade weapons or anything else for hostages nor will we." Six days later, at his press conference, the President repeated that assertion.

Forty-eight hours after that, Poindexter held in his hand an official document, signed by the President in his presence, that directly contradicted what the President had twice solemnly told the American people. Without hesitation he tore it up and put it in his burn bag. In his testimony he expressed no regret, claiming that the finding was "very narrow" and "not fully staffed." He maintained it was a "CYA [cover your ass] finding" for the CIA.

If Poindexter's disclosure of his destruction of the finding hurt the President, he soon made up for it. For months leading up to

Poindexter's testimony, the White House had skillfully created the impression that the important question—indeed, the only question—was whether the President had known of and approved the diversion. Although we rejected the view that knowledge of the diversion was the central issue of the investigation, it was clear that the White House believed that a negative answer to that question—which the White House plainly expected from Poindexter—would end the case and should end the hearings.

Poindexter did not disappoint them. He testified that he approved the diversion and did not notify the President of his decision, because:

I also felt I had the authority to approve it, because I had a commission from the President which was in very broad terms, my role was to make sure that his policies were implemented. In this case, the policy was very clear, and that was to support the contras.

After working with the President for 5-½ years, the last 3 of which were very close, probably closer than any officer in the White House except the Chief of Staff, I was convinced that I understood the President's thinking on this and that if I had taken it to him that he would have approved it.

Now, I was not so naive as to believe that it was not a politically volatile issue, it clearly was, because of the divisions that existed within the Congress on the issue of support for the contras, and it was clear that there will be a lot of people that would disagree, that would make accusations that indeed have been made. So although I was convinced that we could properly do it and that the President would approve if asked, I made a very deliberate decision not to ask the President so that I could insulate him from the decision and provide some future deniability for the President if it ever leaked out.[106]

According to Donald Regan, the President's former Chief of Staff, Poindexter initially painted a markedly different picture of his role in the events. Regan testified:

Early that morning, Tuesday morning [November 25, 1986], I went in to see John Poindexter. He was having breakfast and I said to him,

John, Ed Meese told the President about Ollie North and his involvement here with the contras and the contra funding. What about it? What the hell happened? I'll never forget this. He sort of dabbed at his mouth—he was a precise guy, John—and folded his napkin, adjusted his glasses and said, I had a feeling that something bad was going on, but I didn't investigate it and I didn't do a thing about it. I said, how could you do that—a Vice Admiral in the Navy? He said, I really didn't want to know. Now this may hurt your feelings, but I have to tell you this. He said, I was so damned mad at Tip O'Neill for the way he was dragging the contras around I didn't want to know what, if anything, was going on. And he said, I should have, but I didn't. I said, John, you are going to see the President at 9:30 in your regular meeting. You had better have your resignation with you. I said, there is no way for you to stay here. And that's when he resigned, at 9:30.[107]

In spite of the substantial discrepancy in his past statements, with Poindexter's declaration that he had assumed control in order to give the President "plausible deniability," the hearings appeared to have ended. The $64,000 question had been answered. No smoking gun would be found.

Almost immediately, press and public interest in the hearings began to wane. Within the Committee, those who saw their role as defenders of the President argued insistently that the public-hearing phase of the investigation should be terminated as soon as possible. The other members of the Committee, already exhausted by the punishing pace of the investigation, offered little resistance. Although a few highlights remained—notably the testimony of Secretary of State George Shultz and Attorney General Edwin Meese—the hearings had crested and now began to recede.

But, because of doubts about Poindexter's credibility, the question continues to nag: was he telling the truth when he testified that he did not tell the President of the diversion? Stated another way: was the President telling the truth when *he* said he did not know of the diversion?

For Poindexter, not telling the President was out of character and inconsistent with his past practices. He had never previously

withheld information from a superior in these circumstances and
while in the Navy had been commended for keeping his com-
manding officer fully informed.

On the other hand, from the outset the President has insisted
that he did not know of the diversion, and Poindexter's testimony
was fully consistent with the President's statements.

The lack of documentary evidence bearing on this issue raises
another troubling question. North testified that he had prepared
five or six separate memoranda, one for each proposed shipment
of arms to Iran. Each included a reference to the diversion. He
said that each of them was delivered to Poindexter for his use in
presenting the matter to the President for approval; each contained
a designated space where the President could indicate his approval
or disapproval in writing.

Only one memorandum survived, and that in draft form (five
versions of it were found, but they differ only in minor respects).
North testified that he destroyed the others and that his failure to
destroy the survivor was inadvertent.

Poindexter testified that he could not recall ever seeing any such
memorandum and, to support that statement, said that he "told
Colonel North repeatedly not to put anything in writing on the
transfer of funds to the contras. . . . " North denied ever being
given any such instruction and said that if he had he would not
have written the memoranda.

Had North not destroyed the memoranda, they would have
provided important documentary evidence on the question of presidential knowledge. But their destruction by itself is insufficient
to justify the conclusion that the President knew of the diversion.
North destroyed many documents that had never been intended
for the President. The fact that the five or six crucial memoranda
mentioned the diversion was sufficient motivation for North to
destroy them.

Even if the President saw one or more of these memoranda, it
is entirely possible that he did not see or notice their references
to the diversion. The surviving draft memorandum is five pages

long, typewritten, single-spaced. Although it has often been re-ferred to as the "diversion memorandum," it is actually a detailed description of an entire transaction. The reference to the diversion is eight lines long, buried in the middle of the fifth page. Given the President's work habits, even if he saw the memorandum (and there is no evidence that he did) he could well have skipped over the lines about the diversion. Even if he did read them, he might not have grasped their significance.

Whatever private doubts individual members had, the Com-mittee found no evidence that the President knew of the diversion.

Human memory is such that different people can and do fre-quently recall the same events differently, especially when the events involved are complex and occur over a long period of time. But as the number and importance of conflicts in recollection increase, so also does the likelihood that someone is not telling the truth, rather than simply forgetting or remembering incor-rectly. The line between the two is difficult to draw. Whether or not that line was crossed in this instance requires an individual, highly subjective judgment.

In the immediately preceding pages we have discussed the sharp conflict in testimony between North and Poindexter on whether there existed additional "diversion" memoranda prepared by North and delivered to Poindexter. This was an important conflict in testimony that cannot be ascribed to faulty memory; nor can it be reconciled. If the originals of the five or six memos in fact existed and had not been destroyed, they would have provided important written evidence on the question of whether President Reagan knew of and approved the diversion.

There were other important conflicts in the North and Poin-dexter testimony. North testified that on November 21, 1986, as controversy over the affair was rising, he assured Poindexter in a personal conversation that he (North) had gotten rid of all of the memos referring to the diversion. Poindexter testified that he could not recall any such conversation.

As noted, Poindexter testified that he had instructed North not to put anything in writing about the diversion. North testified that Poindexter had never given him any such instruction; had he received such an instruction, he said, he would not have prepared the memos in question. On this central conflict, North's version is logical, consistent with established practice and strongly supported by the copies of the one memorandum that survived. Poindexter's testimony, by contrast, is inconsistent with established practice and is contradicted by the surviving copies.

North also testified that on November 21 he asked Poindexter whether he (Poindexter) had told the President of the diversion; Poindexter said he had not. When questioned about this, Poindexter said he could not recall any such conversation.

Not being able to recall an event is not the same as denying its existence. Claiming to be unable to recall is the favored course for those who are required to testify under oath, and thus risk a perjury charge for a false statement, but who do not wish to disclose the truth. Who can ever forget Richard Nixon's advice to his subordinates when they faced such questioning: "Just be damned sure you say 'I don't remember; I can't recall; I can't give an honest answer to that that I can recall.' "[108]

On the other hand, claiming not to recall an event when one does in fact recall it is also perjury. Although it is a particularly difficult form of perjury to prove in a criminal trial, and thus presents a lesser risk to a person caught in this difficult position, it can be proved, as Michael Deaver found out. Deaver, one of President Reagan's closest friends and assistants, left the White House to become a lobbyist. Federal law prohibits former government employees from certain forms of lobbying activities for a period of time after leaving office. Deaver was asked about some of his lobbying actions in an appearance before a committeee of Congress. In response, while under oath, he said he couldn't recall them. He was then indicted and convicted of perjury, the charge being that he lied when he said he couldn't recall events that he in fact could and did recall.

Poindexter vigorously denied that he had ever lied, and went so far as to dispute the fact that North had lied to Congress, even after North himself admitted to having done so. No doubt on many, perhaps even most, of the 184 occasions during his testimony on which he claimed he could not recall, Poindexter's claim was truthful. But it is very difficult to accept as genuine his inability to recall major events, such as the five or six memos, his conversation with North about the President's knowledge, or his lunch with Casey on November 22.

North, by contrast, readily admitted lying to the Congress, to the CIA, to the Iranians, to others. Indeed, he appeared at times to be boasting about some of his lies. One would expect, therefore, that North, having admitted that he lied, would be judged a less credible witness than Poindexter. But the reverse was true. North came across to the American people, and to some members of the Committee, as truthful, whereas Poindexter appeared vague and evasive.

Finally, we return to the question that for so many became the reason for the investigation itself—the President's knowledge of the diversion of funds to the Contras. Of course, presidential knowledge of the diversion would have been important, but the absence of evidence that the President knew raised equally serious questions that were not examined. The President cannot be held responsible for unauthorized acts carried out by his agents or employees, but he cannot escape accountability for the acts of agents who reasonably believe they are acting pursuant to his desires.

Did the President lead John Poindexter to believe that he had delegated authority to him to make a decision to divert to the Contras profits from the sale of weapons to Iran? How did Poindexter, after having served as an NSC staff member and then as presidential adviser, come to believe that the President would have viewed the diversion as a mere technicality? Why would the President react to the disclosure of the diversion (and Hakim's nine-point plan) as if he had just been "kicked in the belly"?[109]

Did Poindexter allow the concept of "plausible deniability"—traditionally employed to permit the United States to keep its responsibility for covert activities secret from its adversaries—to be used to keep the President uninformed so as to protect him from domestic political controversy and criticism?

Were we, in fact, witnessing the "fall-guy plan," which North had testified that he and Casey had discussed?

Or was it a case of men embittered by their Vietnam experience simply deciding on their own to rise above the written law to keep faith with the American hostages and the Nicaraguan Contras? Bud McFarlane intimated that North had been deeply seared by his wartime experiences.

> He is quite cynical about government. Ollie is a man that is a veteran of an experience in Vietnam. . . . Now, in the wake of his service there, having to cope with the vivid reminders of how worth it was and how tragic a loss of life of Vietnamese . . . I believe that he committed himself to assuming that he would never be a party to such a thing . . . again if he could prevent it.[110]

Representative Henry Hyde stated that the Committee should take into account the hellish impact the Vietnam War had upon our military men. Hyde was correct in urging us to exhibit compassion and understanding. But understanding should not be confused with tolerance. Veterans who wish to ensure that the American Congress does not repeat the mistakes of the past should give serious thought to running for public office so that they can articulate their views and submit them for approval or rejection by the American people. Senator John McCain (R-Arizona), who spent six years as a prisoner of war in Hanoi, serves as a role model for this course of action.[111] But under no circumstances should we permit a situation to develop whereby military officers, placed in positions of political power, are permitted to substitute their judgment for that of their civilian superiors. To do so invites the inevitable dissolution of constitutional government.

Poindexter's declaration that he believed he was merely implementing the President's policies, and doing so in a manner of
which the President would have approved, draws us back to a
consideration of the bond Poindexter shared with his commander
in chief.

Philip Caputo's *A Rumor of War* offers a poignant account of
his days in Vietnam and relates a tragic account of the intuitive
leaps the human mind can take.

Caputo, a young Marine lieutenant, was frustrated at seeing his
men being blown apart by land mines or picked off one by one
by invisible snipers. Obsessed with the need to retaliate, he decided
to send a squad into a nearby village to capture two Vietnamese
whom he believed to be Viet Cong. He would interrogate them,
beat them if necessary, to learn the location of other enemy units,
which he could then attack. If the two Viet Cong resisted capture, his squad would simply kill them. Caputo did not have
authority to send a squad into the Vietnamese village. But out
there, on that isolated outpost, he decided to do what *he* wanted.

The squad carried out its assignment, but instead of capturing
the two men, it "greased" them with shotgun blasts. It turned
out that one of the men (a boy, really) was an informant for the
Marines. The squad had killed the wrong man!

Court-martial proceedings were brought against Caputo for pre-
meditated murder. Caputo's recorded thoughts are instructive:

> Two men who have shared the hardships and dangers of war come to
> know each other as intimately as two natural brothers who have lived
> together for years; one can read the other's heart without a word being
> said.[112]

> It was true that I had ordered the patrol to capture the two men if at
> all possible, but it was also true that I had wanted them dead. There
> was murder in my heart, and in some way, through tone of voice, a
> gesture, or a stress on *kill* rather than *capture,* I had transmitted my
> inner violence to the men.[113]

As we listened to Poindexter testify, even accepting his testimony at face falue, we wondered whether the President had in fact transmitted—through his daily expressed concern for the American hostages or the cause of the Contras—an unspoken authority to his National Security Adviser to *do whatever was necessary.* Or did Poindexter, caught up by North's passion and emotional commitment to the cause of the Contras, rationalize, as Lieutenant Caputo had:

> But who was the real authority out on that isolated outpost? *I* was. I would take matters into my own hands. Out there, I could do what I damned well pleased. And I would.[114]

The Committee would never know precisely whether Poindexter was acting on his own or reacting to a subliminal message sent by President Reagan.

Caputo's inner reflections of his court-martial ordeal offered a final insight into our own proceedings. Caputo spent days with his attorney preparing for his defense. The two engaged repeatedly in a Socratic dialogue, rehearsing questions and answers to the point where Caputo almost became convinced that he had issued a clear and unambiguous order that his men had flagrantly disregarded. Caputo's attorney had written Caputo's testimony out on yellow legal-size paper.

> . . . not one word of it was perjured. There were qualifying phrases here and there—"to the best of my recollection," "if I recall correctly," "words to that effect"—but there wasn't a single lie in it. And yet it wasn't the truth.[115]

Were Poindexter's words to the Committee the truth in every sense? We don't know. We may never know.

Arthur Liman, in his closing questions to Poindexter, underlined the inconsistency in the Poindexter testimony:

> LIMAN: Now, Admiral, as you sat there and you listened to the press conference and the Attorney General describing the diversion as an aberration in the President's policy, talking about potential political

disaster if it ever came out must have seemed to you to be coming true with a vengeance, right?

POINDEXTER: Mr. Liman, . . . it . . . was several days after that that that began to dawn on me, and that's when I got an attorney.

LIMAN: Well, even before you got an attorney . . . you realized this was now a major political issue as you listened to the Attorney General and you read the newspapers, right?

POINDEXTER: I realized that the . . . media and the newspapers were blowing this all out of proportion and there was significant pressure from Congress for the administration to appoint an independent counsel, and I thought, and still think, that it was a gross overreaction to an issue.

I think with hindsight some mistakes were made in terms of handling the issue in November, and I think that in the effort to make sure that the White House was not accused of cover-up, . . . we moved too fast, and I accept some of that responsibility in that I don't think with hindsight that I should have resigned when I did. We should have stayed around to get to a full explanation as to what we were trying to do and the reasons—

LIMAN: Admiral, you said that one of the reasons you did not tell the President about this was because you realized that it would be controversial and you wanted the President to be able to deny it.

POINDEXTER: That's correct.

LIMAN: Now, all of a sudden the controversy that you had anticipated if this became public when you approved it in February of 1986 had occurred, right?

POINDEXTER: Yes, that is a statement of fact.

LIMAN: . . . can you tell us why you didn't then stand up and say, "I, Admiral Poindexter, made the decision and did not tell the President of the United States"?

POINDEXTER: Mr. Liman, this is a hypothetical question, and before I made the decision to retain attorneys, I was obviously giving it a lot of thought, but I did not want to make that kind of decision until I had had an opportunity to consult with attorneys. And after I did, I followed the advice of my attorneys.

LIMAN: Now, you talked about how much you wanted . . . to provide the President with deniability.

POINDEXTER: Correct.

LIMAN: Deniability usually, in covert operations, has another word, an adjective that precedes it called plausible deniability, right?

POINDEXTER: Yes, that's the usual term of art.

LIMAN: Did you make any contemporaneous record in your notes, or any other place, at the time that you decided to give the President deniability, that you were not going to tell the President?

POINDEXTER: No, I did not write that down.

LIMAN: So that you created a situation where it would be only your word to corroborate that of our Commander in Chief?

POINDEXTER: That is correct.[116]

In the final analysis, the Committee had no evidence that the President knew of the diversion. But Poindexter cast a shadow of doubt that was never removed. The diversion of funds was an important issue, certainly, one that might have pulled down the President if Poindexter had testified other than he did. But the fact that Poindexter did not cripple the President does not mean that he did not damage the presidency. For, if he arrogated to himself the discretion and responsibility that properly belonged to President Reagan, then we understand more fully the implications of his sobering declaration: " . . . the buck stopped with me."[117]

Battle Royal

S ecretary of State George Shultz's appearance before the Committee was as welcome as that of a Saint Bernard at the site of an avalanche. He sat at the witness table alone and spoke with fervor about the need for, and the ability of, public officials to serve their President with candor and respect for the law.

It was Shultz who warned the President against selling arms to Iran and swapping arms for hostasges. It was Shultz who blew the whistle on the attempt by North and Poindexter to cover up their misdeeds by preparing misleading statements to Congress and the American people. It was Shultz who had the courage, and the loyalty to Ronald Reagan, to tell the President that he was wrong in his disastrous news conference of November 19. And it was Shultz who, finally, killed the Iran initiative.

When George Shultz was sworn in as Secretary of State in July 1982, he was one of the best-prepared persons ever to enter a president's Cabinet. After earning a Ph.D. degree in economics, Shultz taught at M.I.T., the University of Chicago, and Stanford University. In the Nixon administration, he served as Secretary of Labor, director of the Office of Management and Budget, and secretary of the Treasury. Between the Nixon and Reagan administrations, he was president of the Bechtel Group, one of the nation's largest construction companies. Before becoming Secretary of State, he was chairman of President Reagan's Economic Policy Advisory Board.

Shultz needed that vast experience during the Iran-Contra affair. On December 4, 1985, Admiral John Poindexter became National Security Adviser to the President. The next day Poindexter briefed the Secretary of State on the Iran initiative. Shultz told Poindexter that it was "a very bad idea," that it amounted to paying for hostages, and that Shultz was opposed to it. Poindexter did not tell Shultz that earlier on that day the President had signed a finding authorizing the secret sale of arms to Iran in exchange for hostages.

Thus occurred the most disastrous foreign-policy adventure of the Reagan administration, approved over the objection of the Secretary of State and then implemented without his knowledge. It is an example of how a government should not conduct foreign policy.

Two days later, on December 7, the President met at the White House with Shultz, Poindexter, Secretary of Defense Weinberger, Chief of Staff Don Regan, and John McMahon, deputy director of the CIA. The purpose of the meeting was to discuss the Iran initiative. Shultz and Weinberger vigorously expressed their opposition to the initiative on both policy and legal grounds. When the meeting was over, both men thought they had prevailed upon the President. Former National Security Adviser Robert McFarlane was asked by President Reagan to go to London to tell the Iranians that there would be no arms. The initiative appeared dead.

But it was not. Neither Shultz nor Weinberger had persuaded the President. He was determined to act contrary to their advice, and in fact had already done so by signing, forty-eight hours earlier, the finding that authorized the shipment of arms to Iran in exchange for the release of American hostages. Thereafter both men were avoided as much as possible. That was difficult, since the initiative involved foreign policy and one of the men to be avoided was the Secretary of State, ostensibly the person in charge of foreign policy. So Shultz was on occasion involved in meetings with the President at which the subject arose; he repeated his objection.

One such occasion was on January 7, 1986. President Reagan, Vice President Bush, Poindexter, Shultz, and other top officials met at the White House to review the Iran initiative. Again the meeting occurred just hours after the President had signed a secret finding approving the shipment of arms to Iran; this signing had taken place on January 6. Again Shultz was not told. Again Shultz argued against the initiative, unaware that it was already in motion.

The same thing happened ten days later. On January 17 the President signed a third finding authorizing the shipment of arms to Iran. On that same day he discussed the Iran initiative with Shultz. Once again Shultz was not told of the finding.

Obviously Poindexter was not alone in keeping Shultz in the dark. The President himself was aware, at both the December 7 and January 7 meetings, that he had just signed an order authorizing the shipment of arms to Iran. Yet on both occasions he permitted Shultz to proceed with his argument against it, leading him to believe on both occasions that he was still considering the matter when in fact he had already made his decision and acted on it.

Earlier in 1985 the President had met with Country Two's head of state. The leader told the President that his nation would contribute an additional $24 million to help the Contras. Immediately thereafter Shultz and McFarlane met with the President to debrief him on his meeting. The President said nothing about the contribution to Shultz or McFarlane.

Shultz cannot bring himself to acknowledge that the President, by intent or inadvertence, contributed to misleading him. That is understandable, since it is painful and embarrassing to him. But however painful and embarrassing it may be, it is clear that he had been misled by the very person he was so loyally serving.

Not all of the members of the Committee viewed Shultz as we did. Representative DeWine criticized Shultz for deliberately ignoring the facts once the President had rejected his arguments. In DeWine's words to Shultz, "You purposefully cut yourself out from the facts. . . . You walked off the field when the score was against you. You took yourself out of the game."[118] Similar criticism of Shultz was made by the three members of the Tower Board.

> Secretary Shultz and Secretary Weinberger in particular distanced themselves from the march of events. Secretary Shultz specifically requested to be informed only as necessary to perform his job. Secretary Weinberger had access through intelligence to details about the operation. Their obligation was to give the President their full support and continued advice with respect to the program or, if they could not in conscience do that, to so inform the President. Instead, they simply distanced themselves from the program. They protected the record as to their own positions on this issue. They were not energetic in attempting to protect the President from the consequences of his personal commitment to freeing the hostages.[119]

Representative Hyde thought that Shultz hadn't tried hard enough to convince the President and should have threatened to resign:

> Now, Mr. Secretary, I can't escape the notion that had you opposed this flawed policy and were willing to resign over this policy difference as Secretary Vance resigned over a policy difference with the previous President,[120] you could have stopped it dead in its tracks and if you couldn't, you and Secretary Weinberger sure could.[121]

Although we did not share either DeWine's or Hyde's view (or that ultimately contained in the "Minority Report"), we think it important to reflect upon Shultz's decision to remain as secretary of State in the wake of the President's rejection of his advice. After all, Shultz had offered to resign on three prior occasions—when called upon to take a lie-detector test, when his access to travel had been curtailed, and when Bud McFarlane had traveled to the Middle East in 1983 on a diplomatic mission without Shultz's knowledge.[122] Surely the Iranian arms sales ranked as high in importance. When Shultz walked away, he knew that the initiative was going forward. There were a number of incidents during the spring of 1986 to alert him that the United States was pursuing a plan that included trading arms for hostages. Robert B. Oakley, a top State Department official, prepared a memo on June 7, 1986, that waved a red flag for Shultz:

> . . . there is no doubt as to what was going on during the last ten days in May. This was in direct blatant violation of basic hostage policy approved, reapproved, stated and restated by the President and the Secretary of State; it was equally in violation of both the policy and the law on arms transfers to certain countries; and it has explosive domestic political and foreign policy implications. There is evidently an assumption somewhere that nothing will ever be known publicly, at least with any reasonable degree of certainty; therefore anything goes for hostage release which is humanitarian and should be popular at home.
>
> In my judgment this is both a *terrible* way to conduct foreign or domestic policy and a naive, unrealistic, *dangerous* disservice to President Reagan. . . . If the truth . . . comes out, [so will] tough questions/criticisms/accusations from certain foreign governments and domestic political circles. In addition to public criticisms, there is the problem—often cited correctly by the Secretary—that those holding our hostages and other potential hostage-taking groups will know of it and will know how to deal with or get things done from the United States. Finally, even if there were to be no outside knowledge of these efforts to ignore fundamental policy tenets, the super-secretive, apparently hypocritical approach to the problem has a significant negative impact upon many of those who are aware of it and who are also involved in doing their utmost in working faithfully for hostage release and on other problems *within* policy guidelines.[123]

Shultz may not have seen this particular memo, but it was clear that he was at least vaguely aware of some of the events described in it.

Having spent six years as Secretary of State, Shultz knew when an argument with the President was over. He often referred to President Reagan as a decisive man. That is a diplomatic way of saying that he is also a stubborn man. Periodically over a six-month period, Shultz (and Secretary Weinberger) used every argument available to dissuade the President from going forward with the plan. The President was absolutely determined to reject their advice. It was open for Shultz to resign in protest. That might have stopped the program, for surely investigative journalists would have probed the reasons for his departure.

One can spin out speculation upon speculation. The competition and conflict between Shultz and Weinberger was well known—particularly in the field of arms control. It is possible that Shultz placed a higher premium upon making progress with the Soviet Union on the Strategic Arms Reduction Talks (START) and Intermediate Nuclear Force (INF) negotiations and did not want to risk having the Secretary of Defense move into a vacuum that would be caused—at least initially—by his own departure.

Shultz may have given serious thought to resigning after the plan was exposed and would have been justified in doing so. But it was precisely at the time when Ronald Reagan was in the greatest danger that Shultz decided to fight against those who had prevailed upon the President in the first instance. Casey wanted Shultz fired for disloyalty because he refused to be a part of the conspiracy to cover up what had occurred. More important, Shultz refused to allow the President to risk destroying his presidency by lying to the American people. He remembered the lessons of Watergate, even if the President's other advisers had forgotten. The easiest thing for Shultz to do would have been to resign and make a point of personal honor. It was harder to stay on—and more loyal—to engage in the battle royal that ultimately rescued Ronald Reagan's presidency from a morass of lies.

A majority of the Committee members rejected DeWine's view of Shultz. Republicans and Democrats alike recognized Shultz's quality and integrity. Unlike Poindexter, who made decisions without informing the President, Shultz had enough respect for Reagan to tell him when he was wrong and to provide him with details.

There is no more telling example of these different approaches than the handling of the nine-point plan. Of all the dangerous activities in the whole affair, none exceeded this incident in foolishness.

From October 6 to October 8, 1986, Oliver North, Richard Secord, Albert Hakim, and George Cave, a Farsi-speaking retired CIA officer, met with Iranian officials in Frankfurt, Germany. The opening American negotiating position was a seven-point proposal prepared by North. It was not acceptable to the Iranians.

The discussions did not succeed until the third day, by which time North, Secord, and Cave had left, leaving Hakim to negotiate for the United States. Hakim was an Iranian-born naturalized American, admittedly involved to make a profit, representing his new country in negotiations with his country of birth. It would be laughable were it not so serious.

Confident of his negotiating skill, Hakim quickly reached agreement with the Iranians on the "nine-point plan," which also was described as the "Hakim Accords." By whatever name, the agreement was not only absurd but dangerous as well, opening the United States to unlimited opportunities for extortion.

The United States was to provide Iran fifteen hundred TOW antitank missiles, spare parts for HAWK antiaircraft missiles, free medicine, and "technical assistance, material and specialized know-how, reorganize the military intelligence, maps and communication links." In exchange, Iran was to pay for the weapons and spare parts and to obtain the release of "one and one-half" of the American hostages in Lebanon. "One and one-half" was explained as the release of one hostage and a special effort to gain release of another.

In addition, one of the provisions stated that, before the one and one-half hostages were released, "Albert [Hakim] will present the plan for the release of the 17 Kuwaitis."

Hakim reported his success to North, who enthusiastically recommended the plan to Poindexter, even though the plan represented a retreat on key points. Shortly thereafter, Poindexter testified, he presented the plan to President Reagan, who approved it.

The Kuwaitis referred to in the agreement were also known as the Da'Wa terrorists. They had previously been convicted of bombing the U.S. and the French embassies in Kuwait, killing four people and injuring eighty-seven more. The release of these terrorists had been an important objective of the Iranian negotiators. Resistance to their release had been an even more important part of the Reagan administration's policy against terrorism.

As Shultz testified, "And here was little Kuwait, very vulnerable standing up to [terrorism]. So we have to support them. They are much more vulnerable than we. If they can stand up for it, doggone it, so should we."[124]

The importance of opposition to release of the Da'Wa terrorists to the antiterrorism policy of the Reagan adminsitration was soon reaffirmed. In response to press inquiries about a posssible trade of the American hostages for the seventeen Da'Wa, the White House issued a statement on October 14:

> We will not negotiate the exchange of innocent Americans for the release from prison of tried and convicted murderers held in a third country, nor will we pressure other nations to do so. To make such concessions would jeopardize the safety of other American citizens and would only encourage more terrorism.[125]

Six days earlier President Reagan had approved a plan under which the United States had secretly done virtually what the White House now denounced. Or had he?

Poindexter testified that he had personally obtained the President's approval of the nine-point plan.

> LIMAN: Did Col. North report to you that part of the plan was for Gen. Secord or Hakim to come up with a plan that the Iranians could use to attempt to convince the Kuwaitis to release the Da'Wa prisoners?
>
> POINDEXTER: I believe he did. That was my understanding, that it was not something that Gen. Secord—I don't, I can't say that I really remember Albert Hakim's role in this, but my recollection would be

that Gen. Secord was to come up with a plan which he could give the Iranians that the Iranians could execute, not that the U.S. Government would do it or not even that Gen. Secord would actually do anything.

LIMAN: Did you clear that with the President?

POINDEXTER: My best recollection is I did.

LIMAN: Did you understand that General Secord was acting in this venture at the request of the United States, namely the NSC?

POINDEXTER: Yes, I did.[126]

But Shultz testified that, when he told the President of the plan, Reagan "reacted like he had been kicked in the belly."[127]

SHULTZ: And I told the President the items on this agenda, including such things as doing something about the Da'Wa prisoners, which made me sick to my stomach that anybody would talk about that as something we could consider doing. And the President was astonished, and I have never seen him so mad. He is a very genial, pleasant man and doesn't—very easy going. But his jaws set and his eyes flashed and both of us, I think, felt the same way about it, and I think in that meeting I finally felt that the President understands that something is radically wrong here.[128]

According to Poindexter, just a few weeks earlier the President had personally approved the very plan to which he now reacted so negatively.

What really happened? There are three possibilities:

1. Poindexter did not obtain the President's approval and lied when he said he did.

2. Poindexter did obtain the President's approval, and the President lied and put on an act for Shultz's benefit when Shultz told him of the plan.

3. Poindexter obtained the President's approval of the plan without describing the negotiators or the details of the plan, particularly the provision about the seventeen Da'Wa.

We believe the third possibility is the most likely. Poindexter's condescending attitude toward the President was displayed in his testimony regarding approval of the diversion without telling the

President. Shultz, by contrast, had sufficient confidence in and loyalty to the President to tell him in detail what had happened, including the unpleasant facts about the Da'Wa terrorists. Then and there the Iran initiative ended, done in by George Shultz.

The Secretary of State offered this assessment of the nine-point plan: "Our guys got taken to the cleaners."[129]

His assessment accurately describes the entire Iran initiative.

Blind Trust

Edwin Meese III was the Attorney General of the United States. He held that office because he is a close personal and political friend of the President. Friendship, in fact, has been one of the primary qualities most presidents have sought when selecting the chief law-enforcement officer. John F. Kennedy, for example, appointed his brother Robert to be attorney general, quipping that Robert needed some on-the-job training. Richard Nixon chose his close personal friend John Mitchell.*

An inordinate amount of controversy has, however, dogged Attorney General Meese, because of the judgment he has exercised relative to his personal finances and the attendant ethical demands of his office. It would require a separate book to tell the complex tale of Meese's financial, ethical, and legal problems.[130]

Unsubstantiated allegations concerning ethical or legal inproprieties should never disqualify any person from holding high public office. A demonstrable pattern of poor judgment exercised on ethical issues, however, ordinarily would preclude an individual from being, or remaining, the head of the Department of Justice. In politics, however, loyalty sometimes outweighs other values. The higher the office, the more at stake, the greater the dependence on the loyalty of others.

Ed Meese has been loyal to the President. Ronald Reagan has more than reciprocated that loyalty. His loyalty to Meese is enduring, perhaps even endearing, but ultimately it blinds him to all other considerations.

*Meese resigned on July 5, 1988.

Just before noon on Friday, November 21, 1986, the Attorney General met with the President in the Oval Office. Also present were Don Regan, the President's Chief of Staff, and Admiral Poindexter.

A crisis atmosphere prevailed. Eighteen days earlier a Lebanese newspaper had disclosed that the United States had sold arms to Iran. A political firestorm immediately engulfed the administration. Against his desire, the President bowed to public pressure and addressed the American people in a nationally televised speech on November 13. Six days later he held a televised press conference. On both occasions the President made statements that were false. Twenty minutes after the press conference concluded, the White House issued a "clarification" correcting one of the President's most serious misstatements.

As he watched the press conference, Secretary of State Shultz became so alarmed by the inaccuracy of some of the President's statements that he telephoned the White House and asked to meet with the President. They met the following day, Thursday, November 20. Shultz had prepared for the meeting a document that identified some of the inconsistencies. It was, according to Shultz, a "long, tough discussion."

So, when the President met with Meese the following day, a meeting requested by Meese, Reagan was already aware of the confusion into which he and his administration had sunk over this matter. Meese suggested that he be authorized, in his words, "to develop a factual overview of the events relating to the Iranian initiative." The President readily agreed. A target date for a report was set for the following Monday.

Although the Attorney General is the chief law-enforcement officer of the United States, Meese later said that he was not acting in that capacity. Rather, he said, he was acting as "legal adviser to the President." Thus began the brief investigation that came to be known as the Attorney General's inquiry into the Iran-Contra affair.

Much has been written about that inquiry, most of it deservedly critical. In a July 27, 1987, interview with *The New York Times*, Rudman gave the most blunt assessment: "I tend to believe it was a case of gross incompetence. I guess it's better to be dumb than crooked."

Rather than attempt to retrace each step taken that fateful weekend, we will discuss the two aspects of the inquiry that raise the most troubling questions, and which lead us to conclude that the inquiry was either grossly incompetent or skillfully conceived and conducted to obscure the truth. Those two aspects are the manner in which Meese conducted personal interviews during the inquiry and his failure to prevent the destruction of classified and other relevant documents that might have revealed the truth.

The purpose of the inquiry was to elicit information, to gather in one place all of the facts about a complex and confusing series of events. From beginning to end Meese dominated the inquiry.

Meese conducted the inquiry haphazardly, without adherence to the most minimal of investigative standards. There was no written report of the results. Meese simply told the President some of what he had learned and then, the following day, in a hastily scheduled press conference, told the American people what he had told the President. Not surprisingly, there were many inaccuracies.

The Attorney General's behavior raises serious and difficult questions: Was he trying to uncover the truth? Or obscure it? Whatever he was trying to do, did he succeed?

We begin with the interviews.

During the inquiry the Attorney General conducted ten interviews involving nine persons, all of them past or present high officials in the United States government. One of them, Robert McFarlane, was interviewed twice, on Friday and again on Monday. President Reagan, Vice President Bush, Chief of Staff Regan, Secretary of State Shultz, CIA Director Casey, Admiral Poindexter, North, and Stanley Sporkin, then CIA general counsel, were interviewed once.

The pivotal interview, with North, took place on Sunday afternoon in Meese's office in the Department of Justice, lasting three hours and forty-five minutes. Meese was present for the first two hours of the meeting. Members of his staff were present for the entire interview. One of them took thirty pages of handwritten notes during the meeting. It was during this meeting that North, in Meese's presence, confirmed the diversion.

Every interview by Meese (except the November 22 interview with Casey), *up to and including* the one with North, was conducted in a precise, professional manner: at least one other person was present (a member of Meese's staff), and detailed, written notes were kept of what was said. The importance of these notes became clear at the hearings, when Meese relied upon them extensively to refresh his recollection.

But every interview by Meese *after* the one with North was conducted in what can only be described as a careless, unprofessional fashion: no one was present other than Meese and the person being interviewed, and no notes were taken. In this way the President, the Vice President, the Chief of Staff, the Director of the CIA, and the National Security Adviser were interviewed. It is especially incredible that the National Security Adviser, Admiral Poindexter, was "interviewed" this way. He had already been identified as one of the central figures in the affair and had been listed by North as one of the three persons in the government who knew of the diversion. Yet Meese, the person in charge of the inquiry, did not regard Poindexter as sufficiently important to interview; instead, he conducted what he called "casual conversations" with Poindexter and the other high officials. Meese explained it thus at the hearings:

In the meetings that I had with Secretary Shultz, the meeting with Mr. Sporkin, the meeting with Mr. McFarlane, the meeting with Mr. North, all of these are what you might call interviews where we were seeking to elicit a great deal of information which we were hearing in each case for the first time.

The other conversations that took place were not for the purpose of eliciting great amounts of information. They were either casual conversations, conversations in which I was the original person present, for example, with the President and Don Regan, in which I don't usually take notes in those quick meetings, or they were meetings in which I was seeing people to confirm information we already had in the long interviews that had already taken place, and it was just by happenstance, in that case it was an accident that nobody was there, because Mr. McFarlane came in just as I was leaving for the White House.

In the case of Admiral Poindexter, I was just trying to confirm what we already knew, and he did in fact confirm it. Had he not confirmed it, I am sure we would have gone through the usual interview process with him and taken a detailed statement from him.[131]

As part of his curious approach to the conduct of interviews, Meese intentionally excluded his principal note-taking assistant from his meetings with Casey. The second meeting occurred on Tuesday morning, November 25, after Meese received a telephone call at home from Casey. Casey asked Meese to come by his house on the way to work, which Meese did, arriving at about quarter to seven. John Richardson, Meese's assistant, was in the car with Meese. Richardson had taken notes at previous interviews, including the thirty pages from the interview with North. But Meese went into Casey's house and met with Casey alone, while Richardson waited in the car.

If the interview process was sloppy, the way in which the Attorney General and his associates mishandled the securing of documents was even more so. The Attorney General's inquiry began at noon on Friday, November 21. One of Meese's early decisions was not to involve anyone from the Criminal Division of the Justice Department. Indeed, Meese explicitly rejected an effort by the head of that division to become involved. Instead, Meese relied on three of his assistants, all of whom were political appointees, none of whom had any criminal-investigative experience, and only one of whom had substantial legal experience.

Either through neglect or design, Meese and his associates took no steps to prevent the destruction of documents. As a result, many documents were destroyed, lost to the inquiry and to history.

The destruction began in earnest soon after North learned of the inquiry. North's deputy, Lieutenant Colonel Earl, testified that he had spoken with North early on Friday afternoon. North told Earl that he (North) had just been at a White House meeting where he had learned that Meese was going to look into activities at the National Security Council. North told Earl he asked Meese, "Can I have or will I have 24 or 48 hours?" Meese said he didn't know if North would have that much time. Both North and Meese testified that they could not recall any such conversation.

In any event, North acted as though he had very little time. He requested the originals of a selected list of classified documents. They were delivered to him by the security officer in charge of documents (except one document that could not be located). North then instructed his secretary, Fawn Hall, to prepare new "originals" of the documents and to destroy the old originals, which she did. He also instructed her to place the new, altered original documents back in the files, which she did not do.

She did not do this because in the meantime North had begun shredding documents, and she joined him at the shredder. For hours the two of them, assisted by Earl, shredded documents. No one will ever know exactly how many or which documents they destroyed.

To them, obviously, it wasn't enough. Later that day Hall, with Earl's help, smuggled several documents out of the building in her clothing. And two days later, late Sunday evening, North returned for a final orgy of shredding.

By then it was clear to North that the diversion had been uncovered. That afternoon he had spent nearly four hours in the Attorney General's office, being asked questions. He had been shown a copy of a memorandum written by him that referred to the diversion. So, at eleven o'clock on Sunday evening, North returned to his office. There, for over five hours, he destroyed documents.[132]

Nothing better illustrated Attorney General Meese's attitude toward this inquiry than his view of what North was doing in his office that night.

> MEESE: Well, we don't know whether those were relevant documents, irrelevant documents, or what they were.
> MITCHELL: Do you think Colonel North spent from 11:00 in the evening until 4:15 the next morning destroying irrelevant documents?
> MEESE: I think he probably did.[133]

Investigators are inquisitive and skeptical, often cynical. Ed Meese is none of those things. To the contrary, he is among the least inquisitive, least skeptical of men. His suspicion is not easily aroused. He attributes to others only the most benevolent of motives. Only such a man could believe that Oliver North, in the midst of enormous controversy over his action, having destroyed scores of documents on Friday and Saturday, only to learn on Sunday that he had missed a crucial memorandum, would return to his office at eleven o'clock on Sunday evening and stay there until four-fifteen the following morning destroying *irrelevant* documents!

At the hearings, Meese vigorously defended his inquiry. His principal argument was that he had uncovered the diversion and made it public; everything else was incidental to that; and by this standard, the inquiry was successful.

The discovery and disclosure of the diversion memo weighs in the Attorney General's favor. That the memo was discovered by Bradford Reynolds, the Assistant Attorney General for the Civil Rights Division, and John Richardson, the Attorney General's Chief of Staff, and was shown to Meese by them in the presence of Charles Cooper, the Assistant Attorney General for the Office of Legal Counsel, makes it unlikely that its existence could have been concealed; the Attorney General did take the responsible course, however. It is plausible to argue that, without the diversion memo, no evidence of wrongdoing would have remained. All reference to the authorization of the shipment of weapons by the Israelis in 1985 had been altered; the December 1985 finding signed by the President, with its retroactive provisions, had been destroyed; the January 17, 1986, finding made no reference to prior U.S. actions. Congress could have challenged the wisdom of a covert arms sale to Iran and the legality of the President's action in not notifying Congress. But it was the evidence of a diversion of funds to the Contras that raised the possibility of criminal wrongdoing and posed a direct threat to Ronald Reagan's presidency.

Some members of the press have speculated that the discovery and disclosure of the diversion memo was planned in advance by Casey or North or both, as a part of the real cover-up.[134] According to this theory, the unsigned diversion memo, coupled with Poindexter's denial of having informed the President, was designed to lead Congress down a blind alley and into a dead-end street. This strikes us as the stuff of fiction rather than fact. Disclosing the existence of a diversion scheme ran the risk that Congress would not only shut down a program dear to the President's heart (Contra aid) but would also reveal the other covert activities contemplated for Secord and Hakim's Enterprise. A simple and safer plan to protect the President would have been to destroy all documentary evidence and let North and Poindexter become the "fall guys."

We do not consider the disclosure of the diversion memo an act of deception. But questions will always remain about the integrity of the Attorney General's inquiry. Some will speculate that those who approved the Iran initiative hoped that North would have enough time to complete his search-and-destroy mission and that Secretary Shultz would join in the effort to construct a wall of lies around the White House. When that did not happen, the center could no longer hold or the story be contained.

Unfortunately, this view is encouraged by the fact that Attorney General Meese (like those who preceded him) wears too many hats—presidential adviser, personal friend, National Security Council member, chief law-enforcement officer—and it was never clear which hat he was wearing during the course of his investigation.

The reason Congress felt compelled to create an office of independent counsel was that it knew the American people would not believe our laws were being impartially administered when an attorney general was called upon to investigate and pass judgment on high officials in an administration of which he is part. This would be especially true of the President, who would have appointed the Attorney General in the first place.

If we are to abolish the independent-counsel law and restore the mantle of impartiality to the Justice Department, we believe it is time for presidents to stop the time-honored practice of appointing their personal friends (or relatives) as this nation's attorney general. We doubt that a restoration of faith in the impartial administration of justice can be achieved until we select independent men and women to serve as the guardians of justice.

Et Tu?

Many of the witnesses who testified before the Committee had a code name. Some had two. Adolfo Calero was "Barnaby" or "Sparkplug"; Robert Owen, "T.C.," "the Courier"; Oliver North, "Steelhammer," "Blood and Guts"; Ronald Reagan, "Joshua"; John Poindexter, "Beethoven." Don Regan did not have a code name. Perhaps those who dispensed such affectionate aliases never considered him a major participant or player in the White House foreign-policy-making apparatus. Indeed, in his testimony, Regan consistently asserted that he stood on the very periphery of national-security decisions.

He maintained that he did not have much more than a surface understanding of either the Iranian or the Contra-aid program. That admission in itself was significant in revealing how the White House was organized and run. For nearly two years Regan rode a wave of generally favorable publicity as Ronald Reagan's chief of staff. He was the President's majordomo, the man who exercised absolute control over the President's schedule, meetings, and speeches. Not a paper or a person slipped into the Oval Office without his approval. He was regarded as the most powerful chief of staff since Sherman Adams.[135]

Regan took visible pleasure in wearing this mantle of power. He appeared with the President in photographs with world leaders. When the President misspoke, Regan corrected the record. He once described himself as chief of the circus parade's "shovel brigade." The image was a crude one, casting the President in a rather ignoble light. The First Lady was furious. Her relationship with the Chief of Staff deteriorated. Then the Iran-Contra scandal broke. The scapegoat was obvious. It was only a question of time before Regan fell.

On February 27, 1987, Regan was replaced by former Senate Majority Leader Howard Baker. At the time Regan looked old, ashen, a broken man. The torch of power had passed. He heard for the first time of his firing when it was announced on CNN television. The prince of power was dead. Long live the prince.

When Regan testified before the Senate Intelligence Committee in December 1987, it was obvious that he was still embittered by his fall from power. He had a reputation as a martinet, a caustic, hard-boiled ex-Marine who either cowed his staff or fired them. Indeed, it was written that he ran the West Wing of the White House as if it were a cross between Merrill Lynch and Quantico. Regan's most memorable gesture to Congress came in the form of a four-letter obscenity to the Senate.

Testifying before the Intelligence Committee, Regan said he knew virtually nothing of the Iran-Contra affair. Poindexter had independent access to the President. Regan did not see or clear the paperwork generated by the NSC staff and presented to the President. Regan offered an organizational chart that displayed the White House chain of command. None of the lines of authority ran to his office. At the time his protestations of disengagement seemed outlandish; members treated his testimony with open skepticism. Yet the Tower Commission concluded, in one devastating paragraph:

> Mr. Regan also shares in this responsibility [disorderly and informal process]. More than almost any Chief of Staff of recent memory, he asserted personal control over the White House staff and sought to extend this control to the National Security Advisor. He was personally active in national security affairs and attended almost all of the relevant meetings regarding the Iran initiative. He, as much as anyone, should have insisted that an orderly process be observed. In addition, he especially should have ensured that plans were made for handling any

public disclosure of the initiative. He must bear primary responsibility for the chaos that descended upon the White House when such disclosure did occur.[136]

When he appeared before the Senate Intelligence Committee, Regan offered testimony on the origins of the weapons sale to Iran that differed sharply from that of Robert McFarlane. Regan testified that President Reagan had never approved the Israeli proposal to transfer weapons to the Iranians. In fact, according to Regan, when the President first learned about the transfer of TOW missiles, he became upset and asked McFarlane to convey his displeasure *privately* to the Israelis. McFarlane testified that at no time did the President tell him to convey his unhappiness to the Israelis, and that the President was quite positive about the release of the Reverend Benjamin Weir.

This was a basic conflict that the Intelligence Committee was unable to resolve. McFarlane's version of the facts seemed more credible, for several reasons:

1. McFarlane's entire career has been one of respect for the line of command. He is the last person who would recommend a course of action that had been rejected by the President of the United States.

2. The Israelis had established a good relationship with President Reagan and would be reluctant to jeopardize it by selling weapons without his explicit approval.

3. The Israelis are extraordinarily sensitive about their security needs and would be reluctant to transfer TOW missiles or any other weapons to the Iranians without a guarantee of their replacement.

4. If the President had expressed to McFarlane his discontent over Israeli actions, it is difficult to believe that the United States would have approved the November 1985 shipment of HAWK missiles to Iran.

5. Regan's dislike of McFarlane was well known. Many believed that he was responsible for forcing McFarlane's resignation as

National Security Adviser. When *The Washington Post* quoted McFarlane as saying it had been a mistake to send weapons to Iran, Regan responded angrily: "Let's not forget whose idea this was. It was Bud's idea. When you give lousy advice, you get lousy results."[137]

Regan offered the Tower Board a possible explanation for McFarlane's *assumption* that he had been authorized to tell the Israelis to proceed with the first shipment of TOW missiles:

> This is only conjecture on my part. I've never discussed it with Bud. All I can say is that Bud, of course, would be hearing from the President, as I said, not always, not every day, but frequently he would be hearing from the President, what's new on the hostages. Anything going on? What about that Iran connection? Anything going on there? So that I could assume that Bud would think there was a sense of urgency here to the extent that the President was concerned about this and wanted something done. He had suggested it. It was his initiative. . . . He could assume, I suppose, that the President wanted this. [Reagan] hadn't raised Cain about the Israeli shipment, so a second try might not be out of order. I can only surmise that.[138]

Regan's speculation was important for two reasons. First, Poindexter had also made an assumption about what the President would have approved—the diversion to the Contras of funds from the sale of weapons to Iran. It is interesting to note that the President did not always have to speak to be understood (or misunderstood). For example, when Attorney General Meese disclosed the existence of the diversion to the President, Don Regan remembered:

> . . . after the Attorney General left, the President—I lingered behind just to try to console the President. I knew he was distraught and saying we would have to take steps to clean up the mess. I said, in my judgment, if all of this hangs together and is true, Poindexter has got to go and we will have to clean house, and *the President didn't comment. He never comments on something of that nature. And by his silence, I took that I had consent to proceed with this.* [Emphasis added.][139]

But if Regan's speculation about McFarlane's assumption is correct, then either the President was sending ambiguous signals to his subordinates, or those who dealt with him on a daily basis were totally inept in comprehending what he wanted. If so, the White House had not been overrun by a cabal of zealots who disregarded clearly defined standards of conduct. Rather, the President's failure to define his goals—and the acceptable means of achieving them—ultimately produced the scandal.

On this point, we would note that other members of the administration appeared eager to read Ronald Reagan's mind. Former White House spokesman Larry Speakes, when asked why he fabricated quotes for the President during Reagan's meetings with Mikhail Gorbachev, stated:

> I could certainly have talked to the President and said, "Mr. President, this has just come up, I want to get right to you and let you know that people have questioned it and I took the liberties and felt very comfortable these were your thoughts and I wanted to get them out." I'm sure he would have said that's all right.
>
> . . . You're in the heat of battle and the rush of events—that's what convinced me I should do it. The time was getting away. I was heading for the briefing room. I had no words of the President's for any impressions except in all the meetings we'd had before. I knew his thoughts, if not his words. So I did it to serve the President.[140]

Second, Regan's version of the initiation of the arms sales to Iran also implied that the Israelis (and McFarlane) were responsible for dragging the United States into this foreign-policy disaster. According to the notes that Regan kept of the November 10, 1986, meeting at the White House, Secretary Shultz confirmed that the Israelis had "suckered us" into the deal. Moreover, North, after the sales had been exposed, suggested that the Israelis take the blame for the transfer. And Vice President Bush, on January 25, 1988, in his controversial interview with CBS anchorman Dan Rather, stated that he had been concerned that a covert action had been under the control of a foreign power (Israel).[141]

Israel, in turn, initially argued that it was simply doing the bidding of the United States. Israel's role in the genesis of the arms sale to Iran has never been fully explored or explained. Although Israel did provide written documentation pertaining to its activities, it exercised its rights as a sovereign nation not to submit its citizens to examination by U.S. officials. It is unlikely that Israel merely served as the obedient handmaiden of the United States in its dealings with Iran, but it is unfair for U.S. officials to try to shove responsibility onto Israel's shoulders for the debacle. Administration officials were fully aware that Israel's objectives in negotiating and trading with Iran were quite different from our own. Still, our interests, while not mutual, nevertheless coincided, and resulted in a full partnership. We used and relied upon each other's resources. But, in the final analysis, Israelis are responsible for the actions of the Israeli government, and Americans are responsible for the actions of the U.S. government.

We had prepared extensive questions for Regan. For example, in a December 1985 meeting at the White House, Regan had joined with Secretaries Shultz and Weinberger in opposing the continuation of the Iran program because "the thing had been a fiasco up to that point . . . had not worked. . . . We were dealing with some very unusual people. We were fooling around for the better part of six months with very little to show for it . . ."[142]

Then, four weeks later, on January 7, 1986, at the meeting attended by President Reagan, Vice President Bush, Attorney General Meese, Secretary Shultz, Secretary Weinberger, DCI Casey, and Admiral Poindexter, Regan reversed his recommendation. He joined Meese, Poindexter, Casey, and Bush in supporting the plan, because Poindexter had assured the President that "there was a whole new lead; a whole new plan and that it might turn things around."[143]

Those who participated in the January 7 meeting assumed the

hostages would be released within thirty to sixty days. This appeared to be the rationale for withholding immediate notice to Congress of the presidential finding signed in its final form on January 17, 1986. Yet, although the plan had proceeded for a full ten months, all of the hostages had not been released. In fact, under this new plan of direct weapons sales to Iran by the United States, the first hostage, Father Lawrence Jenco, was not released until July 26; the second, David Jacobsen, on November 2. What did the Chief of Staff do to satisfy himself that the Iran initiative was still a responsible plan? Why did he not inquire about the financing mechanism that permitted Poindexter and North to inflate the price of weapons to help raise money for the Contras? Did he know about any of the participants involved in the plan or their reliability?

McFarlane returned from Teheran in late May 1986, after spurning an Iranian offer to release two American hostages in exchange for the delivery of twelve pallets of HAWK spare parts that were awaiting shipment in Israel. The Iranian offer included a pledge of subsequent efforts to obtain the release of the other two remaining hostages. When on July 26, 1986, the Iranians released Father Jenco, administration officials feared that, if they did not respond positively, the lives of the remaining hostages might be lost. So the United States responded by sending *all* of the twelve pallets of the HAWK spare parts that McFarlane had refused to send in May. Thus, the United States ended up giving the Iranians, for one hostage, all the parts that we had earlier refused to give for the release of two hostages and an Iranian promise to work for the release of the other two! We pass over the fact that, on September 9, Frank Reed was taken hostage in Lebanon. How did Regan allow the President to get (in Secretary Shultz's words) "taken to the cleaners"?

When the Iran initiative was exposed, what specific steps did Regan take to ensure that the President was fully informed of the facts before he made false and misleading public statements?

Regan said that he was preoccupied with other matters.

COHEN: The operation was under way for about ten full months and still the hostages hadn't been released. . . . Given the fact that months had passed and we had not seen the release of all the hostages that was planned within 30 to 60 days, why weren't you down pounding on John Poindexter's desk or door, saying what's going on, what's happening with the hostages, what are the details, who is involved, why aren't we making progress?

REGAN: Good question. I don't know the answer. Frankly, I had enough on the plate that—I was listening to what was going on but I was more concerned about what was going on in other areas and I just didn't look into it. . . .

COHEN: So this just was left to Admiral Poindexter?

REGAN: That's right. I won't say it was swept aside, but it certainly wasn't very high on the screen.[144]

In May 1986, while Shultz was in Tokyo with the President and Regan, Shultz received a cable from the U.S. Ambassador to Great Britain. According to the Ambassador, an Israeli (Mr. Nir) had approached a British entrepreneur, Tiny Rowlands, in an arms deal that had White House approval and involved John Poindexter as the point man. Rowlands's name was synonymous with syndication—the sharing of financial risks and rewards among a group of investors. If Rowlands was involved, there had to be others. In fact, Adnan Khashoggi and Ghorbanifar were also mentioned in the cable. Shultz wanted to know what was going on. Regan had no answer and sent Shultz to see Poindexter. Poindexter simply denied that the United States was involved or had approved any such approach to Iran. At no time did Regan seek to satisfy himself as to the truth or falsity of the rumor concerning Rowlands.

When Father Jenco was released by his Lebanese captors in July 1986, White House officials feared that, if weapons were not transferred to the Iranians, our remaining hostages would be endangered.

COHEN: Did you play a part in the decision to then go forward and release the weapons to the Iranians?

REGAN: I offered no opposition. I won't say that I played a role in it, because it was more of a passive role. I sat. I heard. I listened.[145]

What thought was given to the fact that McFarlane had returned from Teheran in May, having refused to release a second load of weapons when the Iranians would arrange for the release of only two hostages, not four, and yet just two months later, the Iranians released only one hostage and received all of the weapons?

REGAN: I think people were upset, very disgusted with what was going on. The bait was still there, though, if we could save a life here, a life there. You weigh that sort of thing and it is very hard to—with a degree of finality—say, "to hell with it."
COHEN: You wanted to save the hostages?
REGAN: Definitely. That was the way to get arms [to the Iranians].
COHEN: If it were not for the hostage issue, you agree it is unlikely that the President would ever have agreed to sell weapons to the Iranians?
REGAN: I don't think he ever would have agreed, bona fides, or what have you.[146]

Regan said that during the first week of November 1986, when the story of the U.S. arms sales to Iran broke in the American press, he had urged the President to go public with all the facts. Poindexter argued against him. The President chose to remain silent. Finally, Regan prevailed upon the President to make a public statement. But Regan had little notion of who was gathering the facts. The administration was in a state of angry disarray. At the November 10, 1986, meeting, Shultz believed that the President was being given erroneous information by Casey and Poindexter, who wanted the President to use his communicative skills to "bail them out." Shultz, in turn, was accused of being disloyal.

On November 15 Shultz gave Regan a draft paper calling for the United States to declare an end to any arms sales to Iran. Regan said that the White House was not in a position to adopt it. Shultz's frustration deepened. CBS's "Face the Nation" had invited Shultz to appear on its program the next morning. The

White House wanted him to appear. Shultz's problem was that he didn't know what he could say. British Prime Minister Margaret Thatcher was visiting President Reagan in Washington. Shultz had traveled to Camp David and joined the President and Mrs. Thatcher for lunch. Shultz wanted Regan to clear with the President a statement that he could make the next morning. Things were too hectic. Helicopters were turning their engines. No time, Regan told him. Impossible.

The next day, Shultz said that the United States should discontinue any sales of weapons to Iran. When asked whether he, the Secretary of State, spoke for the administration, Shultz had to respond, "No." He was saddened and embarrassed by having to make this comment. The battle inside the White House intensified. The next day the White House announced that Shultz *did* speak for the administration and that there would be no more sales to Iran.

The President made several erroneous statements during his November 19 press conference. Shultz called the President and met with him and Regan the next day in the President's private quarters in the White House in an attempt to correct the false information the President had been given.

On November 21, when Regan finally saw the chronology that was being prepared under Poindexter's supervision, he realized that the statement of events in 1985 included the false cover story about oil-drilling equipment. By that time, the Attorney General had decided that a full inquiry was needed. Regan's reaction when Meese advised him of the diversion? "Horror, horror, sheer horror." Regan then confronted Poindexter, who allowed that he was vaguely aware of the diversion plan but had simply neglected to pay much attention to it. Regan never inquired whether Poindexter had informed the President of the plan.

The recitation of these events presented a dramatic refutation of the image that Donald Regan had run the White House as if it were either Quantico or Merrill Lynch. Ironically, what proved so extraordinary was not what Regan had to say but how he said it. He breezed into the Senate Caucus Room with an unexpected lightheartedness that disarmed the Committee. It was obvious that he had undergone a personal transformation since the time when he so ignominiously left public office. A ruddy flush had returned to his face. He strode with confidence to the witness table and joked with Committee members. No attorney accompanied him— but, of course, he was not a target of the independent counsel.

With flashes of Irish wit and self-deprecating humor, Regan readily admitted that the stories about his control of White House policy and process had been exaggerated. "I don't mind spears in the chest," he quipped, "it's the knives in the back."[147] Regan seemed to have joined the Committee not for combat but for cocktails. The members were surprised, the press stunned. Was this a new Don Regan? To what should we attribute this change in manner? Perhaps he had "slipped the surly bonds" of public office or was simply levitating now that he no longer had to please Mrs. Reagan.

Whatever the reason, the new Don Regan, through his appearance that day, did two things: he repudiated the "man-in-charge" image that he had earlier cultivated, and he regained some of his prior stature.

At the conclusion of his testimony, a number of Committee members shook his hand and congratulated him. Exiled from public office, Regan had returned to capture the hearts of Capitol Hill. He went on to become an author and part-time commentator for NBC Radio.

Regan's recovery of his reputation was short-lived. He provoked a storm of controversy in publishing his memoir, *For the Record*. Some viewed the books as an honest account of his years in the Reagan administration. Others, however, considered his disclosure of Nancy Reagan's astrological dependencies, which often forced Regan to calibrate the presidential schedule to the alignment of planets, to be spiteful and vindictive. The verity of Regan's far-ranging observations was lost in the charges of his disloyalty. With the book's publication, Regan joined a growing list of trusted

Cabinet members and aides—former Secretary of State Al Haig, former budget director David Stockman, Michael Deaver, and Larry Speakes—who painted a portrait of a president who was passive, pliant, uncurious, and detached from the responsibilities of governance. Regan's response to the charge of disloyalty was blunt and caustic: one act of disloyalty begets another.

Rough Rider

Caspar Weinberger is a dark-haired, round-shouldered man who appears taller than his five feet and six inches, and younger than his seventy years. He is conservative in philosophy and dress: dark suits, white shirts, and regimental ties that are nearly always adorned with a tie clasp bearing the presidential seal. When he served as President Nixon's director of the budget, he earned, for his budget-cutting practices, the nickname of "Cap the Knife." As Ronald Reagan's Secretary of Defense, Weinberger traded his budget knife for a military sword; he became a tireless advocate for a strong military, and the spending necessary for it. He spent hours in the field with military personnel, riding in the open hatches of M-1 tanks or watching night operations aboard an aircraft carrier in the Indian Ocean.

With vast experience in government, Weinberger always proved to be a formidable witness at congressional hearings, where he would idiosyncratically balance two long, sharpened pencils between the middle and index fingers of his right hand. Weinberger came to hearings well prepared and determined to present testimony in a dogmatic and unequivocal fashion. He was a monopolist in hoarding time for answers to questions, speaking rapidly and without pause between paragraphs of Joycean length. He scolded those who attempted to interrupt him as if they were schoolboys caught trespassing in his backyard. Above all else, Weinberger was an unabashed Reagan loyalist and, until his retirement in November 1987, one of the President's closest friends in the Cabinet. Considering all these factors, several of us expected Weinberger to downplay the disagreement in the Reagan administration over the issue of the Iranian arms sales, rather than to speak forcefully about the advice he had given to the President. We were wrong.

Weinberger gave a spirited defense of his actions in criticizing the entire Iran program. At no time did he seek to soften his characterization of the plan's absurdity or the dangerous consequences of its execution. It was clear that he deeply resented the Tower Board's criticism that he had failed to do enough to protect the President from acting on bad advice.

In a strong, stern voice, Weinberger testified that:

• He rejected the Tower Board's conclusion that he had distanced himself from the Iran-Contra affair.

• He insisted that there were no moderates to be dealt with in Khomeini's Iran.

• He had advised the President that we would be opening the United States to blackmail at the hands of the Israelis and Iranians if we agreed to sell arms to Iran.

• He denied that the Iranians were at any time in danger of losing the war to Iraq—contrary to the assertion made by John Poindexter on January 16, 1986, justifying the sale of arms to Iran.

• The chairman of the Joint Chiefs of Staff had never been consulted about what impact, if any, the arms sale might have on the Iran-Iraq war.

• He and Secretary Shultz had been taken off the intelligence distribution list.

• He did not know that McFarlane had furnished intelligence information to the Iranians.

• He disputed the claim by North and Poindexter that the Iranians had stopped engaging in terrorism.

• He had presented to President Reagan alternative options to get our hostages out of Lebanon.

• He could remember no other occasion on which he and the

Secretary of State were united on a foreign-policy issue and their combined counsel was rejected by the President.

Although Weinberger expressed his concern that knowledge of covert actions be confined to as small a group as possible, he also flatly rejected Poindexter's endorsement of extra-legal procedures to achieve desired goals. Poindexter had testified that a "private organization, properly approved, using non-appropriated funds in an approved sort of way, may be a solution to the problem."[148] The Secretary of Defense said:

> I thought that the common law and all of the rules under which civilization is governed grew out of the recognition that the warring private feudal groups could lead to nothing but war, and that the only way you could ever get a peaceful community under the rule of law is to have a government which was the source of, and indeed the repository of, the law.
>
> So I think any of these things that attempt to run private operations of this nature become private governments, is totally wrong and I would be totally opposed to it.[149]

A balance between the need for maintaining secrecy and the need for informing key people in the government must always be struck:

> I certainly include the leadership of the Congress and various others within that. . . . Some people say we pay a price for our freedom— for a free society. Maybe that is true. . . . Whatever it is, it's worth it . . . [150]

Representative Tom Foley focused on the central issue involving the need for notification:

> FOLEY: For the most part, in the absence of prior notification, consultation is difficult or impossible, is it not?
>
> WEINBERGER: Yes.
>
> FOLEY: And would you regard consultation as often a very valuable opportunity for the President?

WEINBERGER: Indeed, yes, sir. Not only because it is very useful to have the advice and I think we need the help of everybody we can get, but I also think that it is important for the longer-range success of any kind of activity, because I have frequently made the point in private meetings that we can't fight a war on two fronts.

We can't fight with the enemy, whoever that may be, and we can't fight with the Congress at the same time.

We need to have the United States government unified if any kind of activity is going to succeed over the long run. . . .[151]

Weinberger was asked whether he agreed with the opinion of Admiral Bobby Inman, the former Deputy Director of the CIA, that an administration had three options in dealing with a process established by law: (1) change the law if it is wrong; (2) challenge the law in the Supreme Court; or (3) comply with the law to make it work. He responded that he was in "complete agreement."

He not only offered a different vision from Poindexter as to how a democratic government should function, but also offered a far different version of what happened at that important December 7, 1985, meeting at the White House also attended by George Shultz, Donald Regan, Robert McFarlane, John McMahon, and President Reagan. Weinberger was concerned about the credibility of the United States and the impact that the sale of weapons might have upon our allies:

I thought that it would certainly cause a great deal of problems because we had denied weapons to Jordan, to Saudi Arabia, to a number of other countries in the area, we had refused to supply them and if it came out we were supplying weapons to Iran, Jordan's mortal enemy, it would be a very damaging thing to us; that Saudi Arabia had a justified fear of Iran because of the type of leadership that was prevalent in Iran and Iran's geographical position and that this [our sale of arms to Iran] would hurt us with countries with whom we needed to have friendly relationships.[152]

Not only would the disclosure of such activity have a negative impact on the effort to stop the export of weapons to Iran by friendly governments, but it was bound to have a similar effect

on private individuals as well. For example, on July 30, 1987, a
federal judge dismissed forty-six of the fifty-four counts that had
been brought against ten defendants in a major $2-billion arms
shipment to Iran. The case had been delayed repeatedly because
of the revelations of the agreement to sell weapons to Iran and the
congressional and independent-counsel investigations that were
under way. All of the defendants maintained that the Reagan
administration had given them approval for their transactions.

It occurred to us that it might be easier for a judge and jury to
find criminal intent on the part of those who sold weapons to the
Iranians for profit as opposed to those who acted out of patriotism. Yet the two private U.S. citizens who had $8 million in a
secret Swiss account, Secord and Hakim, claimed to be motivated
principally by patriotism. The question would be further complicated by an entry contained in Donald Regan's notes on the
November 10, 1986, meeting at the White House. Vice President
Bush had asked, "Is [the New York] case a private or public
endeavor to sell arms to Iran[?]" The answer was "Probably private
with government knowledge."[153]

Weinberger differed with Poindexter in another important respect regarding that meeting on December 7, 1985. Weinberger
concluded that he and Shultz had raised enough legal and policy
objections to persuade the President to discontinue the initiative.

> My impression of the President's reaction was that he was against it
> and had . . . decided not to do it. In fact, when I got back to the
> Department, I told General [Colin] Powell, I believed this baby had
> been strangled in its cradle, that it was finished. That was the strong
> impression I had from his comments.[154]

Secretary of State Shultz's recollection of that meeting was generally consistent with Weinberger's:

> So it was a very vigorous discussion, and it took place in the family
> quarters in a rather informal kind of setting, and I think Secretary
> Weinberger started off by saying something like, "Are you really in-

terested in my opinion?" And the President said, "yes." And so he gave it to him. So did I.

BELNICK: Was the President fully engaged in this conversation?

SHULTZ: Oh, yes. This idea that the President just sits around not paying attention, I don't know where anybody gets that idea. He is a very strong and decisive person.

BELNICK: Was he a strong proponent of the proposed policy at that meeting against your opposition and that of Secretary Weinberger?

SHULTZ: Well, I don't remember that he sort of argued with us. He listened, and you could feel his sense of frustration. He said at one time—because Cap is a particularly good lawyer—he said, "There are legal problems here, Mr. President, in addition to all of the policy problems."

You know how people get sometimes when they are frustrated. He [Reagan] said, "Well, the American people will never forgive me if I fail to get these hostages out over this legal question" or something like that.

And Secretary Weinberger—"but," he said, "visiting hours are Thursday," or some such statement.

So there was that kind of banter. I know people have looked at those notes and wondered if the President was advocating violating the law, and there was no such tone to that at all. It was the kind of statement that I'm sure we all make sometimes when we are frustrated.

BELNICK: Where did you understand that the matter stood when that meeting ended on December 7?

SHULTZ: Well, I wasn't sure. But I felt that between Secretary Weinberger and [me], we had made a real dent and that with the—Don Regan seeing it the same way, we having talked through various aspects of what might be done, that perhaps we had won that argument.[155]

Admiral Poindexter came to a different conclusion:

I have a very vivid recollection of that meeting, and it was in the residence. The President pulled a foot stool up to the coffee table and sat there very quietly, as is his nature, listening to all of the discussion up to that point, listening to Secretary Shultz, to Secretary Weinberger, Mr. McFarlane. I had very little comment. I don't recall the Chief of Staff saying very much. . . .

And the President listened to all this very carefully, and at the end of the discussion, at least the first round, he sat back and he said something to the effect . . . that "I don't feel we can leave any stone unturned in trying to get the hostages back. We clearly have a situation here where there are larger strategic interests, but it is also an opportunity to get the hostages back, and I think we ought to at least take the next step."[156]

Perhaps the President's ambiguous response allowed each person to believe that he had carried the day with the President. Within a month, however, President Reagan, although he did not reveal that he had signed a finding authorizing the continuation of the arms sales, left no doubt that he had rejected Weinberger's and Shultz's advice.

Representative Ed Jenkins asked who, after all of the debate on this issue, had made the best argument for going forward with the sale.

Weinberger gave a telling answer: "Perhaps the President."[157]

Secret Witnesses

F or most Committee members, once Caspar Weinberger left the hearing room and the four leaders of the Committee gave their final summations, the investigation was over. Three more witnesses were scheduled to testify in closed session. But few expressed interest in their testimony. Perhaps the absence of television's klieg lights signified that the curtain had fallen across the congressional stage. Or members may have known that whatever information emerged would not alter what had become in the public's mind the central question of the hearings—the President's knowledge of the diversion. Perhaps fatigue had simply taken its toll. In any case, most of the Committee's members delegated to those who served on the House or Senate Intelligence Committee the responsibility for examining the remaining witnesses.

Tom Polgar, Sr., had argued strongly for the need to call key witnesses from the CIA. He pointed out that the Senate Intelligence Committee had listed the question of the CIA's role in the entire affair as second in importance only to that of the President's. And yet we had done little more than skim the surface of the CIA's activities in both the arms shipment to Iran and the support given to the Contras.

On May 6, the second day of the hearings, when Senator Inouye announced that William Casey, the Director of the CIA, had died, many members expressed privately their belief that the full story of the Agency's activities would never be known. Those who had dealt with Casey in the past knew that, even if he had lived and

249

remained completely lucid and coherent, it was not likely that he would have discussed much beyond that he wanted us to know or thought we would accept.

Casey was a deceptively tough-minded and wily intelligence chief. His penchant for secrecy and his distrust of Congress were well known. He never volunteered information. With Casey, if you did not ask the right question, you simply did not receive the right answer. Even if you did ask the right question, you were never sure that you had received the right answer. Casey spoke as if he had too many oversized teeth that just kept getting in the way of coherency. It was a common joke that the Director of the Central Intelligence Agency had a built-in voice scrambler. Casey took no offense: this spared him the charge of deliberate deception. His congressional overseers could never be sure whether he misspoke or they misunderstood. The Director seemed to relish this capacity for Delphic ambiguity.

Even if Arthur Liman and John Nields had had the opportunity to bring their full talents to bear in pursuing Casey through the rubble of contradictions, inconsistencies, and lies, we doubt that Casey would have revealed the full extent of his advice and activities. After Secretary of State Shultz threatened to resign if Casey provided false testimony during his appearance before the House Intelligence Committee on November 19, 1986, Casey nevertheless insisted falsely that the pilots of the CIA's proprietary aircraft believed the plane was carrying oil-drilling equipment. And, as we were to learn later from the CIA Chief of the Central American Task Force (C/CATF), Casey had once called him into his office and proceeded to deride rumors that Casey was suffering from cancer. "Isn't that the most ludicrous thing you've heard? Do I look like a man with cancer?" Casey asked. The C/CATF confessed that Casey had looked completely healthy.[158] In fact, Casey had been undergoing treatment for prostate cancer for well over a year.

Polgar argued that Casey's death should not diminish the Committee's mandate. In a closed session we had taken the testimony of the Agency's Costa Rican station chief, Joseph Fernandez, whose pseudonym was "Tomas Castillo." Castillo had been caught in an ethical no-man's-land trying to help the Contras, as instructed, without violating the law. But he was merely a foot soldier in assisting the Contras, not the architect of the plan itself. His superiors still had much to account for, because there was little that North did or could do without calling upon the CIA.

Although the Committee had taken the depositions of the C/CATF, Deputy Director of Operations Clair George, and Chief of Counterterrorism Duane "Dewey" Clarridge, their testimony was either incomplete (because we did not at the time know all of the questions to ask) or inadequate. The Committee could pass no judgment upon the CIA's activities based upon their prior testimony.

The Committee's apparent indifference to the CIA's role unintentionally, but predictably, produced a certain disdain by some in the Agency toward our proceedings. The Agency's cooperation had evolved from what our staff described as "mobile stonewalling" to a contemptuous disregard of our requests. It was evident that the CIA had concluded that it had little to fear from our Committee and decided to adopt a narrow and conservative view of what information it had to produce. As of late July, dozens of Committee requests were being ignored. Failure to take the formal testimony of any CIA witnesses (other than Castillo) would not only leave the record incomplete, but would also lend credence to the inevitable criticism that the Committee was contributing to a cover-up of the facts. How could we justify spending an entire day examining Glenn Robinette or Bretton Sciaroni, but fail to call a single high-level witness from the CIA?

Although the Committee was disposed to take testimony from Agency witnesses, two questions emerged: what witnesses should be called, and should the testimony be taken in public or closed session? There was little discussion of either question. Although William Webster, the former Director of the FBI, had been confirmed as the new Director of the CIA, no one thought he was in a position to contribute to our proceedings. The most logical choice was Deputy Director Robert Gates. Gates had been nominated by President Reagan to serve as the Director, but withdrew his name after several Senate Intelligence Committee members criticized him for not knowing more about the sale of weapons to Iran, and for not being vigorous enough in searching out the facts for William Casey's testimony that was to be given to Congress. It was never discussed in such terms, but there was concern among Committee members that, if Gates were called, he could offer little information about the origins or implementation of either the Iran arms sales or the Contra-aid program; the Committee would then be left to focus upon his role in the preparation of Casey's testimony. The Committee decided that Director Webster and the congressional Intelligence Committees were more appropriate to review the propriety of Gates's actions. Instead, the Committee, in closed sessions, would focus upon the following areas:

1. The circumstances of the CIA's involvement with the HAWK missile shipments through Portugal in November 1985. By regulation, the CIA is prohibited from honoring requests from the NSC staff without the specific approval of the Director or Deputy Director of the Agency.

2. The circumstances—or conspiracy—that permitted the routine use of CIA helicopters in resupplying the Contras from Honduras at a time when the Boland Amendment prohibited the activity.

3. The complicity of CIA headquarters personnel in the support provided by Tomas Castillo to the "southern front."

4. The CIA's conduct in withdrawing from responsibility during the operative phase of the Iran arms sales.

When Castillo testified, he struck us as a man who had been left to walk in a forest without a map or a compass. He knew that the Boland Amendment prohibited the CIA from providing any direct or indirect assistance to the Contras. In spite of the law, Castillo assisted Ambassador Lewis Tambs in acquiring land for an airstrip in order to help "open a southern front." When the Boland Amendment was changed to permit the Agency to provide intelligence information, communications equipment, and humanitarian assistance, Castillo suppled flight-vector information and other services to the pilots of Secord's Enterprise to help them deliver lethal supplies to the Contras on the southern front. Assisting the so-called private benefactors was a violation of CIA policy. Castillo maintained that his activities were well known to his superiors. At one point Castillo communicated to CIA headquarters a recommendation from North that would have allowed Castillo to disengage as a middleman in providing assistance to the private benefactors. The proposal was rejected by the CIA. In fact, the C/CATF, in an ambiguous cable, instructed Castillo not to undertake any action that could be misconstrued by Congress.

In January 1986, during the course of an internal investigation conducted by the CIA's Inspector General, Castillo withheld information about his activities. Castillo explained *to the Committee* that he had done so because he had been told by Deputy Director of Operations Clair George that the investigation would be limited in scope. When he was confronted with a broader investigation, he was unprepared and therefore withheld information to protect the Agency. George later denied ever having advised Castillo about such a restricted investigation.

As a result of his conduct, Castillo had been suspended pending completion of the CIA's investigation. Castillo exemplified the human toll exacted from one who believed he was doing what his superiors wanted while knowing that he was walking and perhaps crossing a fine line of legality.

> You may question whether my officers and I understood the legal constraints of the Boland Amendment. Of course we did—or we thought we did—notwithstanding the fact that there were no lawyers assigned to my Station and the cable guidance from Headquarters on these matters was understandably terse and narrow and did not pretend to address every eventuality. The application of the Boland Amendment in humane, rather than legal, terms in the field operational environment led us to feel we were in the middle of a mine field with each step becoming a critical decision. My officers and I diligently tried to

adhere to the constraints of the Boland Amendment as we understood them, and I believe we were generally successful.[159]

Castillo wanted to convey to us his personal anguish:

Since my return to Washington in January, I have experienced some of the worst moments of my life. My [family's] absence, the imposed isolation, the interruption of my command, the unfounded press and media speculation about my participation and possible violation of the law, and the possibility of irreparable damage to a career I cherish and have dedicated the last 20 years of my life to are all factors which have made the last few months very difficult. On the basis of my actions . . . it should not have been so.[160]

When Senator Paul Sarbanes asked Castillo what he was currently doing for the Agency, Castillo wept. His career—his life—had been placed in suspended animation. He was doing nothing but waiting.

Duane "Dewey" Clarridge was the second CIA witness. A former chief of the CIA's European Division and veteran of other major posts, Clarridge enjoys a high reputation among his Agency colleagues. He is considered a protégé of the deceased William Casey.

Clarridge is something of a dandy. He dresses in well-cut clothes, sports a gold bracelet on his right wrist, and tucks a silk handkerchief in the chest pocket of his suits and sport coats. One of our Senate colleagues who previously served on the Intelligence Committee once remarked that "Dewey . . . would parachute anywhere in the world behind enemy lines—provided he could land at a four-star restaurant!"

Clarridge is a graduate of Brown University, highly intelligent and reputed to speak several languages. His reputation, like Poindexter's, made his lack of memory in testimony before the Committee somewhat suspect. There was little he seemed to remember, even about events that had occurred only weeks prior to his previous congressional testimony.[161]

In 1984 Clarridge was directing the CIA's activities in support of the Contras. In his deposition, when asked on two occasions whether he had been aware of any discussions concerning soliciting third countries to assist the Contras, he replied, "No."

After reviewing the cable traffic prior to traveling to Country Six in April 1984, Clarridge changed his answer—but with an important qualification. According to Clarridge's revised statement, the cables indicated that the Agency thought Country Six was offering unprompted assistance rather than responding to an Agency solicitation of assistance. In fact, after traveling there, Clarridge determined that the CIA had misunderstood the nature of that government's intent. No offer was ever made by that country. He said the offer they had intended to make was indirect; they would give aid to a third country, which in turn would assist the Contras; they would do so only if reimbursed. Before the offer was made, the administration decided that it would be politically embarrassing to pursue an arrangement that might make us look beholden to a government whose policy of human-rights abuses was unacceptable to most Americans.

Clarridge testified at length about his role in authorizing the use of a CIA proprietary aircraft to move HAWK missiles to Iran in November 1985. Clarridge maintained that at that time he believed the shipment consisted of oil-drilling equipment. The CIA's station chief in Lisbon had testified that he had learned that the shipment would contain HAWK missiles and that the purpose of the shipment was to secure the release of the American hostages. The station chief had cabled this information to Clarridge, but Clarridge said he had never seen such a cable. The cable, mysteriously, was missing from CIA files.

This was an interesting point of dispute. According to Don Regan, even he and the President knew prior to the shipment that it was to contain HAWK missiles. We found it troubling that an intelligence official who held such a high position and such a distinguished record of service could be so profoundly lacking in curiosity.

Then there was the matter of Richard Secord, the man who became a central figure in both the Contra-aid and Iran programs. When Clair George testified, he was asked about Secord's notoriety.

> GEORGE: It meant what I told you when I took my oath and appeared before the Select Committee in late November of 1986. Secord had been messed up and involved—in some way engaged in activities in the fringes of Tom Clines, Ed Wilson, international arms traffic. I had no evidence then and I have no evidence now that Mr. Secord is violating law; but there's a world of ours in which there are people we do not deal with and Mr. Secord is one of them.
>
> COHEN: The world of yours . . . is it fair to say that people at your level, and I'm talking certainly with Mr. McMahon, Mr. Casey, yourself, Mr. Clarridge, would have knowledge of . . . General Secord's activities?
>
> GEORGE: Absolutely.
>
> COHEN: His is a name that certainly would pop up on the mental screen?
>
> GEORGE: I don't see how you could be in this business and not know the name of Richard Secord.[162]

Clarridge claimed never to have heard either of Richard Secord prior to 1986, or of Secord's past association with the notorious Edwin Wilson—the former CIA agent who had sold weapons and explosives to Libya, a nation which is one of the most notorious sponsors of global terrorism.

Despite Clarridge's alleged insulation from common knowledge, he made a positive contribution in confirming the existence of a philosophic and policy division within the administration pertaining to our foreign policy. Secretary of State Shultz had opposed including any arms as part of an effort to seek a new relationship with Iran. Shultz was charged at that time with promoting among our allies and other friendly nations a project called "Operation Staunch"—the effort to stop the flow of weapons into Iran. That we were engaged in precisely the conduct we were preaching against would not only expose us as hypocrites, but would also undermine our ability to occupy a leadership role in uniting the free world against the scourge of terrorism. Secretary of Defense Weinberger also opposed the sales—but more, it seemed, because he had concluded that it was an absurdity for the United States to deal with an irrational nation, and lunacy to think that we would find any moderates who could be effectual under the Ayatollah Khomeini's extremist leadership. Weinberger obviously fell into that group who, in Clarridge's words, "felt there was no such thing as a 'moderate element' in Iran and that what we really should be doing is teaching the Iranians a lesson."[163]

There existed another group, presumably including men such as Robert McFarlane, William Casey, John Poindexter, Oliver North, Donald Regan, Vice President George Bush, and—most important—Ronald Reagan, who were persuaded that selling arms to Iran might achieve a diplomatic *breakthrough*. As became clear, however, the breakthrough to Iran was secondary and incidental to the *breakout* of our hostages.

An administration so deeply divided cannot long maintain a consistent and coherent policy. In January 1987 the small but oil-rich nation of Kuwait, an ally of Iraq, called upon the United States to protect its tankers from attack by *Iran*. According to the Kuwaitis, the Soviet Union was prepared to protect them if we refused. Eager to demonstrate that we had not abandoned our professed neutrality in the Iraq-Iran war by tilting toward Iran, we proceeded (or at least appeared) to tilt back to Iraq by reflagging eleven Kuwaiti tankers and sending U.S. warships into the Persian Gulf to protect the tankers. The administration made the decision to take this action before an analysis of its consequences had been completed by our intelligence community.

According to Clarridge, the philosophic tug of war waged within the administration was then being dominated by the Weinberger school of thought:

> . . . the group that had been interested in opening up relations with Iran or with some people in Iran . . . that has come to naught and the

group more interested in teaching the Iranians a lesson or finding an excuse to teach them a lesson have now moved into the ascendancy.[164]

It is important to note the irony involved in such a dramatic reversal of policy toward Iran in such a short period of time. It is more important to note the risk posed by covert actions that either run counter to our stated public policy or do not enjoy the support of those principally responsible for formulating foreign and defense policy.

The CIA Chief of the Central American Task Force (C/CATF) is a tall, rangy former college-football standout. The Agency regarded him as a rising star, having awarded him a $20,000 bonus in 1987 for outstanding service. Eager to testify before the Committee to explain his role, and to describe the pressures he had to endure, he was intense as he sat at the witness table and frequently leaned into the microphone, unable to control his anger. He had spent more than ten hours testifying before the grand jury. He had woken up every morning "feeling lousy." His wife had asked him whether they would ever wake up feeling good again.

As C/CATF, he said he had been put in a position of trying to work within the parameters of an impossible law—the Boland Amendment. He suggested that partisan politics played by Congress were responsible for the constant changes in the law. He subsequently backtracked when challenged—first asserting, then denying that disagreement with the policy of assisting the Contras constituted the playing of partisan politics. However one characterized the dynamics of congressional action, all he knew was that he found himself in a "nutcracker"—a word he used repeatedly. He felt trapped between the stops and gos of Contra aid, the ever-shifting boundaries of permissible conduct: no military aid; limited military aid; humanitarian assistance; intelligence information; communications equipment.

It was his judgment that U.S. policy—its formulation and execution—fell on the shoulders of Oliver North.

He was the person that filled the void and who dealt with these things by dint of the void and by dint of personality; and he did it, and he was the person who moved and formulated and pushed and cajoled.[165]

His private assessment of Oliver North?

I never knew Col. North to be an absolute liar, but I never took anything he said at face value, because I knew that he was bombastic and embellished the record and threw curves, speed balls and spit balls to get what he wanted. . . . I have seen Col. North play fast and loose with the facts. . . . But, on the other hand . . . there was a lot of fact in what he said, too.[166]

Whatever doubts he had about the reliability of North's representations, the C/CATF knew that North was deeply involved in assisting the Contras at a time when that assistance was prohibited. Ironically, at the very time when the White House was urging its officials to testify fully and completely before the Senate Intelligence Committee's preliminary inquiry, he and his colleague Clair George evaded questions during their appearance before the Senate Intelligence Committee in December 1986. There might have been a rationale for withholding information about North's activities prior to November 25, 1986, but what justification could there be after North's activities had been puplicly disclosed?

The C/CATF was not one to volunteer information. During a House Intelligence Committee hearing on October 14, 1986, he testified as follows:

We know what the airplanes are by type. We knew, for example, there were two C-123s and C-7 cargos. . . . We knew in some cases much less frequently that they were flying down . . . into southern Nicaragua for the purposes of resupply, but as to who was flying the flights and who was behind them, we do not know.[167]

Yet he maintained before our Committee that his prior statement was not false:

C/CATF: I want to make one thing very, very clear. I don't lie and I don't provide false answers, and if I'm put in a situation that is undeniable, I will find some way to avoid lying. . . . I didn't know who was flying those flights.

CAROME [House Committee counsel]: Or who was behind them, is what you said?

C/CATF: You could have put me on a rack and I couldn't have told you who the pilots were, who was managing them. I at that time suspected, but didn't know that General Secord was involved with them. I had no idea where the money was coming from. . . . It is not a lie.[168]

He said that he had been taken aback when, in his presence, Elliott Abrams categorically assured Congress that there was *no* U.S. government involvement in the Hasenfus plane that was shot down by the Sandinistas in October 1986. He knew Abrams was wrong. But others at the witness table (such as Clair George) also knew that Abrams was wrong. The C/CATF wasn't going to be the first to tell the truth.

I could have been more forthcoming, but I frankly was not going to be the first person to step up and do that. . . . So long as others who knew the details, as much as I, who knew more than I, were keeping their silence on this, I was going to keep my silence.[169]

The last witness to testify was Clair George, a thirty-two-year veteran at the CIA, who served as deputy director of operations (DDO).[170] A colorful man, he speaks as though trained in drama at Yale. Although monitoring the Contra-aid program was not a principal responsibility for George, he was aware that North and the NSC staff were assisting the Contras. He, too, was practiced in the art of precise elocution. At the October 14, 1986, House Intelligence Committee hearing, he stated:

First, I would like to state categorically that the Central Intelligence Agency was not involved directly or indirectly in arranging, directing, or facilitating resupply missions conducted by private individuals in support of the Nicaraguan Democratic Resistance.[171]

George was in error, but unwittingly so according to his later testimony. He offered an apology to our Committee. We then inquired about his silence in the presence of Elliott Abrams's categorical denial of U.S. government assistance in support of the Contras.

> I was surprised Abrams made that statement. It was so categorical. The question is, should I leap up and say, "Hold it, Elliott, what about—excuse me, all you members of HPSCI [the House Permanent Select Committee on Intelligence], but Elliott and I are now going to discuss what we know about"—and I didn't have the guts to do it.[172]

Besides his reluctance to contradict another senior administration official, George revealed a frustrating inability to ward off other identifiable dangers. George outlined how the United States was drawn into the Iran arms sales. Several approaches had been made to the White House to deal with Iran in an effort to get our hostages out of Lebanon. John Shaheen, a former business associate of Bill Casey's;[173] the Israelis; Michael Ledeen, an NSC consultant; and Adnan Khashoggi, the international arms dealer and financier—all had made proposals. Behind each approach stood the same middleman, Manucher Ghorbanifar, a person the CIA believed to be totally unreliable. However, after the Israeli shipment of 508 TOW missiles succeeded in producing the release of Reverend Weir, Ghorbanifar gained credibility at the White House. But CIA doubts persisted, particularly after the November 1985 Israeli shipment of HAWK missiles went astray. Ledeen continued to urge support for Ghorbanifar. The Agency insisted that Ghorbanifar be subjected to a lie-detector test. When the polygraph test was administered, on January 11, 1986, Ghorbanifar flunked with flying colors. According to George, "If memory serves me, Mr. Ghorbanifar could only repeat his name and nationality and pass the machine."[174]

Five days later, on January 16, George sent out a "burn notice" on Ghorbanifar—for the third time. "In our language we send a notice around the world that the individual that we are speaking about should not be dealt with because he's dishonest and untruthful."[175]

In spite of the CIA's absolute distrust of Ghorbanifar, President Reagan signed a finding the very next day. According to George:

> On the 18th, after having sent a cable we will do no more business with Ghorbanifar, I was taken to the White House and giving a finding which in its practical sense said, "You will be doing business with Mr. Ghorbanifar."[176]

George was adamant. He met with Director Casey and said:

> "Bill, I am not going to run this guy anymore," which means in our language, "I will not handle him, he is a bum."[177]

George also criticized using Secord as a commercial cutout to handle the shipment of arms to Iran. Secord "worked the edge of the international arms market. . . . In my mind, as a manager of the American clandestine service . . . [Secord] was an individual with whom I would not do business."[178]

But, according to George, President Reagan, Casey, and North were driven by a determination to get our hostages out of Lebanon. As a result of CIA opposition, Casey shifted responsibility for controlling the operation to North and set up as a CIA liaison an agency official who was inexperienced in covert operations. George told us:

> There couldn't have been a better mismatch. . . . I should have fought with Casey, and said if we are going to handle this guy, . . . I'll get three of the meanest men I know alive and we'll handle him.
>
> You see, all that was unimportant. It didn't matter what I said. It didn't matter whether I said, let my 18-year-old daughter handle him. They were already using him in a major international foreign affairs activity, so as I said yesterday, I'm not playing with the whole deck.[179]

Throughout his testimony, George defended Casey:

> Bill Casey was the last great buccaneer from O.S.S. He was dropping agents into Germany and France and saving lives when most of us

were doing nothing. This was a great guy, Bill Casey, and he saw in Ollie North a part of that, and he liked Ollie. But you could get to Casey and say, "Ollie is crazy," and Casey would change his mind.[180]

George was quick to dispute North's claim that Casey knew about the diversion plan or had ever given North suicide pills to take on his trip to Teheran. When asked how Casey could have ignored all of the warning signals offered by CIA professionals and turned such an important operation over to amateurs, George said:

> Bill Casey fell afoul to a charge in the White House that "come on, Bill, we have enough of those"—as Dick Secord titles us—"shoe salesmen; let's get a real operation together and really do something."[181]

They did something. They turned to Oliver North.[182]

Copilot or Passenger?

The Committee did not focus on the role of Vice President George Bush.

Our first concern was the President's role. In addition, the evidence that was before the Committee gave no indication that Bush was aware of the diversion of funds, and there was no compelling evidence that he knew of the covert resupply operation in Central America. In fact, the evidence showed little significant role for Bush in any of the events under investigation by the Committee.

Bush maintained that, although he was aware of the Iran arms sale, he was not intimately involved in its implementation. Further, he stated that he was unaware that it was arms for hostages until he was briefed by Senator David Durenberger (R-Minnesota), then Chairman of the Senate Select Committee on Intelligence, on December 20, 1986, almost a month after the affair had become public. He has frequently described himself as "out of the loop."

In his autobiography, Bush says of the Durenberger briefing, "What Dave had to say left me with the feeling . . . I'd been deliberately excluded from key meetings involving details of the Iran operation."[183] However, records show that he attended many briefings during which the arms sale and the hostage issue were discussed. McFarlane testified (and White House logs confirm) that Bush was at the August 6, 1985, meeting at which McFarlane reported that Iran wanted one hundred TOW missiles from Israel, in exchange for which four hostages would be released. At that meeting Secretary Shultz told the President that it was "a very bad idea" and "we were just falling into the arms-for-hostages business and we shouldn't do it." Secretary Weinberger also opposed the sale at that meeting. The Vice President was present on January 6, 1986, when Poindexter briefed the President on a plan to send four thousand TOW missiles to Iran in exchange for hostages. At that meeting Poindexter presented a finding to the President, which the President signed. Bush was also present on January 17 when an almost identical finding was signed by the President. The memorandum accompanying the finding, signed by Poindexter and prepared by North, states, "The Secretaries [Shultz and Weinberger] do not recommend you proceed with this plan." At the bottom of the page, Poindexter had written and initialed: "President was briefed verbally from this paper. VP, Don Regan and Don Fortier were present.—JP."[184]

According to White House records and Secretary Shultz's testimony, the Vice President attended the January 7, 1986, meeting at which Shultz "expressed myself as forcefully as I could. That is, I didn't just sort of rattle these arguments off. I was intense."[185]

Bush, however, said he didn't remember "any strenuous objections." He maintained, "If I'd sat there and heard [Shultz and Weinberger] express opposition strongly, maybe I would have had a stronger view."[186]

In testimony to the Committee, Weinberger stated, "I made the same arguments [at the January 7 meeting] with increasing force, but apparently less persuasion, and George Shultz did the same thing."[187] Poindexter also testified about that meeting:

LIMAN: . . . [Is] it true that Secretary Shultz, and Secretary Weinberger again expressed their opposition to the initiative?
POINDEXTER: Yes, they did.
LIMAN: And is it also correct—
POINDEXTER: Very vigorously.[188]

Shultz testified, "It was clear to me by the time we went out that the President, the Vice President and [the others] all had one opinion and I had a different one and Cap shared it."[189]

Bush, in a January 25, 1988, interview with CBS News anchorman Dan Rather, said, "I've heard George Shultz be very, very forceful. And if I were there [and] he were very, very forceful at that meeting, I would have remembered that."[190]

The next day, Shultz, on CBS's "This Morning," reasserted that the Vice President had been at the meeting and that he (Shultz) had strongly opposed the inititative.[191] President Reagan does not remember Bush's being at the meeting.[192]

But Poindexter, testifying in his deposition, volunteered that the Vice President was present at the meeting:

> LIMAN: At that time [January 7] that they were meeting . . . it was Meese and Secretary Shultz and Secretary Weinberger and yourself.
> POINDEXTER: And the Vice President.[193]

And Attorney General Meese similarly volunteered in testimony before the Committee:

> NIELDS: And the [meeting] on the 7th [of January, 1986] included various members of the Cabinet, Director Casey, Admiral Poindexter, Secretaries Shultz and Weinberger, and the President?
> MEESE: Yes, sir, and also the Vice President, I believe . . .[194]

The Vice President was also briefed, at North's request, by Amiram Nir, the Israeli Prime Minister's special assistant for counterterrorism, in Jerusalem on July 29, 1986. Notes were taken by Bush's aide Craig Fuller, who was the third person present. His memorandum memorializing the meeting was published in the Tower Board's report:

> Summary. Mr. Nir indicated that he had briefed Prime Minister Peres and had been asked to brief the VP by his White House contacts. He described the details of the efforts from last year through the current period to gain the release of the U.S. hostages. He reviewed what had been learned which was essentially that the radical group was the group

that could deliver. He reviewed the issues to be considered—namely that there needed to be a decision as to whether the items requested would be delivered in separate shipments or whether we would continue to press for the release of the hostages prior to delivering the items in an amount agreed to previously.

. . . Nir began by providing an historical perspective from his vantage point. He stated that the effort began last summer. This early phase he said "didn't work well." There were more discussions in November and in January "we thought we had a better approach with the Iranian side," said Nir. He said, "Poindexter accepted the decision."

He characterized the decision as "having two layers—tactical and strategic." The tactical layer was described as an effort "to get the hostages out." The strategic layer was designed "to build better contact with Iran and to insure we are better prepared when a change (in leadership) occurs." "Working through our Iranian contact, we used the hostage problem and efforts there as a test," suggested Nir. He seemed to suggest the test was to determine how best to establish relationships that worked with various Iranian factions.

. . . He said "an agreement was made on 4000 units—1000 first and then 3000." "The agreement was made on the basis that we would get the group," Nir said. "The whole package for a fixed price," he said.

. . . A meeting was organized for mid May in Tehran to finalize the operation. The VP asked Nir if he attended the meeting and Nir indicated he did attend. . . . "McFarlane was making it clear that we wanted all hostages released," Nir reported and, "at the last moment the other side suggested two would be released if those at the meeting stayed six more hours." According to Nir, "the Deputy Prime Minister delivered the request (to delay departure) and when the group said 'no,' they all departed without anything."

According to Nir, "the reason for delay is to squeeze as much as possible as long as they have assets. They don't believe that we want overall strategic cooperation to be better in the future. If they believed us they would have not bothered so much with the price right now."

. . . According to Nir, he [the Deputy Prime Minister] told them about 10 days ago he would cancel the deal. Then nine days ago their

Prime Minister called saying that they were taking steps to release one—the Priest. The second one to be released would be Jacobsen. The Prime Minister also said that one would be released and then "we should give some equipment." Nir indicated to the VP that the bottom line on the items involved spares for HAWKs and TOWs. No denial or approval was given according to Nir. Nir said he made clear that no deal would be discussed unless evidence is seen of the release.

. . . Nir described some of the lessons learned: "we are dealing with the most radical elements. The Deputy Prime Minister is an emissary. They can deliver . . . that's for sure. They were called yesterday and thanked and today more phone calls. This is good because we have learned they can deliver and the moderates can't.

". . . Should we accept sequencing? What are the alternatives to sequencing? They fear if they give all hostages they won't get anything from us."

. . . The VP made no commitments nor did he give any direction to Nir. The VP expressed his appreciation for the meeting and thanked Nir for having pursued this effort despite doubts and reservations throughout the process.

By: Craig L. Fuller [initialed] "CF 8/6/86."[195]

Bush, when asked about the meeting, said that he did not fully understand what Nir was saying. Fuller's sworn testimony makes clear that Fuller understood the import of Nir's briefing.

The issue became and remains important because of Bush's quest for the presidency. Former Secretary of State Alexander M. Haig, Jr., then a Republican challenger, repeatedly pressed Bush with this question: "The American people are entitled to know what position he took during this storm that imperiled our nation's vital interests. Where was George Bush during the storm? Was he the copilot in the cockpit, or was he back in economy class?" Bush dismissed Haig. Senator Robert Dole, who was also challenging Bush for the Republican nomination for president, although less caustic, demanded that Bush fully explain his thoughts and his role in this affair.

During the January 25, 1988, CBS News interview, Dan Rather

raised the same issues in what became a controversial newscast. The Vice President challenged Rather's objectivity and selective view of his overall record and complained that he had been misled by CBS into believing that the interview would be a "political profile." A *Los Angeles Times* public opinion poll taken within twenty-four hours showed that Americans were evenly divided on whether Rather had treated Bush fairly.[196] But the question was to remain a major factor in Bush's quest for the presidency: exactly what were his thoughts about the propriety of the covert action itself, and what steps, if any, did he take to satisfy himself about the potential consequence to the United States if it went forward?

A *New York Times* January 29, 1988, editorial drew one conclusion:

> Even with its gaps, the record compels the conclusion that Mr. Bush knew or should have known enough to warn the President against shipping arms to Iran in return for American hostages. To understand why, recall that he heads the Administration's task force on terrorism, which has always insisted on the principle of never bargaining with terrorists.
>
> Then consider the fact that the Vice President attended many national security meetings and had other opportunities to learn, or strongly suspect, that this cardinal principle of antiterrorism was being violated.[197]

The *Times* editorial made an important point, but it is necessary to make another.

Despite the myths that take root in political life, power and position are never quite as great or high as either portrayed or imagined. Donald Regan offered an example of how image can be larger than life. The Vice President of the United States is not the President's partner or alter ego. Vice presidents are often selected as running mates for the geographic and philosophic balance they bring to their political party's national ticket. The presidential candidate and his running mate campaign as a team, publicly

muting their substantive differences, yet allowing the image of
those differences to persist in order to appeal to the broadest range
of voters.

Once elected, however, the President and his top advisers rel-
egate the Vice President to the role of understudy, to be informed
of policies and events rather than actively involved in shaping
them. The philosophic balance that was so important for the political campaign becomes, almost immediately, a potential source
of discord to those who surround and advise the President. The
demand for absolute political loyalty replaces the desirability of
balance. Whatever his personal views, the Vice President cannot
publicly disagree with the President's policies or actions without
fracturing the bond of unity they must maintain. The Vice President lacks flexibility to express his views even in private Cabinet-
level sessions, particularly when deep divisions among officials
exist. For the Vice President to advocate any position might be
construed as either undercutting the value of his advice should
the President reject it, or compromising the President's flexibility
in reaching a decision by forcing him to avoid embarrassing his
own Vice President.

When the Vice President seeks election to the presidency, the
perception of the Vice President as working at the President's
right hand is at war with the reality of his distance from real
decisionmaking in the White House. In most instances it serves
the Vice President, as candidate, to foster and enhance the former
perception. But when the President is unpopular, or the subject
is an administration failure, the Vice President seeks distance from
the responsibility. As columnist Mark Shields has described it,
the problem is claiming to be the coleader on the one hand and
claiming to be the "one person who can clean up the mess we're
in" on the other. Jimmy Carter's Vice President, Walter Mondale,
was saddled with this dilemma in 1984, four years after Carter
had left office. And many analysts believe that Hubert Humphrey's
inability in 1968 to balance loyalty to President Lyndon Johnson
with convincing anti–Vietnam War Democratic voters that he had

privately expressed reservations to Johnson was responsible for his narrow loss to Richard Nixon.

The problem of the public perceptions and the private views of vice presidents is not unique to George Bush. It may account for the fact that, despite the apparent advantages of the office of vice president, no sitting vice president has been elected president since Martin Van Buren in 1836.

The Vice President has refused to disclose the substance of his conversations with President Reagan. It is possible that, in those conversations, Bush cautioned the President against selling weapons to the Iranians. But whatever doubts surround Bush's views, Poindexter was convinced that the Vice President supported the initiative.

On February 1, 1986, more than a week after the meeting in London at which North, pursuant to the finding signed by President Reagan on January 18, agreed to the sale of four thousand U.S. TOW missiles to Iran in exchange for the release of the American hostages in Lebanon, Poindexter stated in a memo to McFarlane:

> George [Shultz] and Cap [Weinberger] still disagree on policy grounds, but are cooperating, Bill [Casey], Ed Meese, Don Regan, and I are fully onboard this risky operation, but most importantly, President and VP are solid in taking the position that we have to try.[198]

Nearly a year after the plans to sell a limited quantity of weapons to Iran was conceived, the Israelis continued to draw a distinction between the strategic goal (better relations with Khomeini's successors) and the tactical result (getting American hostages out of Lebanon). Virtually all of the evidence, however, indicated that President Reagan was consumed with obtaining release of the hostages. And it seemed not to matter to him that the Israelis, who had once argued that they were dealing with Iran moderates, concluded that the United States was now dealing instead with the most radical elements in Teheran. We note also that the Israelis determined that the moderates were impotent because they could not deliver all the American hostages, but that the radicals were unlikely to secure the release of all the hostages because Iran would lose all leverage in obtaining weapons. In addition, the Committee learned that the Israelis' First Channel was reporting to the same Iranian leaders as was the Second Channel!

Vice President Bush considered himself to be on the periphery of this major foreign-policy decision—in Haig's terms, more of a passenger than a copilot. But we think it fair to say that, even if he were a copilot, his position would have remained the same. Lost in the furor over the Bush-Rather exchange and the assessments of who "won" was Bush's response to Rather's question about "arms for hostages":

> I went along with it—because you know why, Dan . . . when I saw Mr. Buckley, when I heard about Mr. Buckley being tortured to death, later admitted as a CIA Chief. So if I erred, I erred on the side of trying to get those hostages out of there.[199]

The Vice President endorsed the weapons sale to Iran either out of loyalty to the President or because he, too, was consumed by the passion to obtain the freedom of the hostages.

PART III

True or False

Real emeralds are worth more than synthetics but the only way to tell one from the other is to heat them to a stated temperature, then tap. When it's done properly, the real one shatters.

I have no emeralds. I was told this by a woman who said someone had told her. True or false, I have held my own palmful of bright breakage from a truth too late. I know the principle.

—John Ciardi
The Birds of Pompeii

The Report

Two Committee reports were filed on November 19, 1987: one by a bipartisan majority of fifteen Democrats and three Republican senators, the other by six House Republicans and two Republican senators. The division between the reports generally reflected the philosophies, interrogation, or speechmaking of the individual members displayed during the hearings. A separate book would be required to relate the tug of war that took place in the preparation of these two reports. Arthur Liman's talent as a negotiator was stretched to its full limit as he shuttled back and forth between the House and the Senate reconciling the substantive and stylistic differences between the numerous drafts of the reports.

The majority's judgments were stated in stark and solemn terms. The responsibility for the Iran-Contra affair was placed directly on President Reagan. Secrecy, suspicion, and disdain for the rule of law were the essential ingredients of the Iran-Contra affair. The President was responsible for setting the standards of conduct for his subordinates. He failed to instill in his aides a proper regard for the law. If he did not know what his top aides were doing, he should have. Administration policy was rife with confusion and contradiction, which invited failure. Secretly trading arms for hostages violated the United States' public policy of refusing to deal with terrorists. The President made a number of erroneous statements to the public. Key administration officials gave false and misleading information to Congress and engaged in a cover-up of

275

U.S. involvement in the shipment of HAWK missile parts to Iran in November 1985. The administration's decision to solicit financial aid from private citizens and foreign governments and the diversion to the Contras of funds from the sale of arms to Iran violated both the letter and the spirit of the Boland Amendments.

The majority report captured the full implications of the Iran initiative in two succinct, powerful paragraphs:

> Too many drivers—and never the right ones—steering in too many different directions took the Iran initiative down the road to failure. In the end, there was no improved relationship with Iran, no lessening of its commitment to terrorism, and no fewer American hostages.
>
> The Iran initiative succeeded only in replacing three American hostages with another three, arming Iran with 2,004 TOWs and more than two hundred vital spare parts for HAWK missile batteries, improperly generating funds for the Contras and other covert activities (although far less than North believed), producing profits for the Hakim-Secord Enterprise that in fact belonged to U.S. taxpayers, leading certain NSC and CIA personnel to deceive representatives of their own government, undermining U.S. credibility in the eyes of the world, damaging relations between the Executive and the Congress, and engaging the President in one of the worst credibility crises of any administration in U.S. history.[200]

Those who signed the minority report denounced the majority for what they called its hysterical conclusions. Representative Henry Hyde, leading the minority's assault, said the investigation had been a witch hunt from beginning to end. Reagan-administration officials, the minority maintained, made mistakes, but "There was no constitutional crisis, no systematic disrespect for 'the rule of law,' no grand conspiracy, and no Administration-wide dishonesty or coverup."[201]

Rather than holding the President responsible, the minority report blamed Secretary of State Shultz for a "record of disengagement" and for not resigning his office after failing to dissuade President Reagan from selling arms to the Iranians. Significantly, no words of criticism were directed to Secretary of Defense Weinberger for failing to resign. Moreover, in the minority's judgment, Congress was largely responsible for the affair, because of its inability to keep secrets and its intrusion into the President's foreign-policy domain.

The criticism of Congress had been fueled by an earlier disclosure that the former vice chairman of the Intelligence Committee had disclosed to NBC an unclassified staff report of the Senate Intelligence Committee's preliminary investigation into the Iran-Contra affair. During the course of our hearings, several House Republicans had seized upon this action as proof that Congress could not be trusted with the nation's secrets. There was a large measure of irony in this argument.

WSC: *First, the staff report contained no classified information. Second, the White House had been conducting an intensive lobbying campaign to persuade the Senate Intelligence Committee to release this report. The White House objectives in my judgment were twofold: (1) to shift the responsibility to Congress for disclosing the details of a major covert operation that either originated with the administration and its ally Israel or was initiated by Israel and subsequently approved by the President; (2) to insist that Congress validate the President's claim that he had no knowledge of the diversion of funds to the Contras. It struck me as being more than curious that the President was demanding that Congress, the very institution that he had avoided notifying and consulting with, had to furnish him with a report describing in detail a plan that was formulated and perhaps executed either in or within a few feet of the Oval Office. Most of the information accumulated by the Committee was readily available to the President through his Cabinet and members of his staff. Almost all of the Intelligence Committee's witnesses had been from the White House or the Central Intelligence Agency. . . .* [202]

Congress cannot remain indifferent to charges that it is violating its obligations. It must be willing to deal as severely with its own members as it does with those in the Executive Branch. Similarly, the answer for the Executive cannot be to use its paranoia as an excuse to turn to a group of black-bag specialists to carry out a secret foreign policy in the name of national security.

There was another element of irony in the minority report's denouncing Congress as a leaky sieve. Two days before both reports were to be officially released, a section of the minority report was leaked to *The New York Times*. It was reminiscent of North's blaming Congress for endangering lives by leaking classified information, only to have *Newsweek* reveal that he was in fact the source for the story.

At the press conference following the official release of the majority and minority reports, Warren Rudman wasted few words on the minority's document or declarations. In a strong, unequivocal voice, Rudman dismissed the minority report. "I'm reminded of Adlai Stevenson's great remark about the press: 'This particular report is one in which the editors separated the wheat from the chaff, and unfortunately it printed the chaff.' It is a pathetic report."

We sat in silence behind Rudman, Inouye, and Hamilton in the packed Caucus Room. We were not surprised by the strength of Rudman's words. We exchanged silent glances of agreement. Rudman had spoken for both of us.

The Aftermath

At the conclusion of the Committee's hearings, President Reagan seemed eager to recognize the failures of his administration and to take corrective action. He had changed White House personnel: Howard Baker, the former Senate Majority Leader, had replaced Don Regan as the Chief of Staff; William Webster had been confirmed as the new Director of the CIA; Frank Carlucci was appointed National Security Council Adviser; and General Colin L. Powell selected to serve as Carlucci's deputy. Through Baker and Carlucci, the President began a series of negotiations with the senior members of the House and Senate Intelligence Committees to establish new guidelines for the implementation of covert actions in the future. The following letter reflected what the President's new approach would be:

THE WHITE HOUSE
Washington

Dear Vice Chairman Cohen:

. . . Frank Carlucci has presented to me the suggestions developed by the Senate Select Committee on Intelligence for improving these procedures. . . .

Specifically, I want to express my support for the following key concepts recommended by the Committee:

1. Except in cases of extreme emergency, all national security "Findings" should be in writing. . . .

279

2. No Finding should retroactively authorize or sanction a special activity.

3. If the President directs any agency or persons outside of the CIA or traditional intelligence agencies to conduct a special activity, all applicable procedures for approval of a Finding and notification to Congress shall apply to such agency or persons.

4. The intelligence committees should be appropriately informed of participation of any government agencies, private parties, or other countries involved in assisting with special activities.

5. There should be a regular and periodic review of all ongoing special activities both by the intelligence committees and by the NSC. . . .

6. In all but the most exceptional circumstances, timely notification to Congress under Section 501(b) of the National Security Act of 1947, as amended, will not be delayed beyond two working days of the initiation of a special activity. . . .

While the President must retain the flexibility as Commander in Chief and Chief Executive to exercise those constitutional authorities necessary to safeguard the nation and its citizens, maximum consultation and notification is and will be the firm policy of this Administration.[203]

This new attitude and willingness to search for ways to establish a healthier working relationship with Congress was welcomed. However, the problem, as revealed in the Iran-Contra affair, involved more than just changing personnel. Bill Casey had been one of the President's most trusted confidants. Don Regan, until he crossed swords with the First Lady, had occupied a place of high regard with the President. And Oliver North and John Poindexter enjoyed the President's praise even after their evasions and cover-up activities had been exposed. The President is the person responsible for setting the standards of conduct he expects from his advisers and subordinates and for supervising their actions. His example and tone give meaning to his constitutional duty to see to the "faithful execution of the laws." A change in Presidential advisers without a change in Presidential attitude would be of little value. In this respect, the President's letter and the National Security Decision Directive (NSDD) that was later implemented do reflect a positive response to the results of the Committee's investigation.

And yet the letter and the NSDD in a key respect placed Congress in a less significant position than it had occupied before the Iran-Contra affair. Under existing law, the President is required to give notice to the House and Senate Intelligence Committees prior to the initiation of a covert action. If he deems it justified by the circumstances, the President can notify only eight congressional leaders instead of the full House and Senate Intelligence Committees. The eight (four of whom are Democrats and four Republicans) are the Speaker and Minority Leader of the House, the Majority and Minority Leaders of the Senate, and the chairmen and vice chairmen of the House and Senate Intelligence Committees.

If prior notice is not given, the President must notify Congress "in a timely fashion." Congress, in enacting this requirement in 1976, intended to provide the President with flexibility in the event it was impractical to notify Congress of a covert action. The phrase "in a timely fashion" contemplated a short time span, a matter of days at most. Yet this flexibility was construed by the Reagan Justice Department to give the President absolute discretion in withholding congressional notification. According to Assistant Attorney General Charles Cooper, notice could be withheld for days, weeks, or months. This interpretation of executive power makes a mockery of Congress's role in exercising its oversight responsibilities. Yet it is a position that President Reagan continued to assert in his letter and NSDD. Although the language employed is conciliatory in tone, it is unmistakable in purpose: the President reserved the right not to notify Congress in what he considered exceptional circumstances.

We had come full circle. The sale of weapons to Iran could be such an "exceptional circumstance." But now the President was seeking to formalize by letter and NSDD a constitutional power (to delay notice indefinitely) that Congress had never accepted.

We recognize, as the Iran-Contra report noted, that "Congress cannot legislate good judgment, honesty, or fidelity to the law."[204] But there are changes that can help make the congressional oversight process function better. On September 25, 1987, we introduced a bill, S. 1721 (the so-called Cohen-Boren bill), to incorporate many of the changes initiated by the administration, such as:

• Providing for the first time specific statutory authority for the President to institute covert actions in support of U.S. foreign-policy objectives.

• Requiring all findings to be in writing unless an emergency exists, in which case oral approval must be reduced to writing within forty-eight hours of a decision.

• Prohibiting retroactive findings.

• Prohibiting covert actions from violating any existing statutes.

• Requiring notice to the Intelligence Committees when third parties, not otherwise under the control of the United States, are to be used in any covert activities.

• Requiring that the Intelligence Committees be notified of a finding before any department or agency—not just the CIA—undertakes a covert activity.

This bill differs significantly from existing law and from the President's NSDD. The legislation continues the requirement that all covert actions must ordinarily be reported to the Intelligence Committees before they are undertaken. In rare circumstances, however, where there is insufficient time to notify the Congress, the bill permits the President to initiate such actions to protect U.S. interests, provided that he notify the Intelligence Committees or the congressional leadership in writing within forty-eight hours of his decision.

The administration withheld from the Congress notice of the finding authorizing the Iran arms sales for a period of ten months after it was signed. Indeed, notice obviously was provided only after the operation had been revealed in a Lebanese newspaper.

It is our view that, if the President has "unfettered discretion"[205] to determine when the Intelligence Committees will be notified of covert actions that have been initiated, the Committees' ability to oversee such activities on behalf of the Congress and the public would be fundamentally compromised. We believe the only alternative available to Congress is to drop the "timely fashion" language in favor of a specific time period. The forty-eight-hour period was chosen because it had previously been the period, informally agreed to by the CIA, in which the Intelligence Committees would be notified of presidential findings.

The administration has argued that an absolute requirement to notify Congress of covert actions within forty-eight hours of their initiation intrudes upon the exercise of the President's constitutional powers and prerogatives. Moreover, it contends, requiring such notice will jeopardize U.S. intelligence-gathering capability.

This is a curious argument for the administration to make. On the one hand, it maintains that it has advised the Intelligence Committees of every covert activity, other than Iran-Contra, initiated or continued during the past eight years. On the other, it asserts that legislating what is now practiced will spell the ruin of our intelligence service. Either the administration has not been advising Congress of every covert action, or our intelligence-gathering capability is in ruins, both of which the administration denies. The administration cannot have the argument both ways.

It is important to understand why we reject the administration's assertion that a fixed notification period is an unconstitutional infringement upon the Executive's powers.

First, the requirement is only to provide notice. Nothing in the bill prohibits the President from acting to protect U.S. interests as he sees fit; indeed, the bill explicitly recognizes this authority as stemming from the constitutional powers and prerogatives of the President. When there is not sufficient time to give Congress advance notice, the President may provide it after the fact, albeit within forty-eight hours.

Moreover, under existing law and under the bill, it is clear that, although notice is required, the approval of the Intelligence Committees (or the congressional leadership) is not required for the President to undertake and carry out a covert action. This means that even if the Committees were unanimously opposed to a particular covert action, the President would be free to go ahead with it if he believed it to be in the best interests of the United States. What the Committees are seeking, in the words of Clark Clifford, is "a voice, not a veto."

Congress shares responsibility with the Executive for covert actions. The Executive may conduct and direct the operations, but, under the Constitution and laws of the United States, it is the Legislative that must authorize and provide appropriations for such activities. The Constitution expressly provides that "No Money shall be drawn from the Treasury, but in consequence of Appropriations made by law." Further, it is made clear by statute that funds that have been appropriated by law may be expended only for purposes authorized by Congress. Covert actions require funding, and it is the Congress alone that must provide such funding. It is that simple.

Equally as compelling, however, is the fact that covert actions inevitably involve actions on the part of the United States that bear directly upon responsibilities given to Congress by the Constitution. For example:

• Congress alone has the authority to declare war. Covert actions sometimes involve the United States in secretly conducting or supporting armed hostilities against foreign governments, actions that could draw the United States into open hostilities. Such actions might also invite retaliatory measures by hostile foreign governments, either against the United States or its allies, also a possibility of which Congress ought to be aware.

• Congress is also charged by the Constitution "to raise and support Armies" and "to provide and maintain a Navy." Covert actions can adversely affect U.S. military strength and readiness. Congress needs to be aware of such possible consequences.

• Congress is solely invested by the Constitution with "all legislative powers," including the power to "make all Laws which
shall be necessary and proper for carrying into Execution the
foregoing powers, and all other powers vested by this Constitution
in the Government of the United States, or in any Department or
Officer thereof. . . . " Covert actions can undermine laws that
have been passed by Congress; this happened in the Iran-Contra
affair. Moreover, they can suggest the need for legislative restrictions, at least for some aspects of proposed or ongoing operations.
Congress, in fact, has occasionally imposed this kind of restrictions. But without knowledge of such operations, it cannot have
the opportunity to evaluate them.

• Notice to Congress is intended in part to provide the President
with independent advice. In a democracy, public policy is made
in public. It is the product of open, competitive debate. There
are two reasons for that. The first is that the American people
have a right to know what their government is doing and why.
The second is our belief that if all points of view are heard, especially opposing points of view, the person making the decision
is more likely to make the right decision, the decision that is in
the national interest.

Open debate is one of democracy's greatest strengths, its absence
one of the great weaknesses of totalitarian societies. When covert
action is necessary, there obviously cannot be an open debate.
That is a loss to the President, the decisionmaker, who is deprived
of the full range of opinion on an important issue. The law tries
to compensate for this to some extent. It requires the President
to notify some congressional leaders prior to initiating a covert
action. One reason is to give the President the benefit of different
points of view. The congressional leaders are elected independently
of the President. They are not subordinate to or dependent upon
him and are therefore more likely to give the President the frank
advice that any president needs in making these very difficult
decisions. It is significant that every person who advised President

Reagan on the Iran-Contra affair was subordinate to and dependent upon him. Only George Shultz and Caspar Weinberger had the courage and wisdom to speak out.

The concern about leaks is a real one. But it leads to a question of balance. How much benefit does the President get from the advice of independently elected congressional leaders? How much is the risk of leaks increased by their knowledge?

Apply that balance to the Iran arms sales. Many people in the Executive Branch of our government knew about the sales. Private American citizens, many without security clearances, knew. Some Israelis knew, among them government officials and private citizens. Some Iranian officials knew; some Canadians knew; at least one Saudi Arabian knew. And Ghorbanifar, described by the CIA as an unreliable liar, knew.

Are we to believe that telling eight of the most experienced elected officials in the United States Congress would increase the risk of disclosure? Against that, how much did the President lose when he was deprived of the independent advice of those eight officials?

Every person will make his or her own judgment on these questions. We are convinced that, if the President had told the congressional leaders of his intention to sell arms to Iran, to swap arms for hostages, to pursue a private policy that directly contradicted his public policy, at least some of them—maybe Lee Hamilton or Dick Cheney or Bob Dole or Bob Michel—would have said before the fact what the American people said after the fact: "Mr. President, we respect and admire your concern for the hostages, but it is a mistake to sell arms to Iran. It is a mistake to swap arms for hostages. Don't do it."

Constitutional and political arguments aside, the reality is that covert actions can have serious repercussions for the United States. As Clark Clifford testified:

> In the last year or so, we have witnessed the recurrence of an all too frequent problem: covert activities that get out of control and embar-

rass the nation and undermine our credibility and capability to exercise world leadership. . . . Moreover, the problem is getting worse, the costs are getting higher and the damage is getting greater. For this reason, I say that, unless we can control covert activities once and for all, we may wish to abandon them.[206]

Controlling covert actions, however, must start with knowledge on the part of the Congress. Without it there can be no check and no balance. Information concerning such activities is ordinarily confined to a relatively small number of officials within the Executive Branch. There is no debate in Congress on either funding or policy; no discussion in the press; no court of world opinion. Public awareness is usually nonexistent. The only check on covert actions outside the Executive Branch is the congressional Intelligence Committees, the members of which necessarily become the surrogates for their congressional colleagues, and for the American people. But they cannot perform this function without knowledge and awareness, and for this they are dependent upon the President.

Since the Intelligence Committees were established in 1976, every administration, including Reagan's, has, as a matter of practice, recognized the Committees' special role, and has cooperated to ensure that they are able to fulfill it.

There have been lives at risk in many of these covert operations. There have been substantial foreign-policy interests at risk. But this has not prevented the administration from notifying the Committees as required by law. Indeed, at their respective confirmation hearings, both the current Director and Deputy Director of the Central Intelligence Agency told the Senate Intelligence Committee that they could not imagine what circumstances would prevent them from notifying the Committees of a covert action. Robert Gates, during his confirmation hearings to be director of the CIA, stated: "I will recommend to the President against withholding prior notification under any circumstances, except the most extreme involving life and death, and then only for a few days, several days."[207] William Webster later commented: "I have trouble imagining any situation that is so sensitive and life-threatening that the Congress cannot be advised of it." When asked whether he would have the same answer if he had doubts about the ability of the Committee to keep the information secret, Judge Webster replied: "I have no doubts at the present time."[208]

Finally, we should note that S. 1721 contains a major concession to the President. It permits the President to limit notice of certain covert actions of extraordinary sensitivity. Under current law, as previously noted, the President can limit notice to the Intelligence Committee chairman and vice chairman in each house, the Majority and Minority Leaders of the Senate, and the Speaker and Minority Leader of the House. The bill gives him the further option, where he believes even this limited notice would pose a problem, to notify only the Majority and Minority Leaders of the Senate, and the Speaker and Minority Leader of the House. In short, he could withhold notice from the Intelligence Committees altogether while particularly sensitive operations were at risk, provided he keeps the elected leaders of the House and Senate advised. Thus S. 1721 provides an important option to the President that is not available under existing law.

At this writing, the fate of S. 1721 is unclear. On March 15, 1988, the Senate approved it with modifications by a vote of 71 to 19. The House of Representatives is expected to pass a similar bill. President Reagan has indicated he will veto the legislation. Even if it becomes law, we harbor no illusions that it will provide a permanent obstacle to future abuses. The struggle for control of policy and the President's ear will continue, as will the suspicions and personality conflicts that are at the core of the human experience. Law cannot legislate morality. The enactment of legislation does not guarantee adherence to its provisions. It can, however, set standards that lawmakers and the American people can reasonably expect to be observed.

The President vs.
the Congress

The President shall be Commander in Chief of the Army and Navy of the United States.

—Article II, Section 2, of the Constitution

The Congress shall have power . . . to declare war.

—Article I, Section 8, of the Constitution

On one level the Iran-Contra affair was a battle in the two-hundred-year-old war between the President and the Congress. Since the nation's founding, Americans have debated the respective powers of the Executive and Legislative Branches.

The men who wrote the Constitution had as a central purpose the prevention of tyranny. They tried to create a system of government in which no individual, no group, no institution could achieve total power. They succeeded brilliantly. The United States has had forty presidents and no kings.

They succeeded in part because they divided the central government into three separate, coequal branches among which they dispersed power. Each has served as a check on the others. None has become dominant.

Although the role of the Judiciary has occasionally captured the nation's attention, the focus of tension has been the relationship between the Executive and the Legislature. As the framers probably anticipated, power has ebbed and flowed between the two branches, depending upon political circumstances, especially the political success and standing of the President. Presidential power has reached its zenith under aggressive presidents who served in times of national crisis—Lincoln and Franklin Roosevelt. It has been at a low ebb under weak presidents in times of national calm—Harding and Coolidge, among others.

Although the Constitution distinguishes the power of the Executive Branch from that of the Legislative, it does not distinguish between domestic and foreign relations. Indeed, the words "foreign affairs" do not appear in the Constitution. Yet it is precisely in foreign affairs that the dispute between the President and the Congress has been the longest and the loudest.

The Constitution grants to the President only three powers that relate directly to foreign relations: he is designated commander in chief of the armed forces, with authority to direct those forces; he has the authority to negotiate treaties with other countries; and he may nominate ambassadors to other countries.

The Constitution grants to the Congress the power to declare war; the power to raise and support armed forces; and the power to regulate foreign commerce. The Senate is given the authority to ratify or reject treaties negotiated by the President and to confirm or reject ambassadors nominated by him. So the only power vested exclusively in the Executive is the power inherent in his designation as commander in chief of the armed forces.

The debate began early. Jefferson believed in the dominance of the Legislature (except, of course, when it interfered with his actions as president), arguing that the President possessed only those powers specifically granted him in the Constitution, all other power residing in the Congress. Hamilton argued the opposite. As was so often the case, Jefferson was right in theory but, as a matter of practice, Hamilton's view has largely prevailed.

The twentieth century has been marked by an expansion of the powers of the presidency that would have surprised and alarmed the men who wrote the Constitution. That expansion has not been unbroken; there have been stops and retreats along the way. But the trend is clear.

Representative Henry Hyde fostered that view in the hearings when he said, "The President is endowed with plenary and exclusive power as the sole organ of the federal government in the field of international relations."[209] But the President does not have "exclusive" power in foreign affairs: the Constitution makes that clear. And an analysis of the relatively few Supreme Court decisions on the subject confirms it.

Representative Hyde, as he acknowledged, was quoting from the Supreme Court case of *United States* v. *Curtiss-Wright Export Corporation* as support for his view of presidential power.[210] Similar views were expressed by Poindexter and North.

The *Curtiss-Wright* case involved a law enacted by Congress that delegated to President Franklin D. Roosevelt the authority to prohibit the shipment of arms to Bolivia and Paraguay if he decided that a prohibition would promote peace between those two countries. The President exercised that authority. Curtiss-Wright ignored his order and, when sued by the government, argued that the decision was legislative in nature and could not be delegated by Congress to the President.

The Supreme Court disagreed and, in 1936, upheld the right of Congress to delegate that authority to the President. The decision was written by Justice Sutherland. In it he made the following statement:

It is important to bear in mind that we are here dealing not alone with an authority vested in the President by an exertion of legislative power, but with such an authority plus the very delicate, plenary and exclusive power of the President as the sole organ of the federal government in the field of international relations—a power which does not require as a basis for its exercise an act of Congress, but which, of course, like every other governmental power, must be exercised in subordination to applicable provisions of the Constitution.[211]

That statement—in particular the words "plenary and exclusive power of the President as the sole organ of the federal government in the field of international relations"—has been cited repeatedly by those who contend that the President has exclusive power in foreign affairs.

But, as the Supreme Court itself later made clear, the words of the *Curtiss-Wright* decision must be confined to the facts of that case. That both the President and the Congress have a role in foreign affairs is clear in the statement from the opinion of now Chief Justice Rehnquist in the 1981 case of *Dames and Moore* v. *Regan*:

> When the President acts pursuant to an express or implied authorization from Congress, he exercises not only his powers but also those delegated by Congress. In such a case the executive action "would be supported by the strongest presumptions and widest latitude of judicial interpretation, and the burden of persuasion would rest heavily upon any who might attack it." . . . When the President acts in the absence of congressional authorization he may enter a "zone of twilight in which he and Congress may have concurrent authority, or in which its distribution is uncertain."
>
> . . . In such a case, the analysis becomes more complicated, and the validity of the President's action, at least so far as separation-of-powers principles are concerned, hinges on a consideration of all the circumstances which might shed light on the views of the Legislative Branch toward such action, including "congressional inertia, indifference or quiescence." . . .
>
> Finally, when the President acts in contravention of the will of Congress, "his power is at its lowest ebb" and the Court can sustain his actions "only by disabling the Congress from action on the subject."[212]

The most succinct expression of the view that power in foreign affairs is shared came from President Reagan himself. In 1983 he said, "The Congress shares both the power and the responsibility for our foreign policy."[213] Unfortunately, the President has made other statements to the contrary. So, in the President's words, and in the country, the debate continues. It will not be settled in our lifetimes, if ever.

There have been several thoughtful analyses of the Iran-Contra affair in the context of the struggle between the President and the Congress for control over the making of foreign policy. One, entitled "An Autopsy," written by Theodore Draper, appeared in *The New York Review of Books*.

After disputing the view (expressed by North and Poindexter, among others) that the President has sole authority to make foreign policy, Draper concluded:

> It is clear, then, that the Constitution does *not* charge the president with "making" foreign policy. It would be more nearly correct to say that the Constitution implicitly charges Congress with making and the president with executing foreign as well as domestic policy. Indeed, in foreign affairs the Constitution limits the president the most with respect to his ability to declare war. Presidents have made war without declaring it, but they have done so by pretending that they were waging something other than war.
>
> Nevertheless, so much has changed since the Constitution was written that a literal interpretation hardly conveys the present-day reality. The Constitution's very terseness on the subject of foreign affairs opened the way for practices and interpretations that have almost invariably benefited the enlargement of presidential prerogatives. The late constitutional scholar Edward S. Corwin asked where the Constitution vested authority to determine the course of American foreign policy. "Many persons are inclined to answer offhand 'in the President,' " he replied, "but they would be hard put to it, if challenged, to point out any definite statement to this effect in the Constitution itself." What the Constitution actually says, he observed, "is an invitation to struggle for the privilege of directing American foreign policy"—a conflict which presidents since George Washington have been winning. Presidents have used and abused their constitutional role of commander in chief to operate "on the very fringes of constitutionality (and arguably beyond that)," a recent study notes. Congress has rarely chosen or succeeded in sharing the responsibility for foreign policy with the President. Congress has in fact been largely craven in

the face of presidential initiatives and has stepped in only after some executive action has misfired or resulted in a debacle. Congressional actions in foreign affairs have usually been cleanup operations, such as these very hearings after the Iran-contra fiasco.[214]

Although the congressional investigation of the Iran-Contra affair was much more than a "cleanup operation," it surely was in part that. The most satisfying evidence that the cleanup worked was the statement issued on February 10, 1988, by Howard H. Baker, Jr., the White House Chief of Staff, and Lieutenant General Colin L. Powell, the President's National Security Adviser. Seven days earlier, the House of Representatives had rejected President Reagan's request for funding to provide additional military assistance to the Contras. A flurry of efforts quickly ensued, directed at raising money from private sources and other governments to keep the Contras alive as a fighting force. In a calm and reasoned manner, Baker and Powell ordered all administration personnel to refrain from participating in such activities. For a time, at least, the lesson had been learned.

Pardon Me

I n December 1986, during the Senate Intelligence Committee's initial inquiry into the Iran-Contra affair, White House officials suggested that the Committee offer to grant North and Poindexter immunity from criminal prosecution in exchange for their testimony. In spite of President Reagan's public request that his aides cooperate in disclosing facts to Congress and the country, both North and Poindexter chose to invoke their constitutional right not to incriminate themselves.

Serious consideration was never given to the White House suggestion. It was regarded as a disingenuous attempt to grant what would be tantamount to a "congressional pardon," which would have effectively terminated the independent counsel's investigation before it began. Several Committee members facetiously suggested that, if the White House wanted to discover the facts, the President should consider granting both men a pardon. We knew, of course, that, whatever the President's personal inclination, he was not prepared to accept the responsibility for such pre-emptive action. Intelligence Committee members were unaware at this time (as later revealed by *The Washington Post*) that North's attorney had already raised the subject of a pardon with some White House officials.

On March 16, 1988, a federal grand jury returned criminal indictments against Oliver North, John Poindexter, Richard Secord, and Albert Hakim. The twenty-three counts in the indictments included conspiracy to defraud the United States, theft of government property, obstruction of justice, wire fraud, false statements, and destruction and removal of documents. Five days earlier, on March 11, Robert McFarlane had pleaded guilty to four misdemeanor counts of withholding information from Congress. He asked that he be sentenced prior to the trials of any other defendants against whom the independent counsel would bring criminal charges.

After Independent Counsel Lawrence Walsh obtained the indictments, the question of presidential pardons surfaced again.

North quickly announced his resignation from the Marine Corps. He stated his resignation was prompted by the need to subpoena documents and testimony for his defense from his superiors, "the highest ranking officials in our government"—a challenge to higher authorities that would be incompatible with his military status. North's public statements, and his attorney's, contained the bold threat that President Reagan and Vice President Bush might be called to testify at North's trial. The implication was unmistakable—the President could avoid the spectacle by granting North (and presumably the other defendants, since they would be no less vigorous in their defense) a full pardon.

We are unable to divine what action, if any, President Reagan will take in this regard. It is clear from his reaction to the majority report that he did not share many, if any, of its conclusions. During the course of our hearings, when asked to comment on the testimony of various witnesses, President Reagan demurred. "Wait until the Committee completes its work," he said. "Then you won't be able to shut me up." But once the Committee filed its report, he maintained an angry reticence. "You wouldn't want to print what I have to say."

No one enjoys bad news. President Reagan is not immunized from a human reaction by the power of his office. He was clearly stung by the criticism in the report that he had failed to take care that the laws were faithfully executed. But, rather than accept the Committee's judgments, as he did with the Tower Board, he publicly stated that he could find no wrongdoing on the part of his aides.

Even after McFarlane's guilty plea, the President continued to refuse to condemn the violations of law or to acknowledge that laws had been violated. On the day the indictments were returned, he responded to a reporter's question, "I have no knowledge of anything that was broken." When asked about McFarlane's guilty plea, the President replied, "He just pleaded guilty to not telling Congress everything it wanted to know." He laughingly added, "I've done that myself."

A few days later the President went even further. He said, "I just have to believe that they're going to be found innocent because I don't think they were guilty of any lawbreaking or any crime."

A public campaign is underway to encourage the President to grant full pardons to those under indictment for their actions in the Iran-Contra affair. Some members of Congress have reportedly spoken of it directly to the President. He is said to have responded that he "liked the sound of those words." The Reverend Jerry Falwell has announced his intention of collecting two million petition signatures urging the President to grant a pardon.

Over 150 years ago, the greatest Chief Justice in the history of the United States, John Marshall, defined the President's power to grant a pardon as the power to "exempt the individual" upon whom the pardon is conferred "from the punishment the law inflicts for a crime he has committed."215

A pardon is an act of "forgiveness."216 Indeed, the acceptance of a pardon generally is considered to be an admission of guilt or of the existence of facts from which a judgment of guilt would follow.217

Until now, the Reagan administration has shared this common understanding of the pardon power. In 1983 the Department of Justice revised the regulations governing the procedure used in pardon cases. These new regulations state that a petition for pardon should not be filed any earlier than five years *after conviction*, seven years in cases involving "serious" crimes such as "fraud involving substantial sums of money."[218] The 1983 Reagan administration pardon regulations are more stringent than those in force under prior administrations.

It would be a mockery for the administration, after adopting stricter regulations for pardons of ordinary citizens—permitting *only* those already convicted of crimes and then only *after* a substantial waiting period to petition for a pardon—to consider pretrial pardons for those who worked in or closely with the White House.

The presidential pardon power was granted to the Chief Executive in the Constitution as an element of the grant of authority exercised by contemporaneous heads of state, most of whom were hereditary monarchs. It was seen then as an "act of grace"— typically the executive's *personal* act of mercy to an individual to reduce or eliminate the punishment imposed after trial and sentencing.

In *The Federalist Papers*, Alexander Hamilton wrote of the pardon power that it should be entrusted to a single person rather than to a legislative body to mitigate criminal law, which, he wrote, "partakes so much of necessary severity that without an easy access to exceptions in favor of *unfortunate* guilt, justice would wear a countenance too sanguinary and cruel [emphasis added]."[219]

But in discussing the use of the pardon power for cases of treason and insurrection, he cautioned that while "there are often critical moments when a well-timed offer of pardon . . . may restore the tranquillity of the commonwealth" advance notice of such an intent could "hold out the prospect of impunity."[220] The grant of pretrial pardons, however, would establish the precedent that a future president's advisers may act outside the law, indeed, even break the law with impunity.

The granting of pretrial pardons would have the lasting effect of creating a dual standard of justice that places presidential advisers above the law. Such a double standard of justice would be a graphic demonstration to all Americans that the promise of equality before the law is illusory. The strength of our system of government and the respect the judicial system enjoys derive from the fact that we all stand equal before the law; that no one, not even the President, is beyond the reach of our law.

The calls for immediate pardons are partly premised on an assertion that these defendants did nothing criminal. But that is an issue for a judge and a jury to decide.

We disagree with those who would short-circuit the truthfinding processes of our judicial system to embrace not merely the presumption of innocence to which every defendant is entitled, but an unappealable declaration of innocence in the face of indictment and before a jury has acted. There simply is no justification, when an indictment has been issued, to allow those who served close to a president to avoid the judicial process. Neither the aides of powerful figures nor powerful figures themselves should be immune to a judicial determination of guilt or innocence.

As members of the Senate Select Committee that investigated the Iran-Contra affair, we have a firsthand appreciation of how complicated these cases will be. Our job, of course, was not to draw conclusions about whether criminal liability was attached to the actions of the individuals named in the pending indictment. But no one who has reviewed the facts in detail could responsibly say that these defendants can or should be excused from culpability at this early stage.

The President himself is plainly of two minds about the facts in this case. On the one hand, he has said he didn't know what actually happened. On the other hand, he has said that North and Poindexter did nothing wrong. The President's ambivalence underscores the very reason that the task of deciding the guilt or innocence of these defendants must be left to the courts. Neither the President nor anyone else outside the criminal-justice system knows what evidence exists to support the charges in the indictments. The independent counsel's investigation is separate from the congressional investigation. The facts uncovered at the congressional hearings are not all of the facts in these cases. Indeed, it is apparent simply from reading the indictments that the independent counsel has gained access to witnesses and documents that were not available to the congressional committees. That being the case, it is particularly inappropriate for anyone, including the President, to reach a conclusion about the innocence or guilt of these defendants until all of the evidence is presented at trial.

These defendants, like all defendants in criminal cases, are entitled to the presumption of innocence. Indeed, in such highly publicized cases, we all have a special obligation to accord them that presumption. But a presumption of innocence is not the same as a pretrial conclusion of innocence.

Rarely if ever has a president been asked to grant a pardon for acts arising out of events in which he personally was involved. President Reagan, of course, was deeply involved in the Iran-Contra affair. North's statement, upon his retirement from the Marine Corps, that he would call as witnesses in his trial the "highest officials of government" was a not-very-subtle message to the President that if he, President Reagan, does not want to testify at a trial, he had better prevent a trial by pardoning North and Poindexter. But were Reagan to do so, it would be seen inevitably as an effort by the President to spare himself the awkwardness of having to testify and to purchase the silence of North and Poindexter for fear of what they might say at a trial.

If these cases go to trial and if those under indictment are convicted of having violated the law, the issue of a presidential pardon will intensify. Pardons, if granted, conceivably could come in the twilight of the Reagan presidency, when the constitutional remedy, electoral disapproval, would be moot. But the potential damage to the integrity of the rule of law could linger for years.

Conservative columnist and author William Safire, once a speech writer for President Nixon, offers a word of caution to those who believe that such pardons are moral imperatives. He suggests that those who support the Contras and identify with North should be wary of pardons. Suppose that one day a liberal president stacks the National Security Council staff with détentists who share their

President's zeal for peace, asks Safire. What if they should engage in the covert transfer of our Star Wars technology to the Soviets in a misguided effort to achieve an arms-control breakthrough? Suppose that the National Security Adviser orders the transfer without seeking the express approval of the President, so that the latter may enjoy plausible deniability? Would such a future president be warranted, the precedent having been set, in granting pardons to those who truly believed that they were simply carrying out the goals of their President?

Safire maintains:

> My conservative colleagues would howl: Yalta betrayal! Usurpation of the powers of Congress! Pinko takeover of the Presidency! They would be right, but they would not have a leg to stand on. The coup that goes unpunished leads to more coups that cannot be punished.[221]

Safire, in a rhetorical flourish, rallied his fellow conservatives to resist the notion that it is divine to forgive the noble but unauthorized acts of the unelected.

> What the President did in going soft and appeasing the Iranian terrorists was stupid, and he has rightly suffered for it; what his agents did in diverting the profits, if criminal, must not go unpunished or we will all suffer for it.
>
> Think about the consequences of going soft again. Do not invite the next crowd to stage a similar coup with impunity.[222]

We agree.

Reagan Redux

T he President stood tall and erect, elegant in a black over-
coat and white silk scarf. In a spectacular scene, on a cool,
overcast day, thousands of dignitaries stood on the South
Lawn of the White House as an American military band played
the national anthem in a measured, stately beat.

But it was not "The Star-Spangled Banner" that was being
played; it was the national anthem of the Union of Soviet Socialist
Republics. And standing next to Ronald Reagan was the General
Secretary of the Communist Party of the Soviet Union, Mikhail
Gorbachev.

The date was December 8, 1987, the opening ceremony of the
Washington summit meeting between the President and the General Secretary. The meeting featured the formal signing of a treaty
in which the superpowers agreed to destroy all of the land-based
intermediate-range nuclear missiles in their arsenals. It was a political and personal triumph for the President, providing him a
respite from the avalanche of bad news that had begun thirteen
months earlier.

The crisis of the previous year had passed. So, too, had the
virulent anti-Soviet rhetoric that fueled Reagan's rise to the presidency and sustained him during his first term. Now Ronald Reagan stood firmly at attention as the Soviet national anthem echoed
off the southern face of the White House.

Some conservatives, bitter and disillusioned, charged that the
very weakness of his presidency at home impelled Reagan to rush

302

into an ill-considered treaty with adversaries he had spent his political lifetime denouncing as liars and cheats, never to be trusted. Whatever the validity of their views on the treaty, the conservatives may have been correct in their assessment of the President's motives for entering into the treaty. In the baffling, unpredictable way in which human history is made, Ronald Reagan's fall inexorably led him to reach for a rope with which he could pull himself to safety—a successful meeting with the Soviet leader featuring a nuclear-arms-control agreement. There were, surely, other motives as well. But the President's urge for arms control may not have been sufficient, on its own, absent his need for political redemption, to produce the treaty. So, in its own way, the disaster that came to be known as the Iran-Contra affair had contributed to at least one important beneficial result.

We reject any suggestion, however, that Ronald Reagan would jeopardize our nation's security just to rescue the remainder of his presidency. Mikhail Gorbachev saw in Reagan's difficulties an opportunity to shore up his own leadership credentials. He knew that a failure to deal with Reagan meant he would have to wait until after the 1988 American elections before he could even hope to reach some accord on reducing nuclear weapons. In all likelihood, a new agreement could not be achieved until 1990 or beyond. Gorbachev's efforts in promoting *glasnost* (openness) and *perestroika* (restructuring) had generated criticism and opposition in the Soviet Union. He, too, needed some tangible sign of success, a substantive—or even symbolic—achievement that would demonstrate to his countrymen that his leadership was worthy of continued support.

Gorbachev reinforced his own leadership by helping to revive President Reagan's. The concessions made were not one-sided. Reagan dropped his insistence that an INF agreement include the resolution of human-rights issues, violations of existing treaties, and the removal of Soviet troops from Afghanistan. Gorbachev agreed to the terms originally proposed by Reagan in 1981 (the so-called zero-zero option), to remove all U.S. and Soviet intermediate-range nuclear weapons from or targeted against NATO countries, consented to on-site inspection measures, and dropped his insistence that the INF treaty include a termination of President Reagan's Strategic Defense Initiative.

It was a valuable lesson on the many paradoxes involved in the possession and exercise of power. When leaders of militarily powerful nations are politically strong and secure, conventional wisdom holds that they are in the best position to negotiate with their adversaries: mutual strength provides the basis for mutual concessions. But at the Washington summit we bore witness to the corollary that, when superpower leaders must both bolster their respective positions, such mutually shared need can also provide the basis for an equitable treaty.

As we stood side by side on the White House lawn, shifting our feet in a futile effort to ward off the cold, we were also reminded of how quickly the tide turns in American politics and how resilient are the powers of the presidency. We were truly gratified to see President Reagan confidently standing next to the vigorous Soviet leader at the Washington summit and plan for another summit, in Moscow, the following June. We did not, however, want the celebratory mood of this very important event to sweep into oblivion the painful lessons of another.

Conclusions

Walter Lippmann reminds us that a central function of democracy is to allow a free people to drag realities out into the sunlight and demand a full accounting from those who are permitted to hold and exercise power. Congress provides a forum for disclosing the hidden aspects of governmental conduct. But, as the Iran-Contra investigation revealed, in exercising its oversight responsibilities, Congress remains accountable for its own flaws and deficiencies as well.

The congressional hearings provided the American people with a number of lessons. It is unlikely that we will avoid repeating past mistakes or avoid committing new ones. Future congressional investigations of Executive Branch abuses undoubtedly will occur. But we hope that such investigations can profit from what we learned on the Iran-Contra Committee.[223]

First: The intensity of partisanship in the House of Representatives, not likely to diminish in the near future, makes joint hearings undesirable. Committees of each house better reflect the strengths of their institutions. If, as in the case of the Iran-Contra investigation, eliminating duplication is imperative, a single joint committee of manageable size, no more than eleven members, should be formed to carry out a major investigation.

Second: Congress must not seek to exploit for political advantage the Executive's mistakes or improprieties it is investigating. In asserting its responsibility to help shape foreign policy, Congress must recognize its institutional limitations as well. Moreover, it must demonstrate as clear a willingness to discipline the errant actions of its own members as it does in condemning those in the Executive Branch. The American people will not place trust in those who hurl bricks from houses of glass.

Third: Congress must guard against attempts by witnesses or their attorneys to seize control of or manipulate the proceedings. Witnesses should not be accorded special deference because they are heroic, glamorous, or espousing what they believe to be a patriotic cause. Attorneys should be restricted to providing legal advice to their clients. Constant interruptions and expressions of contempt for the proceedings should not be permitted. If attorneys are allowed to berate Congress's counsel, to instruct members when their time for questioning has expired, and to use other such tactics, the integrity of the investigative process will be undermined.

Fourth: Setting fixed deadlines for the completion of congressional investigations should be avoided. But such decisions are often dictated by political circumstances and the need to avoid the appearance of partisanship. In this case a compromise was struck between those who believed an adequate investigation could be completed within two or three months and those who believed no time limitation was necessary. We hope that in future cases such an artificial restraint on the pursuit of the facts will not be necessary.

Fifth: Congress should recognize that, as long as it investigates activities that involve allegations of criminal wrongdoing, it will be entwined in continuing tensions with the Justice Department or an independent counsel. The Iran-Contra Committee could have granted Oliver North immunity at the inception of its investigation as some had advocated. That would have allowed the Committee to take North's private testimony by deposition and to schedule him as one of the very first witnesses. Had the Committee done so, however, it would have effectively precluded the independent counsel's investigation. Moreover, an early grant of immunity, before the Committee itself had conducted any investigation, would have rendered the Committee incapable of evaluating the truth or falsity of North's testimony. Without the testimony of other witnesses, without possession of relevant documents, the Committee would have had no background against which to test North's credibility.

The Committee also might have acceded to the independent counsel's request not to grant immunity until after he had determined whether North had committed an indictable offense. Such deference might, as events have demonstrated, have extended our hearings well beyond President Reagan's term of office. The Committee compromised. Whether it was unwise and unproductive to do so remains a debatable question.

By deferring its grant of immunity to North for a reasonable period, the Committee altered the timing of North's testimony and the degree of his cooperation. It may have been a mistake to do so—or to have failed to call his and Brendan Sullivan's bluff on North's refusal to provide a prehearing deposition—but the fact remains that North's testimony was crucial, if only because he disclosed the existence of the so-called off-the-shelf covert capability that is so inimicable to our concept of democracy.

Future congressional investigatory committees will be faced with similar choices for which there are no fixed rules.

Sixth: Congress must take into account the power of television and yet resist (as the Committee did) the pressure to conform its behavior to television's demands.

The Committee rejected the temptation to call witnesses likely to be sensational but lack credibility; did not force witnesses who invoked their rights under the Fifth Amendment to do so before the cameras in an effort to embarrass them or suggest something was being hidden; and followed its established procedures even as it realized that some of the witnesses and their counsel were using television in a manner that placed us on the defensive. Indulging in provocative techniques might have enhanced the theatrical appeal of the hearings, but it would have trivialized the Committee's responsibilities in the process.

The role of Congress is to inform, not entertain. And television is a powerful and useful tool in serving this end as well. As the Committee struggled to, in Lippmann's terms, drag realities into sunlight, the sunlight was all the brighter through the medium of television. The short-term advantage yielded to those who would exploit the medium was in the end worth it. Television enabled the American people to judge for themselves.

More significant than how we investigated was *what* we investigated, and the lessons to be learned from it. Prior to the Committee's hearings, the sale of weapons to Iran had been described as an act of folly and the diversion of profits to the Contras an abberational by-product of President Reagan's loose management style.

The facts that emerged from our investigation revealed a more complicated set of circumstances and an insidious chain of events. The sale of weapons to Iran was confirmed to be a foreign-policy fiasco. But the establishment of a secret, off-the-shelf capability to fund and carry out future covert activities was a calculated deceit of immense consequences to our democratic form of government. Activities might be undertaken with or without the President's knowledge, yet surely without the knowledge and consent of Congress. The selective use of "nonappropriated" funds to carry out undisclosed activities struck at the very core of government accountability, one of the fundamental tenets of the Constitution.

The use of private citizens, who stood to make millions of dollars, to carry out the traditional functions of government officials and agencies, revealed how easily greed and cupidity can corrupt government policies—especially those that are covert and undisclosed, where oversight is either minimal or nonexistent.

The Reagan administration protested that it was largely unaware of how funds were being generated and weapons delivered to hold Nicaraguan Contras together "body and soul." The hearings revealed that, on the contrary, the administration had set out to circumvent the Boland Amendments with every artifice it could conceive.

Finally, when the covert activity in selling arms to Iran and raising funds for the Contras could no longer be contained, we bore witness to a plan of deceit and misrepresentation that, if carried out, might have unraveled Ronald Reagan's presidency.

There is no doubt that President Reagan was motivated by a sincere desire to free our hostages in Lebanon. More than any other factor, particularly that of establishing an improved relationship with Iran, this desire became the driving force behind the arms sales to Iran. The nobility of one's motives, however, cannot obscure the folly of one's actions. To carry out a highly complex mission of dealing with unidentifiable elements in Iran, the President turned to a private, amateur network of international operatives. In so doing, he displaced the institutional mechanisms designed to provide checks and balances against rash and impetuous conduct. These foreign-policy free-lancers drew a nooselike circle of suspicion and secrecy around the White House. While carrying out one misguided initiative, they conceived another— the diversion of profits to the Nicaraguan Contras, a separate covert program that was of equal importance to the President. In the name of national security, lies were permitted to masquerade as truths before Cabinet officials, congressional committees, and ultimately before the American people.

In the final analysis, the Iran-Contra affair remains a story about power—who has it, in what measure and how it is to be exercised. The Founding Fathers decided that power necessarily had to be "entrusted to someone, but that no one could be trusted with power." History and experience taught them that power unchecked led to its arrogant use and inevitable abuse, and so they diffused it deliberately and set up institutional checks and balances.

Certainly we need people who can take action and cut through red tape. But the fact is that speed of action was never the absolute goal of democracy. A king will always be faster than a congress-man.

The Founding Fathers decided that in a democracy, public policy should be determined through debate, deliberation, discussion, and even dissent, so that the leaders might at least have the opportunity to act wisely, rather than simply quickly and passionately.

The Constitution defines the distribution of powers in broad language. Structures that are too rigid tend to crack under pressure. In avoiding rigidity, the architects of our nation recognized the need to provide a young and dynamic country with enough flexibility so that it could absorb the turbulence produced by the dynamic flow of ideas and interests among a free people. But it does not follow that powers that are not defined with specificity have no identifiable limits.

A central lesson of the Iran-Contra affair is that, though Congress and the Executive may debate and disagree, neither can afford to deceive the other. Congress must accept the limits of its role in formulating foreign policy and the need to restrain and discipline those members who would exceed it. The Executive, in turn, cannot seek to achieve by deception what it cannot accomplish by persuasion.

We think it is clear that, in deciding to include arms as a part of the package to obtain release of the hostages, the President made a serious mistake. But we also think it is clear that the American people did not want to see President Reagan pilloried or politically paralyzed for being human. They wanted, and deserved, an acknowledgment of the truth.

During the hearings a great deal was said about the strategic location of Iran and Nicaragua. No one can dispute the geographic importance of either nation. But we suggest that the most important piece of real estate in the world is not found in the Persian Gulf or in Central America, but in the sixteen blocks that run from the White House to Capitol Hill. Those who visit our nation's capital often express surprise upon seeing the steel-and-stone barricades that surround the White House and the Capitol. These barricades provide safeguards for the President and members of Congress against terrorists and serve to remind us of the dangerous times in which we all live. But they are also symbolic of another kind of warfare that threatens us. For too long the President and Congress have been engaged in constructing an imaginary Maginot Line across Constitution Avenue. It has come at an infinite cost to our national interest. If we continue to lie to each other, or withhold information, or leak information, alter or shred documents, or put them in burn bags, if we continue to interrupt the flow of truth and trust across the sixteen blocks that separate us, then the loss of Persian Gulf oil or Central America to communist forces will be irrelevant, because we will have entered into a permanent state of guerrilla warfare, and the damage that we will inflict upon ourselves would be as suicidal and destructive as any that has taken place in the Middle East.

Somewhere between lives and lies, between compliance with and defiance of the law, there is a place for the truth, for national security, and for the bipartisan formulation of foreign policy.

Twice in the past fifteen years our government has been virtually paralyzed because rules were stretched, laws broken, and policies twisted in an effort to avoid complying with restrictions thought by presidents to be either unwise or unconstitutional. Congress responded to revelations of Executive Branch wrongdoing by turning up the temperature, trying to determine whether synthetic stories were being foisted upon the American people in the name of national security. The struggle for power between the Executive and Legislative Branches is destined to continue. But that struggle, inherent in a system of calculated checks and balances, must be waged in a spirit of good faith, one that recognizes that the responsibilities of each require mutual accommodation, and sometimes compromise. We need not hold in our hands the bright breakage of truths too late. We know the principle.

NOTES

Introduction

1. The Tower Board (formally The President's Special Review Board), established by President Reagan on December 1, 1986, named after its Chairman, John Tower, formerly a Republican senator from Texas. The other members were Edmund Muskie, formerly Secretary of State and a Democratic senator from Maine, and Brent Scowcroft, who had been National Security Adviser to President Ford. The Tower Board issued its report on February 26, 1987.

2. The independent counsel, appointed by a panel of three federal judges, is Lawrence Walsh, himself a former federal judge and Deputy Attorney General in the Eisenhower administration.

PART I

3. *Olmstead* v. *United States*, 277 U.S. 438 (1928) (Brandeis dissenting), p. 479.

Here Come the Judges

4. Liman immediately brought in one of his partners, Mark Belnick, an extremely capable lawyer who possesses a remarkable capacity for digesting and organizing voluminous amounts of information. Liman designated Belnick as his executive assistant. Paul Barbadoro, whom Liman named deputy chief counsel, had served in the New Hampshire Attorney General's office and later as Senator Rudman's counsel to the Senate Governmental Affairs Permanent Subcommittee on Investigations. He is a superlative trial attorney whose youthful good looks and low-key manner belie both his experience and his tough-mindedness.

Inouye and Rudman decided that each senator should have the right to appoint one attorney to the Committee staff. This was an egalitarian gesture on their part, one designed to assure Committee members that the investigation was not going to be a two-man show organized and structured to run over and flatten

313

out the philosophies or political leanings of the individual senators. The decision could have proved disastrous. Senators received dozens of applications (and phone calls in support of them) for each position, once it became known that Committee members would have this prerogative. The appointees selected might have been either inferior or have been responsive exclusively to the senators who appointed them instead of for the Committee as a whole. Fortunately, with very few exceptions, the associate counsels proved to be extraordinarily talented and dedicated, with backgrounds ranging from experienced civil and criminal litigators—including partners from reputable law firms and respected federal and state prosecutors—to senior congressional staffers. These associate counsels worked for the full Committee and formed the core of its staff.

Five younger lawyers served as assistant counsels, each participating in virtually all phases of the investigation. Finally, a University of Texas law professor with prior national security experience was hired as legal counsel to the Committee.

The Committee's investigators came from backgrounds even more varied than the associate counsels. Two of the Senate investigators were former FBI agents, who were regarded as skillful interrogators.

Tom Polgar, Sr., a former CIA station chief with key assignments in Vietnam, West Germany, and Mexico, was one of the most controversial members of the investigative team and one of its most important. Rudman had personally recommended Polgar and vouched for his integrity and professionalism. But when members of the Washington press corps learned of his selection, they suspected the CIA had an agent in place, one who would expertly seal off any doors that might open into improper CIA activity.

We rejected the criticism, believing that only a person who had served with the CIA would begin to understand its operating procedures and techniques and be sensitive to nuances and subtleties that indicated irregularities and deviations. We also knew that investigative reporters were wired into contacts inside the intelligence community who would press an alert button if they saw Polgar or anyone else trying to brush away CIA footprints from the scandal.

The Committee's judgment proved correct. While Polgar remained respectful of the Agency he once served, he was not a blind loyalist. He was deeply troubled by the lack of professionalism that contributed to the CIA support role, in both the sale of weapons to Iran and the aid provided to the Contras. His expertise led directly to the discovery of a number of irregularities in intelligence reporting and a missing CIA cable.

The Senate Committee also had access to a full complement of auditors from the General Accounting Office. Armed with a bank of computers, they spent weeks crunching numbers and tracing the labyrinthian financial transactions among the various shell corporations designed to obscure the origin and destination of money that flowed to and from the Hakim-Secord Enterprise and from domestic private sources to the Contras. They were also instrumental in helping Mark Belnick in locating the missing $10 million contribution given by the Sultan of Brunei, and with the assistance of the FBI investigators traced the traveler's checks that Contra leader Adolfo Calero had given to North.

Each senator on the Committee also had one or more "designated liaison staffers" to help prepare him for the hearings and keep him informed of developments in the investigation. These were individuals who served in senior positions on the senator's personal staff or on one of his committees who, because of their close association with the senators, would focus on specific areas of interest and closely follow the public and private proceedings throughout. These liaisons also participated actively in the preparation of the Committee report.

A House Divided

5. The "cloture rule" in the Senate is technically Paragraph 2 of Rule XXII of the Standing Rules of the Senate. Absent unanimous consent, under normal circumstances in the Senate, ending debate and bringing an issue to a vote when even one senator still wishes to continue debating requires a three-fifths vote of the Senate membership (sixty votes). The procedure for cloture requires that a special petition signed by sixteen senators be filed, and even then, a vote on the cloture motion will not occur until two days later. (All rules in the Senate are subject to, and often are, modified by unanimous consent.) Even if cloture is then invoked, however, there is a whole range of parliamentary maneuvers that can result in what have come to be called "post-cloture filibusters." Even though in 1979 the Senate placed an overall one-hundred-hour cap on debate after cloture has been voted, and in 1986 the Senate reduced the cap to thirty hours, the whole process is still so time-consuming and is sufficiently burdensome that, except in the most intractable of cases, some degree of compromise with adversaries is by far the more productive course for getting things done in the Senate. In fact, more often than not, the mere threat of filibuster is enough to bring the parties to the table to discuss working out an accommodation.

Another important aspect of cloture is that it imposes a "germaneness" rule on consideration of the matter before the Senate. Under normal circumstances, there are no restrictions on the subject of amendments that are offered to legislation in the Senate. This can make the consideration of issues very disorderly and confusing and sometimes a "rider," on a different subject, can be added to a bill, which makes its passage much more difficult. After cloture is invoked on a bill, however, only amendments that are germane—that deal with the same subject matter—are in order.

Deadline Blues and Designated Hitters

6. The Senate Resolution (S. Res. 23) establishing the Select Committee, passed by the Senate on January 6, 1987, in Section 9(a)(1), set the deadline for the Committee's report as August 1, 1987, with special expedited procedures for an extension to October 30, 1987. This extension (and another short one granted by the Senate) proved necessary. The report was filed in the Senate on November 17, 1987. (Rules of Procedure of the Select Committee on Secret Military Assistance to Iran and the Nicaraguan Opposition [Washington, D. C.: Government Printing Office, 1987, p. 19].)

7. The schedule called for the hearings to be divided into two segments. Phase One would be devoted to exploring sources and methods used by the administration to raise and funnel money and arms to Nicaraguan resistance forces; matching administration activities with the various congressional actions to restrict or prohibit such aid (Boland Amendments); determining what legal basis existed to support the sale of weapons to Iran and to provide military and financial assistance to the Contras; tracing the origins of the sale of weapons to Iran and the actions taken pursuant to presidential directives; following the trail of money that had been generated by the arms sales to Iran to determine exactly how much had been "diverted" to the Contras and what disposition had been made of the remaining amounts; and discovering what actions administration officials engaged in to conceal both the sale of weapons to Iran and aid to the Contras after the operation had been exposed.

Each of the witnesses selected to testify in Phase One was believed to possess information and/or documents pertaining to the Committee's areas of interest. Their depositions (private, prehearing examinations under oath) would reveal in advance whether they could in fact contribute to a full explanation of the events under examination. The witnesses were allocated between the two Committees. For example, North was designated a "House witness," giving House Committee members and staff the lead responsibility for examining him both in private and during the public hearings. Admiral Poindexter was a "Senate witness." At the end of approximately five weeks, the Committee would recess for two weeks in order to digest and assess the information acquired during Phase One and use that time to prepare for the most critical part of our investigation, Phase Two.

Phase Two was reserved for the top officials in the Reagan administration and those who we knew would be the chief targets of the independent counsel's investigation into possible criminal activities.

Prosecutors or Potted Plants?

8. The Committee staff (at one time numbering as many as seventy) was handicapped in several important respects.

First, the Committee never had access to adequate numbers of stenographers with top-secret security clearance to take or transcribe depositions. Throughout July, depositions were canceled or delayed because of the inability to locate a reporter with the proper clearances. The House Committee, which had its own set of cleared reporters, grew more and more resistant to the Senate's request to use their reporters and ultimately rejected our requests altogether.

By the beginning of August, the taking of classified depositions was at an absolute gridlock. This dearth of official reporters had a significant impact upon the investigation. At the completion of the public hearings in August, our staff was preparing to complete depositions of several important witnesses. Their efforts had to be terminated. With respect to the CIA alone, at least a dozen depositions remained incomplete or were cancelled.

Another fact of the deposition gridlock was that depositions were not transcribed for, in some instances, months after the testimony was taken. Unless the questioner took impeccable notes, therefore, he or she had to rely on memory to resurrect the deposition. In some instances, the depositions were barely transcribed in time to be used and cited in the Committees' report.

Up the White House Ladder

9. The basic purpose of the independent-counsel law, initially passed in 1978, is to promote public confidence in the impartial investigation of alleged criminal wrongdoing by high-ranking Executive Branch officials.

The independent-counsel (formerly called "special prosecutor") provisions of the Ethics in Government Act were a direct product of the upheaval and controversy associated with the so-called Saturday Night Massacre, in which President Nixon directed the Department of Justice to fire Archibald Cox, the special prosecutor who had been appointed by then Attorney General Elliot Richardson to investigate allegations of criminal misconduct by Nixon-administration officials.

The charter governing Mr. Cox's appointment provided that the Attorney General would not interfere with Mr. Cox's decisionmaking. Despite this assurance of independence, an order to fire Mr. Cox arose from his refusal to obey earlier presidential directives that he halt his efforts to obtain access to presidential materials for his investigation. After Attorney General Richardson and Deputy Attorney General William Ruckelshaus resigned rather than fire Mr. Cox, then Solicitor General Robert Bork issued the desired order.

Prompted by these events, the Congress concluded that a statutory process was necessary to guard against the conflict of interest that exists when the President calls upon his Attorney General to investigate alleged criminal activities by members of his or her own administration. After lengthy debate, the Congress decided upon a system of temporary, outside counsels appointed by a special court and removable by the President only for good cause.

In adopting the independent-counsel system, the Congress recognized that the dangers of conflict of interest were not unique to Watergate, but are inherent in our system of government. The Attorney General is an appointee of the President, at times a close friend and adviser to the President, and part of a political party that aspires to re-election. Thus an attorney general may be placed in a difficult situation when called upon to investigate allegations against senior administration officials.

Even when an attorney general makes unbiased decisions in investigating officials, the public may perceive actions as having political motivations. As former Prosecutor Archibald Cox testified before the Senate Judiciary Committee in 1975: "The pressure, the divided loyalty, are too much for any man, and as honorable and conscientious as any individual might be, the public could never feel entirely easy about the vigor and thoroughness with which the invesitagation was pursued. Some outside person is absolutely essential."

Ironically, there is also a danger that, in other cases, an attorney general may bend over backward to prosecute a high-ranking official if he or she believes that the public will be critical of a decision not to go forward with an investigation.

In these cases, justice would not be served by having the Attorney General conduct the investigation, either, for his doing so could result in a stricter, harsher application of criminal law against government officials.

A fundamental tenet of our democratic system is that all citizens be treated equally and fairly under the law. No one is so powerful or privileged as to be above the law, no one so poor in stature or means as to fall below it. In cases where conflicts of interest exist, or where the public perceives there to be such conflicts, public confidence in the prosecutorial decisions, as well as in our basic system of government, can be eroded, if not totally lost. The independent-counsel process promotes public confidence by taking these cases, in very limited situations, outside the Department of Justice and giving them to a prosecutor who is not beholden to the administration under investigation. In this way, we are able to assure the public that its officials are being investigated fully and fairly, and that no person, no matter how close to the President, is above the law. (On January 22, 1988, the Federal Appeals Court in the District of Columbia, by a two-to-one decision, declared the independent-counsel law unconstitutional. "The act as a whole, taking into account its appointment, removal and supervisory provisions, so deeply invades the president's executive prerogatives and responsibilities and so jeopardizes individual liberty as to be unconstitutional," stated the majority opinion, written by Judge Laurence Silberman.

On June 29, 1988, the Supreme Court ruled 7–1 to reverse the Appeals Court and uphold the constitutionality of the independent counsel.

10. One year to the day later, Robert McFarlane pleaded guilty to four counts of withholding information from Congress. Five days later, on March 16, 1988, a twenty-three-count indictment was returned against Oliver North, John Poindexter, Albert Hakim, and Richard Secord. On June 16, 1988, U.S. District Court Judge Gerhard A. Gesell ruled that "The great bulk of evidence was clearly known to [Walsh] before any defendant received use immunity" and that ". . . there is strong indication that the decision to indict was in no respect tainted."

Déjà Vu—All Over Again?

11. Hearings Before the Select Committee on Presidential Campaign Activities—Testimony of John Dean, p. 984.

12. U.S. Constitution, Article II, Section 4, states: "The President, Vice-President and all civil officers of the United States shall be removed from office on impeachment for, and conviction of treason, bribery, or other high crimes and misdemeanors."

13. Report of the Committee of the Judiciary, House of Representatives, on the Impeachment of Richard M. Nixon, President of the United States, August 20, 1974, p. 7.

14. Charles L. Black, Jr., *Impeachment: A Handbook* (New Haven: Yale University Press, 1974), p. 33.

15. William F. Buckley, Jr., "The Most Damaging Statement," *Washington Post*, July 30, 1987, p. A19.

16. On April 29, 1987, Channell pled guilty to a one-count criminal information charging that he conspired to defraud the IRS and deprive the Treasury of revenue to which it was entitled. Channell named Oliver North and Richard R. Miller as coconspirators.

17. The CIA began advising the House and Senate Intelligence Committees in 1981 that it was using uncommitted funds available to it to fund the Contras. This led to the passage on September 27, 1982, of a classified section of the Intelligence Authorization bill (P.L. 97-269), which, according to a statement later made on the House floor by Representative Boland, Chairman of the House Committee at the time, prohibited the CIA from using its funds for "the purpose of overthrowing the government of Nicaragua" (*Congressional Record*, December 8, 1982, p. H9146).

On December 21, 1982, the Congress enacted the first Boland Amendment, which came to be referred to as "Boland I," and which, according to Representative Boland, contained substantively the same language as the earlier classified prohibition in the Intelligence Authorization. This language, contained in the Defense Appropriations Act, P.L. 97-377, section 793, stated:

> None of the funds provided in this Act may be used by the Central Intelligence Agency or the Department of Defense to furnish military equipment, military training or advice, or other support for military activities, to any group or individual, not part of a country's armed forces, for the purpose of overthrowing the Government of Nicaragua or provoking a military exchange between Nicaragua and Honduras.

On December 8, 1983, the Congress enacted the Defense Appropriation Act for fiscal year 1984, P.L. 98-212, which, in Section 775, stated:

> During fiscal year 1984, not more than $24,000,000 of the funds available to the Central Intelligence Agency, the Department of Defense, or any other agency or entity of the United States involved in intelligence activities may be obligated or expended for the purpose or which would have the effect of supporting directly or indirectly military or paramilitary operations in Nicaragua by any nation, group, organization, movement, or individual.

By the summer of 1984, the $24,000,000 appropriation began to run out. This fact coupled with the language prohibiting expenditure of additional funds raised the issue for the administration, which was determined to aid the Contras, of the meaning of the phrase "agency or entity of the United States involved in intelligence activities." The administration and its defenders would argue that the National Security Council staff was not covered by this language; its critics would argue that it was.

On October 1, 1984, Congress passed an "interim Continuing Resolution," P.L. 98-441, which, in Section 106(c), contained a prohibition against Contra aid. This language came to be known as "Boland II":

> No appropriations or funds made available pursuant to this joint resolution to the Central Intelligence Agency, the Department of Defense, or any other agency or entity of the United States involved in intelligence activities may be obligated or expended for the purpose or which would have the effect

of supporting, directly or indirectly, military or paramilitary operations in Nicaragua by any nation, group, organization, movement or individual.

On October 12, 1984, in the "permanent Continuing Resolution" for fiscal year 1985, P.L. 98-473, in Section 8066, Congress applied this same prohibition to all of FY 1985 with the added provision that the restriction would be removed after February 28, 1985, if the President certified that Nicaragua was continuing to supply rebel forces in El Salvador *and* Congress passed a joint resolution funding assistance to the Contras. Such certification was later made by the President, but the resolution was defeated in the House of Representatives, leaving Boland II in effect for FY 1985.

In the International Security and Development Cooperation Act of 1985, P.L. 99-83, signed into law on August 8, 1985, the Congress, in Section 722(g), appropriated $27 million for "humanitarian assistance" to the Contras. These funds could not be administered by the CIA or the Department of Defense. Also, in Section 722(g), the Pell Amendment prohibited any agreement that conditioned foreign or military aid upon aid to the Contras by a third nation.

On December 4, 1985, "Boland III," contained in the Intelligence Authorization Act for fiscal year 1986, P.L. 99-169, Section 105, became law. Boland III stated:

> (a) Funds available to the Central Intelligence Agency, the Department of Defense, or any other agency or entity of the United States involved in intelligence activities may be obligated and expended during fiscal year 1986 to provide funds, materiel, or other assistance to the Nicaraguan democratic resistance to support military or paramilitary operations in Nicaragua only as classified Schedule of Authorizations referred to in Section 102, or pursuant to Section 502 of the National Security Act of 1947, or to Section 106 of the Supplemental Appropriations Act of 1985 (P.L. 99-88).
>
> (b) Nothing in this section precludes—(1) administration, by the Nicaraguan Humanitarian Assistance Office . . . of the program of humanitarian assistance to the Nicaraguan democratic resistance provided for in the Supplemental Appropriations Act of 1985 or (2) activities of the Department of State to solicit such humanitarian assistance for the Nicaraguan democratic resistance.

Boland III permitted support of the Contras only in particular ways, which included communications equipment and training and intelligence information.

On October 18, 1986, the President signed P.L. 99-500, the Continuing Appropriations for Fiscal Year 1987, which, in Section 201, appropriated $100 million for the Contras, including $30 million in humanitarian assistance. The remaining $70 million could be used for military aid.

These various provisions, and others, were enacted often as compromises between the administration and Congress or between the houses, in conference committees. The House generally opposed Contra aid and the Senate, which then had a Republican majority, generally supported Contra aid. Virtually all of the votes were extremely close and were widely reported by the media and closely watched by the public.

18. House Judiciary Committee, Debates on Proposed Articles of Impeachment, July 30, 1974; Debate on Proposed Article on Concealment of Information About Bombing Operations in Cambodia.

Show Time

19. *Joint Hearings on the Iran-Contra Investigation—Testimony of Richard V. Secord*, 100-1 (Washington, D.C.: Government Printing Office, 1987), pp. 1–4.

20. Ibid., pp. 4–7.

21. Ibid., p. 208.

22. Ibid., pp. 23–24.

Good Copp/Bad Copp?

23. *Joint Hearings on the Iran-Contra Investigation—Testimony of Richard V. Secord*, 100-1 (Washington, D.C.: Government Printing Office, 1987), p. 132.

24. See p. 85.

25. Seventeen Kuwaiti prisoners, connected to "al-Dawa," an Iranian revolutionary group, convicted and imprisoned for their part in the December 12, 1983, attack in Kuwait on the U.S. Embassy, a U.S. civilian compound, the French Embassy, and several Kuwaiti government facilities. (*Report of the Congressional Committees Investigating the Iran-Contra Affair* [Washington, D.C.: Government Printing Office, 1987], p. 8.)

26. See pp. 100–101.

27. *Joint Hearings on the Iran-Contra Investigation—Testimony of Richard V. Secord*, 100-1 (Washington, D.C.: Government Printing Office, 1987), p. 208.

28. Ibid., p. 266.

A Crowd of Sorrows

29. On March 11, 1988, Robert McFarlane pled guilty to four counts of withholding information from Congress.

30. Hedrick Smith, *The Power Game: How Washington Really Works* (New York: Random House, 1988), pp. 600, 608, 630.

31. *Joint Hearings on the Iran-Contra Investigation—Testimony of Robert C. McFarlane*, 100-2 (Washington, D.C.: Government Printing Office, 1987), p. 237.

32. Ibid., p. 5.

33. *Report of the President's Special Review Board*, February 26, 1987, p. B-115.

34. Ibid., p. B-116.

35. *Joint Hearings on the Iran-Contra Investigation—Testimony of Robert C. McFarlane*, 100-2 (Washington, D.C.: Government Printing Office, 1987), pp. 106–107.

36. *Report of the Congressional Committees Investigating the Iran-Contra Affair* (Washington, D.C.: Government Printing Office, 1987), p. 121.

37. *Joint Hearings on the Iran-Contra Investigation—Testimony of Robert C. McFarlane,* 100-2 (Washington, D.C.: Government Printing Office, 1987), p. 208.

Couriers and Contras

38. *Joint Hearings on the Iran-Contra Investigation—Testimony of Gaston J. Sigur,* 100-2 (Washington, D.C.: Government Printing Office, 1987), p. 311.

39. Ibid., p. 316.

40. *Joint Hearings on the Iran-Contra Investigation—Testimony of Robert W. Owen,* 100-2 (Washington, D.C.: Government Printing Office, 1987), p. 365.

41. Ibid., pp. 335–36. See also Ibid., Exhibit RWO-3, pp. 780–82.

42. Ibid., p. 440.

Baksheesh—Coin of the Realm

43. *Joint Hearings on the Iran-Contra Investigation—Testimony of Albert Hakim,* 100-5 (Washington, D.C.: Government Printing Office, 1988), p. 194.

44. Ibid., pp. 214–15.

45. As of the date of his testimony, Hakim had not filed his tax returns for 1986.

46. Secord maintained the money for the Porsche was a loan from Hakim (even though he signed no note and paid no interest) and the airplane money was a consulting fee. Hakim testified that in both cases he took the funds from Secord's profit share. (*Report of the Congressional Committee Investigating the Iran-Contra Affair* [Washington, D.C.: Government Printing Office, 1987], p. 344.)

47. *Joint Hearings on the Iran-Contra Investigation—Testimony of Albert Hakim,* 100-5 (Washington, D.C.: Government Printing Office, 1988), p. 269.

48. Ibid., p. 295–96. See also Ibid., Exhibit AH-22.

49. *Joint Hearings on the Iran-Contra Investigation—Testimony of Oliver L. North,* 100-7, vol. I (Washington, D.C.: Government Printing Office, 1988), p. 330. See also transcript of the Frankfurt meeting.

50. Transcript of the Frankfurt meeting, C371 and C382. See also *Report of the Congressional Committees Investigating the Iran-Contra Affair* (Washington, D.C.: Government Printing Office, 1988), p. 255.

51. *Joint Hearings on the Iran-Contra Investigation—Testimony of Oliver L. North,* 100-7, vol. I (Washington, D.C.: Government Printing Office, 1988), p. 288.

52. *Joint Hearings on the Iran-Contra Investigation—Testimony of Albert Hakim,* 100-5 (Washington, D.C.: Government Printing Office, 1988), p. 389.

53. Ibid., p. 297.

Out on a Limb

54. *Report of the President's Special Review Board,* February 26, 1987, p. B-124.

55. *Joint Hearings on the Iran-Contra Investigation—Testimony of Elliott Abrams,* 100-5 (Washington, D.C.: Government Printing Office, 1988), Exhibit EA-25.

56. Ibid., Exhibit EA-28.

57. Transcript of Proceedings before the Senate Select Committee on Intelligence—Briefing on Nicaragua, Tuesday, November 25, 1986, pp. 14–15.

58. Transcript of Proceedings before the Senate Select Committee on Intelligence—Testimony of Elliott Abrams, Monday, December 8, 1986, p. 38.

59. *Joint Hearings on the Iran-Contra Investigation—Testimony of Elliott Abrams,* 100-5 (Washington, D.C.: Government Printing Office, 1988), p. 162.

60. Ibid.

The Perfect Spy

61. *Joint Hearings on the Iran-Contra Investigation—Testimony of Glenn Robinette,* 100-6 (Washington, D.C.: Government Printing Office, 1988), p. 39.

The Law Men

62. *Joint Hearings on the Iran-Contra Investigation—Testimony of Charles Cooper,* 100-6 (Washington, D.C.: Government Printing Office, 1988), p. 330.

63. Ibid., p. 314.

Beauty and the Beasts

64. *Joint Hearings on the Iran-Contra Investigation—Testimony of Fawn Hall,* 100-5 (Washington, D.C.: Government Printing Office, 1988), p. 139.

65. Ibid., p. 163.

66. Ibid., p. 150.

67. Ibid.

68. John Mortimer, *Clinging to the Wreckage* (New York: Penguin Books, 1984), p. 79.

69. *Joint Hearings on the Iran-Contra Investigation—Testimony of Fawn Hall,* 100-5 (Washington, D.C.: Government Printing Office, 1988), p. 150.

70. Ibid.

71. Ibid., pp. 164–65.

Time Out

72. Louis Nizer, *Reflections Without Mirrors* (New York: Doubleday, 1978), p. 215.

PART II

Top Gun

73. See *Report of the Congressional Committees Investigating the Iran-Contra Affair* (Washington, D.C.: Government Printing Office, 1988), pp. 687–88.

74. *Joint Hearings on the Iran-Contra Investigation—Testimony of Oliver L. North*, 100-7, vol. I (Washington, D.C.: Government Printing Office, 1988), p. 4.

75. Ibid., p. 9.

76. Ibid., p. 10.

77. Ibid., pp. 126–28.

78. Ibid., vol. II, p. 198.

79. Ibid., vol. I, p. 236.

80. *Joint Hearings on the Iran-Contra Investigation—Testimony of Charles Cooper*, 100-6 (Washington, D.C.: Government Printing Office, 1988), pp. 290–291.

81. *Joint Hearings on the Iran-Contra Investigation—Testimony of Oliver L. North*, 100-7, vol. II (Washington, D.C.: Government Printing Office, 1988), p. 172.

82. Ibid., vol. I, p. 232.

83. Ibid., pp. 235–36.

84. Ibid., p. 134.

85. Ibid.

86. Ibid., vol. II, pp. 27–28.

87. Ibid., vol. I, pp. 190–91.

88. Ibid., vol. II, pp. 42–44.

89. Ibid., p. 43.

90. William Shakespeare, *Henry VI, Part 2*, Act IV, Scene 2.

91. *Joint Hearings on the Iran-Contra Investigation—Testimony of Oliver L. North*, 100-7, vol. I (Washington, D.C.: Government Printing Office, 1988), p. 320.

92. Hearings of the Committee on the Judiciary, House of Representatives, Debate on Articles of Impeachment, Pursuant to H. Res. 803, Impeachment of Richard M. Nixon, July 24, 25, 26, 27, 29, and 30, 1974, p. 111.

93. *Joint Hearings on the Iran-Contra Investigation—Testimony of Oliver L. North*, 100-7, vol. II (Washington, D.C.: Government Printing Office, 1988), pp. 124–25.

94. Ibid., pp. 96–97.

95. Ibid., pp. 66–67.

96. Ibid., pp. 90–92.

Lives or Lies?

97. *Joint Hearings on the Iran-Contra Investigation—Testimony of Oliver L. North*, 100-7, vol. II (Washington, D.C.: Government Printing Office, 1988), p. 30.

98. Ibid.

99. *Newsweek*, July 27, 1987, p. 16.

100. "The Ollie We Knew," *The Washingtonian*, July 1987, p. 77.

101. David Halevy and Neil C. Livingstone, "The Ollie We Knew," *The Washingtonian*, July 1987, pp. 140–41.

102. *Report of the Congressional Committees Investigating the Iran-Contra Affair* (Washington, D.C.: Government Printing Office, 1987), pp. 311–13.

Beethoven's Fifth

103. *Joint Hearings on the Iran-Contra Investigation—Testimony of John M. Poindexter*, 100-8 (Washington, D.C.: Government Printing Office, 1988), Exhibit JMP-110.

104. Liman, who deposed Poindexter in private session in early May, knew what Poindexter would say about presidential knowledge of the diversion of the funds from the arms sales to Iran to the Contras. If this were the only relevant question for the Committee, and if Poindexter's testimony definitively answered the question, the hearings might never have gotten off the ground.

First, as this chapter discusses, Poindexter's testimony alone cannot lay to rest doubts about what the President may have known. Second, Poindexter's deposition preceded North's testimony and there was no way to know what North would say and how that might affect Poindexter's testimony. But, third, and most important, what the President knew about the diversion was not the only significant question facing the Committee. The American people deserved to be told where the money went, who was involved, and who authorized these actions. And the hearings as they proceeded raised disturbing new issues. Testimony about the privatization of covert operations, the so-called "fall-guy plan," the "off-the-shelf, full-service" entity North told of, and the details of the negotiations with the Iranians brought to light these and many other serious concerns.

105. *Joint Hearings on the Iran-Contra Investigation—Testimony of John M. Poindexter*, 100-8 (Washington, D.C.: Government Printing Office, 1988), p. 18.

106. Ibid., p. 37.

107. Testimony of Donald T. Regan to the President's Special Review Board, January 7, 1987, pp. 57–58.

108. Richard M. Nixon to H. R. Haldeman and John Dean, Transcript of March 21, 1973, "Transcripts of Eight Recorded Presidential Conversations," Hearings Before the House Committee on the Judiciary on H. Res. 803, A Resolution Authorizing and Directing the Committee on the Judiciary to Investigate Whether Sufficient Grounds Exist for the House of Representatives to Exercise Its Constitutional Power to Impeach Richard M. Nixon, May–June 1974, Serial No. 34, p. 120.

109. Shultz testified that, when he told the President about the inclusion of the Da'Wa prisoners in the nine-point plan ("Hakim Accords"), "He reacted like he had been kicked in the belly" (*Joint Hearings on the Iran-Contra Investigation—Testimony of George P. Shultz*, 100-9 [Washington, D.C.: Government

Printing Office, 1988], p. 62). Regan testified that when the President, on November 24, 1986, was told by Meese of the diversion of funds from the arms sales to the Nicaraguan Contras, "... it [was] like a person was punched in the stomach" (Deposition of Donald T. Regan, Taken by the House Select Committee on Covert Arms Transactions with Iran, July 15, 1987, p. 62).

110. *Joint Hearings on the Iran-Contra Investigation—Testimony of Robert C. McFarlane*, 100-2 (Washington, D.C.: Government Printing Office, 1987), p. 146.

111. Senator John Kerry (D-Massachusetts), like McCain, is a graduate of the U.S. Naval Academy and fought in the Vietnam War. Kerry, however, became a leader in the protest against the war. He also entered elective office, becoming junior senator from Massachusetts in January 1985.

112. Philip Caputo, *A Rumor of War* (New York: Holt, Rinehart and Winston, 1977), p. 317.

113. Ibid., p. 326.

114. Ibid., p. 316.

115. Ibid., p. 330.

116. *Joint Hearings on the Iran-Contra Investigation—Testimony of John M. Poindexter*, 100-8 (Washington, D.C.: Government Printing Office, 1988), pp. 121–22.

117. Ibid., p. 38.

Battle Royal

118. *Joint Hearings on the Iran-Contra Investigation—Testimony of George P. Shultz*, 100-9 (Washington, D.C.: Government Printing Office, 1988), p. 181.

119. *Report of the President's Special Review Board*, February 26, 1987, p. IV-11.

120. Former Secretary of State Cyrus Vance resigned in April 1980, when President Jimmy Carter ordered the "Desert One" mission, an effort to rescue the American hostages then in Teheran. The rescue effort failed.

121. *Joint Hearings on the Iran-Contra Investigation—Testimony of George P. Shultz*, 100-9 (Washington, D.C.: Government Printing Office, 1988), p. 131.

122. Secretary Shultz testified that he had resigned or threatened resignation on three occasions: (1) In August 1986 he sent a letter of resignation to the President. At that time, he said, he knew that "the White House was very uncomfortable with" him. He particularly cited his difficulties in getting his travel approved by the White House, naming Jonathan Miller as a particular problem. (2) In the "middle of 1983" Shultz resigned when he discovered that Bud McFarlane, then deputy National Security Adviser, was sent on a secret trip to the Middle East (Saudi Arabia, Syria, Israel, Jordan, and Egypt) without his knowledge. He said, "When the President hangs his shingle out, he'll get all the business." (3) In late 1985 Shultz resigned over the issue of lie-detector tests. He testified that he reconsidered on that occasion because McFarlane had just left and he felt it would be unfair to the President to have Shultz leave at the same time.

123. *Joint Hearings on the Iran-Contra Investigation—Testimony of George P. Shultz,* 100-9 (Washington, D.C.: Government Printing Office, 1988), Exhibit GPS-27.

124. Ibid., p. 62.

125. *Report of the Congressional Committees Investigating the Iran-Contra Affair* (Washington, D.C.: Government Printing Office, 1987), p. 258. *Report of the Congressional Committees Investigating the Iran-Contra Affair,* Appendix A: Vol. 1, Source Documents (Washington, D.C.: Government Printing Office, 1988), p. 1563.

126. *Joint Hearings on the Iran-Contra Investigation—Testimony of John M. Poindexter,* 100-8 (Washington, D.C.: Government Printing Office, 1988), p. 68.

127. *Joint Hearings on the Iran-Contra Investigation—Testimony of George P. Shultz,* 100-9 (Washington, D.C.: Government Printing Office, 1988), p. 62.

128. Ibid., p. 5.

129. Ibid., p. 72.

Blind Trust

130. The Iran-Contra matter was not the first investigation into Meese's conduct. As early as 1984, Jacob A. Stein was appointed as a special prosecutor to look into a number of allegations concerning Meese's conduct.

Stein conducted *eleven* separate investigations concerning Meese. Several involved Meese's financial dealings with people who received federal jobs; there were also assertions that Meese had obtained special treatment from government agencies for businesses in which he had an interest, and allegations involving inadequate financial-disclosure statements of reimbursements for travel expenses.

Stein said he found no basis under federal law for prosecuting Meese. He noted that, as a matter of jurisdiction, he did not address the question of whether Meese's conduct had been ethical.

In 1985 David Martin, head of the Office of Government Ethics, said that, although Meese had not violated any ethics codes in accepting loans from his tax counselor, John McKean, he had created the appearance of impropriety.

In February 1985 Senator Mitchell, speaking against confirmation in the debate on the confirmation of Meese to serve as attorney ageneral, stated:

> Mr. Meese accepted two unsecured loans totalling $60,000 which were arranged by his tax counselor, John McKean. Meese paid no interest on these loans nor any of the principal until 26 months after first receiving the money, and then only after a press story revealed their existence. McKean was twice appointed to the Postal Board of Governors and now serves as chairman. Mr. Meese personally took part in clearing these appointments.
>
> Mr. Meese was aided in selling his California home by Thomas Barrack. Barrack, who received no commission, advanced the seller a $70,000 loan to consummate the deal, paid the mortgage for a period of time, and finally absorbed an $83,000 loss on the sale, according to the report of the Independent Counsel. Within a week of arranging that sale, Barrack met with Mr. Meese in connection with his efforts to seek a Presidential appointment. He was subsequently appointed to two Federal positions. Mr. Meese could

not recall that meeting until he was shown a note confirming it, and denies any relationship between Barrack's $83,000 contribution on Meese's behalf and Meese's help in getting Barrack an important Federal job, even though both Meese and Barrack acknowledged that they had never met prior to this transaction.

Mr. Meese failed to disclose an interest-free $15,000 loan to his wife on four separate annual disclosure statements. The creditor, Edwin Thomas, first became Meese's immediate subordinate at the White House, and later Regional Director of the General Services Administration in San Francisco. Thomas's wife was first employed at the White House and subsequently appointed to the Federal Merit Systems Protection Board. Mr. Meese claims it never occurred to him that this loan should be reported on the disclosure form.

Mr. Meese obtained a combination of mortgage loans, bridge loans and rescheduled loans from a bank, for a total indebtedness of $420,000. Payments were in arrears on some of these loans for up to 15 months. Four officers of the bank were subsequently appointed to Federal positions. All of these appointments were among those Mr. Meese reviewed. Mr. Meese claimed that he was unaware of the connection.

Mr. Meese accepted preferential promotion to colonel in the Army Reserve, even though the Secretary of the Army had personally called the irregularities in the promotion to his attention. Mr. Meese says he cannot recall that conversation, although he contacted Secretary Weinberger to support the reappointment of the general who approved his promotion.

Mr. Meese accepted a $10,000 check for the Presidential Transition Trust for moving expenses, even though during his initial confirmation hearings last year he testified that he had paid for his moving expenses out of his pocket. When he was advised that the payment of moving expenses was probably illegal, he asked somebody at the trust to alter the check to reflect consulting expenses.

In 1987 federal indictments for racketeering, conspiracy, and mail and wire fraud were brought against three individuals, including E. Robert Wallach, who has been Meese's personal lawyer. Wallach helped represent Meese in 1983, when Independent Counsel Jacob Stein cleared Meese of criminal wrongdoing in accepting loans from friends who were given government jobs, and he was Meese's counsel during his attorney-general confirmation hearings. Also indicted was W. Franklyn Chinn, who managed investments for Meese.

In January 1987 four officials of the Wedtech Corporation pleaded guilty to bribery charges involving millions of dollars in contracts, saying that they had bribed as many as twenty government officials. Chinn was a member of Wedtech's Board of Directors, and both he and Wallach represented the corporation.

Special Prosecutor James McKay said he has no current plans to seek charges against Meese on the Wedtech matter, but added that he might resume the inquiry later and that he would continue his investigation of Meese in other, undisclosed matters.

McKay said, "There is insufficient evidence as of this date [December 22,

1987, that Meese] knowingly participated in criminal activity in connection with his Wedtech actions."

Those indicted have asserted Fifth Amendment rights rather than testify before the federal grand jury investigating Meese. McKay said he might still seek their testimony about Meese after their trial is completed. McKay stated, "There are a number of unresolved questions concerning his involvement with the Wedtech Corp. and other matters."

McKay has declined to describe the "other matters," which reportedly include $55,000 that Meese and his wife invested, at Wallach's suggestion, in a trust handled by Chinn. The Meeses realized more than $35,000 in profits from speculative one-day stock trades that Chinn carried out over a two-year period.

In an ethics filing, Meese disclosed that Chinn on several occasions had invested significantly more funds than was in their investment account, although he and his wife deny any knowledge of the transactions at the time they took place.

The Senate Government Affairs Oversight Subcommittee hearings on July 9, 1987, focused on Meese's partnership with Chinn. Meese referred to the Chinn arrangement in his 1985 and 1986 financial-disclosure statements as a "limited blind partnership." David Martin stated, "We do not recognize 'blind' arrangements created by a filer's own action."

The partnership did not appear on a May 24, 1985, list of Meese's interests included in a memo entitled "Recusal Policy" (initialed by Meese), which was circulated within the Department of Justice.

Senator Carl Levin (D-Michigan), chairman of the Subcommittee, questioned at the hearings how Meese could have omitted the partnership, which supposedly equaled all of Meese's previous stock holdings in value and for which the final legal documents had been signed just one day earlier. Meese replied that the partnership had been "omitted inadvertently."

Meese's July 6, 1987, financial disclosure showed the partnership's legal name to be "Meese Partners." In his earlier disclosure statements, Meese had referred to the partnership as "Financial Management International." He explained at the hearing that the latter name actually referred to the legal entity Chinn owned and used to participate in the partnership.

Levin noted that by using the latter name Meese misled the analysts in the Office of Government Ethics. Martin had earlier testified that the longer name suggested a "pooled arrangement and as such did not raise a red flag in our office until after it had become notorious." Martin said that, if the name "Meese Partners" had appeared instead, "it would have triggered an automatic review."

McKay was named as an independent counsel in February 1987 to look into Lyn Nofziger's involvement with Wedtech. The investigation was expanded to Meese's activities in May, when Meese acknowledged that he had interceded in Wedtech's behalf at Wallach's request in 1982 (when Meese was counselor to the President). On May 11, under pressure from members of Congress and press reports, Meese asked the special prosecutor to look into his relationship with Wedtech. Wedtech was seeking a no-bid $32 million Army engine contract under an SBA minority contractor program. (Wedtech is the third-largest contractor in dollar volume in the history of the SBA program.)

According to the indictment, the conspiracy began in 1981. After receiving memos from Wallach, who was serving as a consultant, adviser, and lobbyist for Wedtech, Meese ordered a White House review that led to Wedtech's obtaining the no-bid contract.

Meese has defended this action as simply seeking to assure that Wedtech received a "fair hearing."

The indictment alleges Wallach received more than $2 million in money and securities from Wedtech to influence Meese.

McKay was also investigating Meese's involvement in a billion-dollar Iraq-to-Jordan pipeline project.

The probe focused on whether Meese was aware of a scheme to bribe Israeli government officials in order to convince them not to interfere with the pipeline project. A memo written in 1985, and sent "eyes only" to Meese by Wallach, referred to $650 million to $700 million in proceeds over a ten-year period to go to Israel—some of which would "go directly" to "Mr. Peres's Labor Party."

Meese and the Israeli Prime Minister reportedly exchanged handwritten letters on the subject of the pipeline, and Meese also arranged a meeting at the request of Wallach with then National Security Adviser Robert McFarlane for Bruce Rappaport, an Israeli-born Swiss businessman who was involved in the project.

Press reports charged that a $150,000 payment of legal fees to Wallach for his work on the project was placed in Meese's stock-trading account. The fee went through two accounts before being deposited, in October 1985, in the account called "Meese Partners," which Chinn managed for Meese's benefit.

Meese has denied any wrongdoing and has stated that his investments were placed in a blind trust and that "at the time of my investing in that firm, I knew nothing about this money [from Wallach] being paid."

On April, 1988, McKay stated that he had found "insufficient evidence to warrant a prosecution" of Meese on charges concerning the Iraqi pipeline matter.

No indictments in any of these matters have named Meese. The Attorney General's spokesman, Terry Eastland, was quoted as saying, "Someone who has been investigated as thoroughly as this person [Meese] has, ought to get some credit for having come through all these investigations clean, at least to this point."

131. *Joint Hearings on the Iran-Contra Investigation—Testimony of Edwin Meese, III*, 100-9 (Washington, D.C.: Government Printing Office, 1988), pp. 332–33.

132. *Joint Hearings on the Iran-Contra Investigation—Testimony of Oliver L. North*, 100-7, vol. I (Washington, D.C.: Government Printing Office, 1988), p. 258. See also *Testimony of Oliver L. North*, 100-7, vol. II, Exhibit OLN-155.

133. *Joint Hearings on the Iran-Contra Investigation—Testimony of Edwin Meese, III*, 100-9 (Washington, D.C.: Government Printing Office, 1988), pp. 336–37.

134. Walter Pincus and Dan Morgan, "Are Deeper Secrets Still Being Hidden?," *Washington Post*, September 6, 1987, p. A1.

Et Tu?

135. Bernard Weinraub, "How Donald Regan Runs the White House," *New York Times Magazine*, January 5, 1986, pp. 12–54. Fred Barnes, "Don't Underestimate Don Regan," *Reader's Digest*, July 1985, pp. 140–44. Ellen Hume and Jane Mayer, "The Rise and Fall of Don Regan," *Regardie's*, January 1987, pp. 96–105.

136. *Report of the President's Special Review Board*, February 26, 1987, p. IV-11.

137. *Washington Post*, November 21, 1986, p. A1.

138. Testimony of Donald T. Regan to the President's Special Review Board, January 7, 1987, pp. 13–14.

139. Deposition of Donald T. Regan, Taken by the U.S. House of Representatives Select Committee to Investigate Covert Arms Transactions with Iran, July 15, 1987, p. 68.

140. *Washington Post*, April 18, 1988, p. B2.

141. "CBS Evening News," January 25, 1988.

142. Deposition of Donald T. Regan, Taken by the U.S. Senate Select Committee on Secret Military Assistance to Iran and the Nicaraguan Opposition, March 3, 1987, p. 59.

143. Ibid., p. 60.

144. *Joint Hearings on the Iran-Contra Investigation—Testimony of Donald T. Regan*, 100-10 (Washington, D.C.: Government Printing Office, 1988), p. 48.

145. Ibid., p. 49.

146. Ibid.

147. Ibid., p. 36.

Rough Rider

148. *Joint Hearings on the Iran-Contra Investigation—Testimony of John M. Poindexter*, 100-8 (Washington, D.C.: Government Printing Office, 1988), p. 58.

149. *Joint Hearings on the Iran-Contra Investigation—Testimony of Caspar W. Weinberger*, 100-10 (Washington, D.C.: Government Printing Office, 1988), p. 248.

150. Ibid., p. 207.

151. Ibid., pp. 208–209.

152. Ibid., pp. 136–37.

153. Ibid., Exhibit DTR-41A.

154. Ibid., p. 137.

155. *Joint Hearings on the Iran-Contra Investigation—Testimony of George P.*

Shultz, 100-9 (Washington, D. C.: Government Printing Office, 1988), pp. 31–32.

156. *Joint Hearings on the Iran-Contra Investigation—Testimony of John M. Poindexter,* 100-8 (Washington, D.C.: Government Printing Office, 1988), p. 25.

157. *Joint Hearings on the Iran-Contra Investigation—Testimony of Caspar W. Weinberger,* 100-10 (Washington, D.C.: Government Printing Office, 1988), p. 241.

Secret Witnesses

158. *Joint Hearings on the Iran-Contra Investigation—Testimony of C/CATF,* 100-11 (Washington, D.C.: Government Printing Office, 1988), p. 171.

159. *Joint Hearings on the Iran-Contra Investigation—Testimony of Tomas Castillo,* 100-4 (Washington, D.C.: Government Printing Office, 1988), p. 3.

160. Ibid., p. 4.

161. The Senate Select Committee on Intelligence on December 2, 1986, asked Clarridge about a meeting he had attended on November 25, 1986. Clarridge could not remember who was there or what was said.

162. *Joint Hearings on the Iran-Contra Investigation—Testimony of Clair George,* 100-11 (Washington, D.C.: Government Printing Office, 1988), p. 262.

163. *Joint Hearings on the Iran-Contra Investigation—Testimony of Dewey R. Clarridge,* 100-11 (Washington, D.C.: Government Printing Office, 1988), p. 61.

164. Ibid., pp. 61–62.

165. *Joint Hearings on the Iran-Contra Investigation—Testimony of C/CATF,* 100-11 (Washington, D.C.: Government Printing Office, 1988), p. 89.

166. Ibid., p. 171.

167. Hearings of the House Permanent Select Committee on Intelligence, October 14, 1986.

168. *Joint Hearings on the Iran-Contra Investigation—Testimony of C/CATF,* 100-11 (Washington, D.C.: Government Printing Office, 1988), pp. 121–22.

169. Ibid., p. 122.

170. At the conclusion of his testimony, Clair George was to comment: "I could be . . . a trivia question some day. Who was the last person to ever appear before the Iran-contra Committee?" (*Joint Hearings on the Iran-Contra Investigation—Testimony of Clair George,* 100-11 [Washington, D.C.: Government Printing Office, 1988], p. 274.)

171. Hearings of the House Permanent Select Committee on Intelligence, October 14, 1986, p. 4.

172. *Joint Hearings on the Iran-Contra Investigation—Testimony of Clair George,* 100-11 (Washington, D.C.: Government Printing Office, 1988), p. 217.

173. See Ibid., p. 191. Shaheen had offered to help secure the release of hostages in Lebanon through an Iranian expatriate, Cyrus Hashemi, if the administration would help in getting criminal charges against Hashemi dropped.

174. *Joint Hearings on the Iran-Contra Investigation—Testimony of Clair George,* 100-11 (Washington, D.C.: Government Printing Office, 1988), p. 257.

175. Ibid., p. 190.
176. Ibid., p. 213.
177. Ibid., p. 212.
178. Ibid., p. 243.
179. Ibid., p. 213.
180. Ibid., p. 269.
181. Ibid., p. 267.
182. C/CATF resigned in March 1988. Clair George resigned in December 1987. Dewey Clarridge resigned in June 1988 to become an executive with General Dynamics; he was among those who were reprimanded by CIA Director Webster. Joseph Fernandez, who was fired by the CIA in December 1987, was indicted on June 20, 1988, by the grand jury investigating the Iran-Contra affair. The five-count indictment charged Fernandez with defrauding the government and lying to government investigators.

Copilot or Passenger?

183. George Bush with Victor Gold, *Looking Forward* (New York: Doubleday 1987), p. 240.

184. *Joint Hearings on the Iran-Contra Investigation—Testimony of John M. Poindexter*, 100-8 (Washington, D.C.: Government Printing Office, 1988), Exhibit JMP-28.

185. *Report of the President's Special Review Board*, February 26, 1987, p. B-63.

186. *New York Times*, January 29, 1988, Section A, p. 1.

187. *Joint Hearings on the Iran-Contra Investigation—Testimony of Caspar W. Weinberger*, 100–10, (Washington, D.C.: Government Printing Office, 1988), p. 139.

188. *Joint Hearings on the Iran-Contra Investigation—Testimony of John M. Poindexter*, 100–8, (Washington, D.C.: Government Printing Office, 1988), p. 31.

189. *Report of the President's Special Review Board*, February 26, 1987, p. B-64.

190. "CBS Evening News," January 25, 1988. ("Text of Dan Rather's Interview with George Bush," *Washington Post*, January 27, 1988, Section D, p. 4.)

191. *Washington Post*, January 27, 1988, Section A, p. 1.

192. Ibid.

193. *Report of the Congressional Committees Investigating the Iran-Contra Affair*, Appendix B: Vol. 20, Depositions (Washington, D.C.: Government Printing Office, 1988), p. 1138.

194. *Joint Hearings on the Iran-Contra Investigation—Testimony of Edwin Meese, III*, 100–9 (Washington, D.C.: Government Printing Office, 1988), p. 203.

195. *Report of the President's Special Review Board*, February 26, 1987, pp. B-145–47.

196. The poll found that 44% believed Bush was treated fairly and 44% thought he had not. A large majority of those interviewed (78%) had seen or heard about the interview. Forty-nine percent believed that Bush had done a good job and 37% a bad job. Fifty-five percent agreed that Bush "should reveal more about Iran-Contra." Rather's favorability rating among Republicans dropped eighteen points. (*Los Angeles Times*, January 29, 1988, Section 1, p. 20.)

197. "What Is George Bush Hiding?," *New York Times*, January 29, 1988, Section A, p. 34.

198. *Report of the Congressional Committees Investigating the Iran-Contra Affair*, Appendix D: Vol. 2, Testimonial Chronology (Washington, D.C.: Government Printing Office, 1988), Entry No. 86/02/01-100.

199. "CBS Evening News," January 25, 1988. ("Text of Dan Rather's Interview with George Bush," *Washington Post*, January 27, 1988, Section D, p. 4.)

PART III

The Report

200. *Report of the Congressional Committees Investigating the Iran-Contra Affair* (Washington, D.C.: Government Printing Office, 1987), p. 280.

201. Ibid., p. 437.

202. *Congressional Record*, January 12, 1987, pp. S596–98.

The Aftermath

203. Undated letter to Intelligence Committee Chairman Senator David Boren and Vice Chairman Senator William S. Cohen from President Ronald Reagan.

204. *Report of the Congressional Committees Investigating the Iran-Contra Affair* (Washington, D.C.: Government Printing Office, 1987), p. 423.

205. *Joint Hearings on the Iran-Contra Investigation—Testimony of Charles Cooper*, 100-6 (Washington, D.C.: Government Printing Office, 1988), Exhibit CJC-21, "Memorandum for the Attorney General: The President's Compliance with the 'Timely Notification' Process Requirements of Section 501(b) of the National Security Act," December 17, 1986, p. 24.

206. Hearings on S. 1721, Senate Select Committee on Intelligence, December 16, 1987, p. 62.

207. Hearings on the Nomination of Robert M. Gates, Senate Select Committee on Intelligence, February 17, 1987, p. 54.

208. Hearings on the Nomination of William H. Webster, Senate Select Committee on Intelligence, April 9, 1987, p. 140.

The President vs. the Congress

209. *Joint Hearings on the Iran-Contra Investigation—Testimony of Bretton Sciaroni*, 100-5 (Washington, D.C.: Government Printing Office, 1988), p. 30.

210. *United States* v. *Curtiss-Wright Export Corporation*, 299 U.S. 340 (1936).

211. Ibid., pp. 319–20.

212. *Dames and Moore* v. *Regan*, 453 U.S. 654 (1981), pp. 668–69 (quoting in part *Youngstown Sheet and Tube Company* v. *Sawyer*, 343 U.S. 579 [1952], pp. 637–38).

213. "Address on Central America" by President Ronald Reagan to a Joint Session of Congress on April 27, 1983.

214. Theodore Draper, "An Autopsy," *New York Review of Books*, December 17, 1987, p. 74.

Pardon Me

215. *United States* v. *Wilson*, 32 U.S. (7 Pet.) 150, pp. 160–61 (1833).

216. Ex parte Wells, 59 U.S. (18 How.) 307, pp. 309–310

217. 11 Ops. Atty. Gen'l., 228 (1865).

218. 28 C.F.R. 1.2 (1987).

219. *The Federalist* No. 74.

220. Ibid.

221. William Safire, "Punish the Guilty," *New York Times*, August 4, 1987, Section A, p. 23.

222. Ibid.

Conclusions

223. See Joseph Nellis, "Contra Iran-Contra: Six Rules That Congress Forgot," *American Politics*, October 1987, pp. 21–24.

INDEX